...Ask What You Can Do For Your Country

The Memory and Legacy of John F. Kennedy

Also by Dan B. Fleming, Jr.:

Kennedy vs. Humphrey, West Virginia, 1960: The Pivotal Battle for the Democratic Presidential Nomination

"By the Good People of Virginia..." Our Commonwealth's Government
(Coauthor)

Virginia History and Government
(Coauthor)

...Ask What You Can Do For Your Country

The Memory and Legacy
of John F. Kennedy

by Dan B. Fleming, Jr.

Foreword by Mary McGrory

VANDAMERE
PRESS

Published by
Vandamere Press
P.O. Box 17446
Clearwater, FL 33762
USA

ISBN 0-918339-61-8

DEDICATION

To my father, Dan B. Fleming, who like John F. Kennedy, devoted his life to public service.

Acknowledgments

I would like to thank the many people who helped make this book possible, particularly those who shared their memories of John F. Kennedy. My wife, Beverly, my daughter, Elizabeth, Phyllis Albritton, Thomas C. Hunt, and Elizabeth Ritchey assisted in locating contributors. The *Irish Times* and the *Roanoke Times* were of great assistance in locating contributors. Allan Goodrich and James Hill from the John F. Kennedy Presidential Library provided invaluable service in locating photographs. I also received valuable aid from the staffs at the Jimmy Carter Presidential Library, the Gerald Ford Presidential Library, the Lyndon B. Johnson Presidential Library, and the University of Northern Colorado Library. Special thanks are also due to Melody Miller for her sympathetic ear and suggestions.

Publisher Art Brown was extremely helpful in organizing and structuring the book and in serving as a sounding board for ideas. Pat Berger did a painstaking job in editing, and Tammie Smith provided valuable assistance in manuscript preparation.

Contents

Foreword

By Mary McGrory

Dan B. Fleming, Jr., a Virginia Tech emeritus professor, has made a sentimental journey, figuratively speaking, around the world to recapture the universal shock and lamentation that followed the assassination of President John F. Kennedy. He records the distress of students in Thailand; Peace Corps volunteers; a former shipmate on a vessel carrying the wounded home, who saw Kennedy haunting the ship's library and heard him talk of his dream of peace; the bugler who played taps at the grand funeral; and the heartbroken Irish farmers who had greeted Kennedy with such palpable pride and love, that Kennedy, who was often considered more English than Irish, responded in kind.

The passing of 39 years has not loosened Kennedy's grip on the world's imagination. Myth and legend have only grown. He was improbably handsome, witty and charming; his wife was exquisite, his children, beguiling. He held press conferences every other week and enjoyed them. He read voraciously, never stopped inquiring and learning. His legacy? He made public service, at home and abroad, seem worthy and attractive to an entire generation. In some mysterious way, perhaps because of his almost miraculous survival in the war and his win-by-a-whisker over Richard Nixon—and religious prejudice—he gave people of all circumstances hope and faith in the system.

There is no criticism of Kennedy in this book. It would be as out of place as at a wake, which is what this book is for those who were not born when the assassination occurred.

I lived through those four traumatic days. I was lucky in that I had work to do. I was a reporter for the *Washington Star* at the time, and I had to go everywhere, from Andrews Air Force Base where I saw the light fall on the edge of the casket and knew that the unthinkable deed had been done, to Arlington Cemetery. It is all printed in my mind—especially when presidential aide Kenneth O'Donnell emerged from the shadows of the grand foyer during the White House wake and told me he would love me forever because I had written that he would have died for Kennedy. "Everyone knows that, I told him."

People would have died for him. This book tells you why.

Mary McGrory, has been a columnist for the *Washington Post* for the past 18 years. Her syndicated column of political commentary appears in more than 125 papers around the country. She won the Pulitzer Prize for her coverage of Watergate in 1974, and her prose in the *Washington Star* about the death of President Kennedy touched the hearts of millions. She has received numerous other journalism awards including the prestigious Lifetime Achievement Award from the National Society of Newspaper Columnists.

Preface

The genesis of this book occurred in 1990 while I was attending a conference in Williamsburg, Virginia. While chatting with a colleague, I happened to mention another meeting I had attended in Columbus, Ohio, where I learned that President Kennedy had been assassinated. My friend then related his recollection of the same event when he was a classroom teacher in Rhodesia. I was moved by his account of the strong impact Kennedy's death had on his students and told him his story was one that should be shared with others. Perhaps, I thought, people today could gain some insight into why John F. Kennedy, was then, and still is today, so revered around the globe. Thus, I began my personal pilgrimage to try to ascertain what qualities John F. Kennedy possessed that endeared him to people in every cross-section of life, from the penthouse to the factory assembly line, from remote parts of the world, such as Nepal, to the Kennedy ancestral home in Ireland.

I began seeking perspectives from many different persons and asked them to tell me what it was about John F. Kennedy that, decades after his death, still gripped their thoughts. Some interviewees began crying as they described their feelings for Kennedy, and several claimed their lives had never been quite the same since his death.

At social gatherings, when I asked people what they remembered best about John F. Kennedy, it was surprising how many individuals seemed to freeze on the spot. You could almost hear their mental wheels turning as they reflected back in time to his life and death. Their sincerity of responses clearly indicated that for most of them, President Kennedy held a special place in their hearts and minds.

My personal connection to JFK began when I was working during the summer of 1958 in a camp on Cape Cod. I had just finished reading JFK's book, *Profiles in Courage*.[1] While waiting for a flight in the tiny Hyannis Airport, I heard an annoyed sounding voice from a customer at the counter. It was an irate Senator John F. Kennedy expressing his displeasure that his flight to Washington, D.C., was an hour late. Seizing my chance, I introduced myself and complimented the Senator on his book. He was quite gracious, particularly considering that I was a stranger and he was not in a very good mood.

From that chance encounter, I was hooked as a Kennedy admirer. Upon learning in 1960 that he would be running for the Democratic nomination for President against Hubert Humphrey in my home state of West Virginia, I volunteered to help. I ended up as a young, inexperienced county campaign chairman for Kennedy. Several friends told me I was wasting my time because his campaign would never go anywhere because he was too young and a Catholic. Of course, Kennedy won in West Virginia, thus proving a Catholic could win in an overwhelmingly Protestant state. This victory ensured him of the Democratic nomination in Los Angeles in August, 1960.

In 1962-63, as part of the Congressional Fellowship Program of the American Political Science Association, I worked as a legislative assistant in the House and Senate. I was able to see JFK in action on frequent occasions.

Nearly all the vignettes offered here are drawn from personal interviews, letters, diaries, documents and speeches gathered over a two-year period.

...Ask What You Can Do For Your Country

The Memory and Legacy of John F. Kennedy

Chapter One

A Trip to Dallas

The question concerning where you were at 1:30 P.M., EST, on Friday, November 22, 1963, still causes people to pause and ponder on that fateful moment described by Theodore H. White as one of those rare times in history that "crease the memory" forever.[2] I used this tragic memory as a vehicle to lead people into recalling not only John F. Kennedy's death, but also those happy memories that demonstrate what it was about him that inspired so many people.

If you were standing among excited people on a warm and sun-lit day on Dealey Plaza in Dallas, Texas, you were an eyewitness to one of the saddest events in our nation's history. The shots that rang out that day reverberated around the world.

William Manchester in *The Death of a President* [3] described America as a result of the President's death as an "…enormous emergency room, with the shocked world waiting outside." The following four days found the nation traumatized in front of their television sets watching events unfold. A form of national paralysis set in culminated by the state funeral and dramatic march to Arlington Cemetery where the President was laid to rest on Monday, November 25, 1963.

The worldwide reaction to the President's death caught even the most veteran political figures off guard. Israel's Prime Minister David Ben Gurion said: "It was the first world mourning in history."[4] Even in remote parts of Africa, reports came in of natives walking miles to express their sorrow over the death of a friend. Clearly the youth, charm, and idealism of President John F. Kennedy had captured the hopes of the people of the world beyond anything ever anticipated.

The recollections contained in this book not only review the tragedy of Kennedy's death, but also go well beyond this event by informing the reader of the worldwide impact of John F. Kennedy on people still living today. These vignettes allow individuals to share their memory of JFK with those too young to recall his death. They suggest why people loved and respected him, not only as Kennedy the President, but as Kennedy the man. As journalist Robert J. Donovan so aptly put it, "He was a hell of a guy."[5]

In this current age of anxiety and uncertainty, Americans seem more than ever to be seeking heroes as part of the cement that binds our nation together. This book helps in that search. John F. Kennedy is now an American hero for the ages. In current public opinion polls, he consistently ranks among our greatest Presidents. The memory of John F. Kennedy and the "brief shining moment" of a political Camelot still burn brightly throughout the world. These personal recollections in this book attempt to capture the feelings that people everywhere had for Kennedy, his life, and his death, and in particular, they emphasize his call of hope through public service to others.

The following accounts recall the fateful visit to Dallas by several people present at the time. Betty Harris describes some of the planning for the Dallas visit, and Secret Service Agent Paul Landis, recalls riding behind the car of President Kennedy when he was shot. Bob Donovan, an onsite journalist at the time of the assassination, reflects on Dallas and his previous contacts with John F. Kennedy, relating to his authorship of the book, *PT 109.*[6] Reverend Bob Davis describes the hectic events at Parkland Hospital, and Colonel James Swindal relates his memory of the gloomy flight back from Dallas to Washington as pilot of *Air Force One.*

Betty F. Harris, Business Woman, Dallas, Texas

Betty Harris was a key player in planning for the President's ill-fated trip to Dallas. She describes the planning process, including the concerns about the possible response of the right-wing groups in the city to the visit. She later regrets sharing in making decisions that may have contributed to the President's death.

Decades later, I still remember in every detail that fateful day in Dallas. For years afterwards I would wake in a cold sweat convinced that something I had done, or had not done, had contributed to the death of President Kennedy. Although the President was only to spend a few brief hours in Dallas, I was responsible for many of the trip's details. I still reflect in horror that I did something wrong in the plans that were made, such as the schedule that was carefully gone over, minute by minute. Even decisions about whether we should have publicized the parade route he took would haunt me.

Although not a native of Dallas, I had lived there for a number of years and was actively involved in Democratic politics, helping establish the Citizens for Kennedy/Johnson Committee for Dallas County in 1960. In 1961 I took a job at the Peace Corps where I got to know fellow Texan and Deputy Director, Bill Moyers. In 1963, I returned to Dallas to resume my business career.

My involvement with President Kennedy's visit to Dallas came about through Vice-President Johnson's associate Bill Moyers. He called me on November 13, 1963, and asked for my help in making the trip preparations in Dallas. I agreed to do so after first refusing. I didn't want to harm my work by getting involved in the tangled and rancorous infighting of Texas politics. I then prepared a long memo offering a rundown on the situation in Dallas. The next day, Moyers flew to Dallas where he stopped to pick up my memo and then continued to Austin where he remained the next week planning the Kennedy/Johnson visit.

Moyers also asked me to contact Sam Bloom, head of the Bloom Advertising Agency and a key figure in the powerful Dallas Citizens' Council. The Council really ran Dallas and was composed of 100 or so corporate leaders. My job was to discuss with him how to keep peace among the warring factions of Texas Democrats during Kennedy's visit, no easy task I might add. One immediate problem concerned who should be invited to the Friday luncheon for Kennedy, hosted by the Citizens' Council.

On Sunday morning, November 17, I met with Sam and, from that point on, was heavily involved in planning for the presidential visit. Even today, I regret the moment when I changed my mind and became, ipso facto, the political advance man in the Dallas segment of the trip. That same day, I met the major figure in the planning team, Secret Service Agent, Winston Lawson. Lawson had come down from Washington on November 8 to begin planning for the President's visit and working closely with the Dallas police department.

Win and I had dinner Sunday night where I learned that plans were still in flux for the site for the luncheon, which related to the parade route chosen. I also learned that the bubble top used on the President's Lincoln only kept out the weather, not bullets. There was considerable debate by the Secret Service about whether to use the bubble top in Dallas. We also discussed two previous episodes in Dallas with Johnson in 1960 and Adlai Stevenson a month earlier. Both were jostled and threatened by right-wing conservatives. United Nations Ambassador Stevenson had come to Dallas to speak on UN Day. Afterwards, he was greeted by a jeering crowd and was hit by a placard carried by a woman protester. Many city leaders were fearful about Kennedy's impending visit and the local enforcement agencies were nervous as well.

I worked closely that week with Dallas police chief, Jesse Curry, and with Win Lawson and Sam Bloom. Sam and the two Dallas newspapers worked to head off possible words or deeds that might embarrass the city. When Chief Curry wanted to park black police vans known as Black Marias on every corner along the route, I opposed this idea because it had a police state flavor to it and made the President look bad. Unfortunately, I won the argument; the vans were not used. Another action that I pushed was having the two Dallas newspapers run maps of the parade route to encourage a large turnout. Both ran the maps and I was pleased. This was another decision that I still regret, but at the time, thought it was a good idea.

Friday morning, November 22, began with a light drizzle. I arrived at the airport and joined the welcoming party in a revamped Quonset hut near where *Air Force One* would land. Mayor Earle

Cabell and his wife, Elizabeth, were there. Mrs. Cabell had a bouquet of Texas red roses to give Mrs. Kennedy. I was given a brown lapel pin by Win Lawson that identified me as part of the presidential party.

Just before the plane arrived, the sun broke through and a very large and happy throng greeted the President's arrival. That day, my heart almost burst for pride as *Air Force One* touched the runaway.

After some last minute switches about who would ride where in the motorcade, we got underway at 11:30 A.M. downtown on an eleven-mile trip to the luncheon at the Trade Mart. I rode in a VIP bus along with other members of the President's staff and with a

President Kennedy and Jackie arrive at Love Field, Dallas, November 22, 1963.

Courtesy of the John F. Kennedy Library

close friend of mine on Johnson's staff, Liz Carpenter. The streets were heavily lined with cheering people. Everything seemed to be going even better than I had hoped for.

And then what happened next is well known to all the world. Later at Parkland Hospital, I watched Mrs. Kennedy, her pink suit splashed with blood, sitting there numb and unmoving. I noticed that she wore printed gloves which I thought strange for an impeccable dresser like Mrs. Kennedy. Then I realized they were white gloves "printed" with blood from her husband's wound. Dave Powers stood by Mrs. Kennedy comforting her with a hand gently on her shoulder.

Win Lawson was nearby stricken both by grief and by the knowledge that the President had been slain on "his watch." While waiting, I saw Dr. Kemp Clark, chief neurologist, say a few words to Mrs. Kennedy. Then he walked over to me as I asked, "How badly was he hurt." Clark replied, "It was lethal." In my hands, I held a pair of gloves, and I twisted them so hard, I split the seams.

The people of Dallas were in a total state of shock after the President's assassination. Although a few unattractive remarks and incidents were reported, everyone I know was stunned. The city of Dallas, including its leaders, didn't know what to do. The great majority of people seemed deeply grieved by Kennedy's death and were equally concerned about the image Dallas presented to the world as being a center of right-wing fanatics.

Looking back at that sad day in Dallas, I always try to remember the happiness that filled my being when President and Mrs. Kennedy first arrived in Dallas. It was a bright and shining moment that I never shall forget.

Paul Landis, Secret Service Agent

Landis was in the car riding behind the President when he was shot. Even today, he worries that he could have done something more to prevent the tragedy.

In 1987, I made my first return to Dallas since that unforgettable day in November 1963. As I took a solitary walk across Dealey Plaza and gazed up at the Texas Book Depository, my mind was flooded with memories from that tragic day 24 years ago.

In 1963, I was a Secret Service agent in Dallas assigned to protect Mrs. Kennedy. When the President was shot, I was riding on the right rear running board of the car following the President's limousine. Riding inside my car were two of his aides, Ken O'Donnell and David Powers. When we drew near the Book Depository Building, I did my usual eye scan, trying to detect any suspicious activities in the building. The windows seemed closed, and I didn't have a clear view of the upper stories of the Depository. I knew at once the popping sounds I heard were gunfire. I turned my head after the first shot but couldn't see anything. I then looked back at the President and saw him take a hit in the head. Fellow agent, Clint Hill, was riding on the running board on the other side of our car and rushed to Mrs. Kennedy who seemed to be crawling out of the back seat of the limousine. Hill was barely able to leap on the back of her car. By his thumbs down signal, I believed the President was a goner.

The next 24 hours were a blur of uncertainty and activity. I followed the President to Parkland Hospital and later witnessed the swearing in of Lyndon Johnson as the new President on *Air Force One*. At the hospital, I spotted a sizable piece of a bullet on the back seat of the President's car and gave it to someone there. I worried at the time whether I should leave it in the car or not.

When we arrived back at Andrews Air Force Base in Washington, I helped carry the coffin off the plane and rode in the ambulance to Bethesda Naval Hospital. After being up all night, I was exhausted by Saturday afternoon and collapsed in a chair in the map room of the White House. My two shift replacements had to virtually carry me out. Ironically the chair in which I had been sitting was Kennedy's rocking chair in the process of being taken away. I guess I was the last person to ever use it in the White House.

My final small part in the funeral took place on Monday, the day of the President's burial in Arlington Cemetery. I walked near Mrs. Kennedy in the procession from the Capitol to St. Matthew's Cathedral and then on to Arlington National Cemetery for the final ceremonies. We stood a distance from Mrs. Kennedy to allow her and the rest of the family some degree of privacy.

Some 20 years later, I returned to President Kennedy's burial site at Arlington Cemetery with my daughter. Only a few people were there that day. As I gazed at his grave, it was hard for me to realize how much time had passed since the events of Dallas and subsequent days, but these events were still so fresh in my mind.

I first began working as a Secret Service agent with the White House detail in October, 1959, when "Ike" was President. I still remember my first close-up look at John F. Kennedy about the third day after he was sworn in as President in January 1961. He merely nodded as he passed by me on duty at my post; we were not introduced. A day or two later, he again came by and much to my surprise, he said, "Hello Mr. Landis. How are you?" I was very impressed that a new President, swamped with so many things to do, had taken the trouble to learn the names of his new staff. During the years I worked in the White House, I found both President and Mrs. Kennedy to be very fine people. We were treated with courtesy by the President, although we were all well aware of the great power residing in his hands. Despite his high office, he still maintained respect for the feelings of the staff and was easy to work for.

One of my favorite personal experiences with the President took place in Palm Beach, Florida. His father Joe was in the hospital there, and the President and his daughter, Caroline, came to visit him. On their way out, Caroline spotted a bubble gum machine and asked her father for a penny to use in the machine. As President Kennedy was often known to do, he checked his pockets and didn't have any money. I was delighted to loan the President a penny to get him off the hook.

My overall impression of the Kennedys was that of a loving and happy family, despite all the heavy pressures of the presidency. After the Dallas assassination, I stayed on in the Secret Service for another six months assigned to Mrs. Kennedy. While most people are acquainted with the Kennedys from the image created by the press, I remember them as real people whom I liked and respected very much.

As an agent on duty at the President's murder in Dallas, I still have remorse over our failure to protect the President. I took the President's death very hard and personally. I will always carry with me the question: Was there anything that I could have done to prevent the tragedy?

Robert J. Donovan, **Los Angeles Times**

Bob Donovan authored PT 109[7] *recording Kennedy's wartime activities in the Pacific. He describes the events in Dallas and offers some of his recollections of writing* PT 109 *and the subsequent making of the film based on the book.*

Like most of my fellow journalists, I became a great admirer of President Kennedy for his wit, intellect and willingness to talk to people. As a reporter, I found it refreshing to be able to talk to Kennedy occasionally alone in his office. Truman and Eisenhower were not accessible in that way. Kennedy seemed to really like reporters and they enjoyed him in return.

On November 22, 1963, I was riding on the second press bus in Dallas. Even today, I still have a copy of my notes from that sad day. We went from Dealey Plaza, where JFK was shot, to the Parkland Hospital where the President had been taken. I rode in a photographer's station wagon, and we hurried up to the presidential car still outside the hospital. I will always remember the crumpled red roses on the backseat. I was particularly aware of the roses because on earlier stops in Texas, Jackie had received yellow roses from California. I had just written a little piece about it. I was therefore surprised when I saw Jackie handed red roses at Love Field in Dallas.

At the hospital we soon learned the President was dead. After this terrible announcement, I returned to Dealey Plaza to fix the scene in my mind, as I could not in the earlier tumult of the motorcade. I was numb as a human being could be. I still remember how, only a short time earlier, I had received a bright smile from the President at Love Field from only a few feet away as he left his plane for the motorcade. Both he and Jackie sparkled that day. I never saw them more dazzling than they were that late morning in Dallas.

JFK was a man who had everything: wealth, fame, power, a beautiful wife and family. Yet, a short time later he had nothing. If this was not a morality play, I never saw one. My contacts with Kennedy were happy ones. I got to know him fairly well when he was running for President in 1960 and I was a reporter for the *New York Herald Tribune*. With his election, the Kennedys became a hot item with the public, and publishers were frantic for articles and books about their lives.

Early in 1961, an editor from McGraw-Hill approached me to write a book on Kennedy's wartime exploits in the Pacific as a PT boat commander. The editor was in a hurry and thought I might provide quick access to the new President. At the same time the *Saturday Evening Post* wanted to run a series.

I got to Kennedy quickly enough in the White House, and he tried to talk me out of the project saying, "You're beating a dead horse" and "all that's been covered before," referring to an article written by John Hershey in the *New Yorker* in 1944 and reprinted in the *Reader's Digest*.[8] I persuaded him that by telling the account in a book he would greatly lengthen the life of the event for the future; he bought that argument. He had his aide, Ted Reardon, contact the Navy to help me out. Much to my chagrin, I soon learned the Navy had nothing at all on the story.

Before I was done, I went to the South Pacific and retraced the trail of John F. Kennedy throughout the Solomon Islands. On the way out, I went to Australia to meet Reginald Evans, the coast watcher who organized the rescue of Kennedy and his crew. Evans's records from that period gave me the indispensable knowledge of the chronology of those events. When I reached the Solomons, I was amazed to find that all ten of Evans's wartime scouts were still living. They were willing to reenact the events following the sinking of PT 109. With the help of the British, who once colonized the Solomons and who provided me a so-called copra scow, I explored the islands where Kennedy had been shipwrecked and even swam in the same waters as Kennedy had after his ship was rammed.

Next I went to Tokyo and interviewed the officers and crew of the destroyer, the *Amagiri,* that sank PT 109. Everything I learned convinced me that Kennedy had behaved very bravely. I don't think Kennedy considered himself a hero, but the members of his crew thought he was. That is probably what really counts about his actions as the skipper of PT 109 and later PT 59 as described in my book, *PT 109, John F. Kennedy in World War II*.[9]

By late summer 1961, I was hurrying to get my writing completed in time for the *Saturday Evening Post*'s deadlines for their serialization of the book. I sent a rough draft for Kennedy to read for any necessary corrections. Instead I received a call from the Ambassador. It was JFK's father, Joe Kennedy, chewing at me about my book saying, "I'm bored to death with it. Why do you have all these islands? Why do you have all those Japs in there?" He also said "Ted didn't like it, and neither did Jackie". It turned out that he was wrong on both counts. "The movie people will make duck soup of the PT 109 episode." I was real-

Naval Lt. John F. Kennedy with his ship, PT 109, 1943.

Courtesy of the John F. Kennedy Library

ly angry by this point and told him, "I don't give a damn about the movies." He replied, "That was why reporters never make any money." The picture was released in 1963.

To review for errors, I was able to show the galleys of the book to JFK and was amazed to see him scan hundreds of pages in some 30 minutes or less. He had mastered speed reading. He made some minor points but never challenged my account of the events in which he was involved. He did not mention it then, but later left me in no doubt that he liked the book.

During the Thanksgiving holiday, I was surprised to receive a call from the President telling me so. I asked him about his father's opinion and he replied, "Ask him yourself." Suddenly I was on the phone with Joe who told me, "Well, you have a great book. You did just what I told you and remembered the pace." This was a big change from Joe Kennedy's earlier tirade and it greatly amused me. If there was any credit to go around, he wanted a share of it.

One meeting I enjoyed with the President in the White House was in September1962. It was with the English-speaking native, Ben Kevu, who had saved the lives of Kennedy and his crew by carrying messages between Kennedy and the Australian coast watcher. Kevu was escorted to the White House meeting by former PT 109 crew member, Barney Ross. Since Ben was not used to Western clothes, he was quite a sight wearing a necktie hanging below his waist. The President showed Ben the coconut shell on his desk on which he had scratched the SOS message that the natives carried to Reginald Evans at his secret post on an island several miles away. Kennedy also gave Ben several PT 109 tie clasps for his children.

When I recall those exciting thousand days of the Kennedy presidency, I still remember him with deep fondness and respect. Perhaps the greatest tragedy of all was that President Kennedy was just hitting his stride when he was slain. I will always think of him as one hell of a guy.

Reverend Bob Davis, Parkland Hospital
As a young minister in residence in Dallas, Bob Davis had the

unique experience of not only consoling Mrs. Kennedy after the President's death, but a few days later also found himself repeating a similar role with the mother of Lee Harvey Oswald after he was shot in a Dallas jail. Ironically both Kennedy and Oswald were brought to the same hospital.

In November 22, 1963, I was a 25-year-old minister originally from a small town in the Texas panhandle, Hereford. I was completing my residency in clinical pastoral education at Parkland Hospital in Dallas. The hospital was the largest in Dallas and averaged several hundred emergency cases a day. In 1963 the hospital was segregated by race. There were separate but equal facilities for blacks and whites, even separate chapels, although church services were integrated.

On November 22, 1963, I was eating lunch in the hospital cafeteria with my boss, Dr. Ken Pepper, Director of the Department of Pastoral Care and Dr. James "Red" Duke, a resident in trauma services. We were joking about how we were missing out on all the excitement because of President Kennedy's visit and motorcade through the downtown to the Trade Mart.

Suddenly a series of emergency calls came over the loudspeaker. Dr. Duke immediately left, realizing something major must be taking place since so many staff were being summoned. Soon we learned that the President and Governor Connally had been shot and were in our emergency room. Ken and I were wanted there at once. In the corridor outside the entrance to the trauma area, I stopped for a moment and was startled to see the double doors suddenly open and a person come flying through the air bouncing off the wall beside me. It turned out it was an FBI agent who had just been ejected by a Secret Service agent because he lacked the proper ID. Clearly emotions were running very high.

I went inside and vividly remember seeing Mrs. Kennedy seated by herself outside the trauma room appearing in a state of shock. She was wearing a cranberry colored suit and hat and you could see the bloodstains on her lap. Ken Pepper tried to console Mrs. Kennedy. I spent my time with Mrs. Nellie Connally and later with a very upset Mrs. Evelyn Lincoln, the personal secretary to the President. I also tried to minister to the concerns of the student nurses and patients in the area. The African American patients were particularly upset because of their great love for the President. The patients were watching TV in the lounges and could see all the turmoil going on outside their hospital.

The grief of the patients took quite different forms, ranging from stunned disbelief that this can't be happening to being distraught and sobbing noisily. One series of incidents that irritated me was the efforts of some in the community, including clergymen, business people and doctors, to get into the hospital claiming they had business there when I believe they were only curiosity seekers. My personal reaction was that I really wished I wasn't even there and that none of this was actually happening. Because I was so tremendously busy during all of this, I had little time to think about my own emotions over the loss of the President, or that I was in the midst of a significant event.

One impression that remains with me was the graciousness of Mrs. Connally, who was a kind and gentle person. Even while she was greatly concerned over the status of her husband, Governor John Connally, whom she believed to be seriously wounded, she was extremely distressed over the President's death and the condition of Mrs. Kennedy. She displayed a great deal of composure amidst all the turmoil surrounding her. I found her to be a very impressive person. Another concern we had was that there might be some sort of conspiracy underway and that perhaps someone might still open fire in the hospital. Our security in those days was pretty minimal and we were relatively unprotected at the time.

That terrible day passed, but little did I know that only two days later, I would once again be summoned to duty in an ironic quirk of fate to minister to a family in distress. On Sunday, November 24, I was again called back in to help my supervisor, Ken Pepper, with the family of Lee Harvey Oswald. Oswald had been rushed to Parkland Hospital after he was shot. He died there a short time later. Ken was already with the family when I arrived to find Lee Harvey Oswald's wife, Marina; two little daughters; his mother, Marguerite Oswald, and his brother, Robert, in various stages of distress. Because of worries over their security, they were placed in a storeroom using stacks of canned goods to form a wall to provide a modicum of security and privacy. It was feared someone would attack the family. The scene was unreal, like something out of a novel or movie. Mrs. Marguerite Oswald kept demanding that her son be buried in Arlington National Cemetery because he had given his life for his country. She was very much out of control and ranting. Adding to the confusion, Robert received an emergency telephone call from his employer informing him that he had been fired. Marina was pretty quiet through all of this because of her difficulty with language, accentuated by all the stress she was undergoing. She was also busy caring for her daughters and was accompanied by baby bottles and a diaper bag. While we were trying to minister to the Oswalds, Ken and I were also busy trying to make arrangements for the Oswald funeral. Not surprisingly, it was not a popular task. We finally were able to make arrangements for the burial in Ft. Worth, Texas.

Despite any personal feelings I might have had about the alleged actions of Lee Harvey Oswald, I had the job to minister to the Oswalds for their loss as with any other family. Their grief was also very sad and heart-rendering. In some ways their grief was more complicated than the Kennedy family's because of the guilt and shame associated with Oswald's act.

From this weekend, I learned an important lesson. I was involved in two quite different, yet strikingly similar events. Both Mrs. Kennedy and the Oswalds were stricken with grief. Yet, somehow they were connected by a level of humanity, thus making grief very democratic.

Colonel James B. Swindal, Pilot, Air Force One

Colonel Swindal relates the events surrounding the flight to and from Dallas and the final flyover of Air Force One *saluting Kennedy at his funeral at Arlington National Cemetery.*

Although I made many flights as the pilot of *Air Force One*, none came even close to being as sad and traumatic as my last flight with

President Kennedy's body from Dallas to Andrews Air Force Base. I began my stint as the pilot of the flying White House, *Air Force One,* when Kennedy took office and flew every flight he took but one until the last.

Although ours was a professional relationship, I felt a certain kinship with the new President since we both served in World War II in the Pacific and were nearly the same age. He always called me Captain, a carryover from his Navy days. Since I was a native of Alabama, we definitely had different accents. One of his staff kidded him about how he ended up with a pilot from Alabama and he responded, "I don't care where he comes from if he can fly the plane." During our nearly three years flying together, I grew to like and respect both President and Mrs. Kennedy, as did the rest of the crew. We found them to be friendly and easy to get along with. In fact, we often thought of President and Mrs. Kennedy as an American version of royalty because of the great reception they received on overseas trips.

President Kennedy congratulates James Swindal on his promotion to Colonel.

Courtesy of the John F. Kennedy Library

When we flew to Texas on November 21, I was aware of some apprehension on the part of the Kennedy staff over what kind of reception the President would receive because of a recent incident involving Adlai Stevenson. In Fort Worth, the President and Mrs. Kennedy were greeted by such a warm and enthusiastic crowd that everyone seemed to relax at that point. When we landed at Love Field on a lovely day in Dallas, another large, happy and lively throng greeted us there as well.

While the Presidential motorcade went on its way, I remained on the plane checking on details concerning our next flight to Austin, Texas. *Air Force One* had a sophisticated communications system on board and we kept constant radio contact with the President's party. I was halfway listening to the Secret Service agents chattering on the radio when I suddenly heard the voice of Roy Kellerman, the Secret Service agent riding with JFK, shouting. This was followed by other very disturbed voices. One said: "Dagger cover Volunteer," referring to the code name for the agent guarding LBJ, the Vice President. Then the voices became incoherent and the radio went dead.

At this point I was baffled. I knew something had really gone wrong, but had no way of knowing what. Soon we received a frantic call from Parkland Hospital. I was told to make preparations to fly back to Washington while dropping the Austin visit. This puzzled me, but I soon learned he had been shot.

Those of us on the plane circled the TV set and watched in a state of stunned shock. When the rest of our crew returned, we learned the President was dead. I think all of us felt like we had been hit by a sledgehammer. For a very brief time, we were like zombies, but then we knew we had serious work to do. Shaking off our personal feelings, we rushed into action to get ready to leave.

We still didn't know who was coming when. Then two cars escorted by motorcycle police came tearing up carrying Vice-President Johnson, his wife, Lady Bird, several Secret Service agents and others. The shades of the plane were pulled shut in case a sniper was lurking nearby.

Upon learning that President Kennedy's body would go back with us, we frantically yanked out several passenger seats to make room for the casket, rather than place it in the cargo hold. We barely made it before the hearse arrived, and we struggled to get the heavy bronze casket into the plane. I then thought we were ready to go and had one engine started when I received word to stop. We had to wait briefly for Judge Sarah Hughes to come on board to swear in Lyndon Johnson as the new President. There was some confusion amidst the mixed crowd of Kennedy and Johnson people, grief-stricken, dazed, and unsure of almost everything.

Despite later reports of open hostility between the staffs of JFK and LBJ, I observed no such problem. If such emotions existed, they were well hidden. I walked up and down the plane and spoke to everyone. I saw no signs of hard feelings. We all were hurt, but I believe accounts of open enmity between the staffs were greatly exaggerated.

The brief swearing-in of Johnson as the new President took place in a crowded, hot, small room. Watching from the cabin doorway, I knew I was witnessing a great moment in history, but still didn't realize the impact of what I was viewing.

As we prepared to take off, I faced a momentary crisis that could have been a potential nightmare under the circumstances. The plane was so heavily loaded with fuel and added passengers that I was slightly concerned over our takeoff. As we taxied out, we hit a soft area on the taxiway. The plane began to sink a little, and it took all the power we had to pull us through a small sinkhole. All we needed at that point would be to return to unload.

We had an uneventful flight back. A day or so before the funeral, I received a call from General McHugh, Kennedy's Air Force aide. Mrs. Kennedy had requested that *Air Force One* be part of the burial ceremony. It was decided that we would fly over Arlington Cemetery just before the President's burial.

On Monday, with a full crew aboard, we left Andrews Air Force Base and made our last flight for JFK. All the crew wanted to come along as their contribution to honor their late Commander in Chief. As we flew low over the cemetery, I could see all the people gathered below. During our flyby, I dipped the wings of *Air Force One* as a salute and last farewell to our fallen President. I was told later by those on

LBJ being sworn in as President by Judge Sarah Hughes.

the ground that it was a moving sight to see the beautiful plane offering tribute.

  Reflecting back on my experiences with President Kennedy, I only regret he didn't have more time in office. I thought he was doing a great job as President and respected and admired him professionally and personally.

Chapter Two

Reaction in Washington

Washington area residents and officials were staggered by the President's death. Members of the U.S. Senate, including J. William Fulbright, Barry Goldwater, George Smathers, and Margaret Chase Smith offer their memories in this chapter. Fulbright warned Kennedy, "Dallas is a dangerous place," and told him, "Don't you go." Senator Smith offered her last remembrance for the fallen President: a red rose, a flower always associated with her. Jeane Dixon made her most famous prophecy as she tried to no avail to get the White House to listen to her fears for the President's life. Dick Scammon recalls in his account his final visit with JFK. The last words he heard from JFK were, "Gentlemen, I will see you when I get back from Dallas."

Several personal friends of the President were out of town that Friday, November 22. Paul "Red" Fay, then acting Secretary of the Navy, shares his first meeting with JFK in 1942. Senator George Smathers also tells us that Kennedy was bothered over his upcoming Texas visit, saying to Smathers, "God, I wish I didn't have to go to Dallas." Secretary of Agriculture, Orville L. Freeman recalls the long return trip from the Pacific with several others from the President's cabinet. George Reedy, Special Assistant to Vice-President Lyndon Johnson, offers a perspective from that of a Johnson staffer placed in an awkward position during the turmoil of the presidential transition. Then Representative Gerald Ford shares his memories of JFK and offers his thoughts on his work with the Warren Commission investigating the President's assassination.

Courtesy of the John F. Kennedy Library

President Kennedy and Senator Barry Goldwater at a ceremony in the White House Rose Garden, 1963.

Barry M. Goldwater, U.S. Senator

At the time of Kennedy's assassination, the late Senator Goldwater was the leading candidate for the Republican presidential nomination.

My relationship with John F. Kennedy meant a great deal to me. I think my respect and friendship for Jack were reciprocated by him. Even though we disagreed in political philosophy, on a one-to-one basis, we were friendly adversaries.

I first met Jack at the end of World War II when he was recuperating from wartime back injuries at a ranch near Benson, Arizona. A friend of mine invited me down to meet him and we had a cordial visit together. Little did I know then, that in January 1953, we would begin serving together in the United States Senate. We were both assigned to the Labor Committee and got to know each other quite well over the next several years.

When Jack was President, he often invited me to the White House to seek my opinion on issues, such as the Bay of Pigs incident. He, of course, would not always take my advice. Although I think Kennedy made some mistakes as President, as we all do, by 1963 he was looking forward to the 1964 presidential campaign. Since he thought I was the likely candidate to oppose him, he discussed with me the possibility of the two of us campaigning together. Our plan was to fly to a city where each of us would present our policy views to the public, taking turns on going first at each stop. We would take the campaign to the American people focusing on the big issues, rather than trivial distractions as is so often the case. We both thought this proposal would greatly improve presidential campaigns in our country. I still think such an approach was badly needed then and is even more needed today.

I learned President Kennedy was shot while on my way to Muncie, Indiana, for my mother-in-law's funeral. By the time our plane arrived in Muncie, the President was dead. I was shocked by the news but unable to leave for Washington until my wife's mother was buried. Unfortunately Walter Cronkite reported on the "CBS Evening News" that I was giving a political speech in Indiana and wouldn't attend the services for President Kennedy. I called Cronkite and told him what I thought of his completely inaccurate account. Later he apologized on his show. I was so dispirited with the media and the events surrounding Kennedy's death, I concluded at that point I wasn't going to run for President. Of course, I later changed my mind.

When I think back on my relationship with Jack Kennedy, I recall him as a witty, charming, and very intelligent man. He would sop up information like a sponge. A few minutes after coming into a committee meeting, he would sound as if he knew the subject intimately. There is no doubt that Jack Kennedy loved his country, and our mutual patriotism drew us together. Politically, Kennedy saw politics as a kind of game like touch football and he always wanted to win. I also think he was far more conservative than people thought. He told me several times that it was his father's influence that made him a little bit conservative.

As a Republican and a conservative, I thought John F. Kennedy made a hell of a good President. As his friend, I still remember him as a hell of a good man, and I think people all over the world viewed him the same way. His death was a great loss to us all.

J. William Fulbright, U. S. Senator

The late Senator Fulbright worked closely with Kennedy as a fellow Senator and took special interest in Kennedy's role in international affairs as Fulbright was Chairman of the Senate Foreign Relations Committee.

That Friday, I was in the F Street Club just finishing lunch with Gene Black, former head of the World Bank. While we were drinking coffee a man came in and blurted out that the President had been shot in Dallas. A nearby friend recalled that I threw down my napkin, jumped to my feet and shouted, "God damn it! I told him not to go to

President Kennedy and to the left, Senator William Fulbright, 1963.

Dallas." Only a few days earlier, I had traveled with President Kennedy to Little Rock and then Heber Springs, Arkansas, to dedicate a dam. I warned him then that "Dallas is a dangerous place" and that, "I wouldn't go there." I told him, "Don't you go." Arkansas borders Texas, and when I ran for reelection to the Senate in 1962, I was the target of scathing attacks by the *Dallas News* because I was considered to be a liberal. In retrospect, I probably had a kind of childish prejudice about Texas from my background that included playing football there as a student from the University of Arkansas. From my youth I still carried this image of Texas as an assertive and vainglorious state.

My earlier association with Senator Kennedy as a fellow member of the Foreign Relations Committee left me concerned about him as a presidential candidate in 1960. When I became Committee Chairman in 1959, I found Kennedy, as a junior member of the committee, to be an inactive participant with a poor attendance record. He really was heavily involved in running for the presidency and made his priority the Senate racket hearings that were widely covered by the press. I was an admirer and supporter of Governor Adlai Stevenson and would have been pleased to have him as a candidate again in 1960. However, when Kennedy received the nomination, I campaigned hard for him and was very impressed by the way he conducted himself throughout the campaign. I was delighted when he won because I believed Congress and the new President would work together in union and we could make progress on all fronts

One of the highlights for me during the Kennedy administration was that I was able to help the President obtain ratification of the Test Ban Treaty as floor leader for the treaty's approval. By a vote to 80-19, the Senate consented to the ratification of the treaty on September 24, 1963. I agreed with the President that this was an important step in lessening world conflict.

In retrospect, there was one piece of advice I gave the President that went unheeded. It was something he should have listened to more thoroughly. I was not privy to the early planning for the Bay of Pigs invasion. At the last minute, I learned of it and wrote a strong memo to the President urging him to abort the invasion. When I hitched a ride to Palm Beach with the President in his plane, I gave the memo to him to read during the trip. He read it without comment and the topic was dropped. When we returned to Washington, I was asked by the President to attend a small and informal meeting of top officials to review the final details for the Bay of Pigs. After several spoke forcefully on behalf of the invasion, including Allan Dulles, head of the CIA, I denounced the project in no uncertain terms. I lost the argument. However, a few days later after the unfortunate event was over, the President told me, "Well, you're the only one who can say I told you so."

One of Kennedy's best qualities was his flexibility and ability to learn from his mistakes, such as the Bay of Pigs disaster. I had high hopes by the time of his death that he would try to make peace with the Soviets and lessen the chance for a nuclear war. He was very bright and learned quickly. His image of youth and energy created expectation worldwide that we were beginning a new day. He was beginning to fulfill the great promise I saw in him when he was struck down. As a person, I liked him and got along well with him. He was very approachable and had an unusual way with people, showing them courtesy regardless of their standing in life. As I observed him in meetings with representatives of other nations, I found him to have a sensitivity to foreign people that I have not observed in any other President. I think he conveyed to people that we in the United States were a civilized people and that he was a civilized man. Looking back at his brief years in office, I was very proud of the way he represented our country.

Jeane Dixon, Psychic and Columnist

Probably no stranger story relating to the Kennedy assassination can be found than that of the psychic forecast of the late Jeane Dixon. Her prediction of Kennedy's death, ignored at the time, turned out to be only too true.

Over my lifetime I have had many psychic visions, but none received more publicity than one I had in 1952. In that year, when I began my morning meditations in St. Matthew's Cathedral and began to kneel in prayer, a vivid image of the White House appeared before my eyes with the numbers 1960 formed about it. As I watched, a darkness drifted over the White House and a person standing in front of it. This figure was a tall, young man with bushy brown hair and blue eyes. I then heard an inner voice telling me that the man was a Democrat who would be elected President in 1960 and would be assassinated while in office. The entire vision was like watching a motion picture. Later I realized the person I had seen was John F. Kennedy.

From that point on I continued to see a dark cloud hanging over the White House and I told many people that my vision would come to pass. I later saw the name Oswald associated with Kennedy's death. By the fall of 1963, my apprehension over the President's life continued to deepen. Friends noticed my obvious discomfort. Several used their contacts with the administration to attempt to warn the President of my fears and to take them seriously. My most direct effort to warn the President was made to Kay Halle, an intimate family friend of the Kennedy family for some 50 years, as well as to the Churchills. I visited Kay's Georgetown home while she was having lunch with Mrs. Alice Roosevelt Longworth and I told her, "You're a close friend of the Kennedys and you've got to tell the President that he must not go to Dallas. If he goes, it's going to be fatal." Kay responded, "Well if it's predestined, why tell me such a thing?" She went on to comment that President Kennedy was a "very brave man" and wouldn't listen to this kind of thing. If anything, it would challenge him to go there. She promised to get word to the President of my grave concerns, but apparently my warnings went unheeded.

On November 22, I was having lunch in the presidential dining room in the Mayflower Hotel. I still remember how upset I was as we began lunch because I knew something dreadful was going to happen to the President that day in Dallas. Suddenly the orchestra stopped playing during lunch and the conductor came to our table and told us the President had been shot. I told him the President was dead. Despite his reassurances to the contrary, I was sure President Kennedy had died. Unfortunately, I was correct. Ironically, the day Kennedy was killed, Mrs. Longworth was the one who called Kay Halle and told her," what Jeane Dixon told me has happened." By then they were believers, but it was too late.

Looking back at John Kennedy's brief years in the presidency, I believe his greatest contribution was to be able to kindle a desire to serve in the hearts of his fellow Americans rather than pursue personal gain. There was something about this youthful and vital man that caused you to care about him. He gave people everywhere self-confidence and inspired them to do better than they thought they could. I admired both President and Mrs. Kennedy and I still miss him today.

Richard M. Scammon, Director, Bureau of the Census

The late Dick Scammon was considered the nation's leading authority on voting demographics. His opinion on political affairs was highly regarded by the White House.

That fateful Friday in November was just another normal working day at the Census Bureau until an office worker rushed in with the news that the President had been shot. We immediately gathered around the radio and soon learned that the President was dead. That evening my wife and I, although we are Unitarians, went to a Catholic church and said a prayer for the President and felt better for it.

I had been appointed Director of the Census Bureau by Kennedy in 1961. It really was not a true political appointment. Rather, the choice was based on my work in election research and statistics. My last contact with the President was ten days before his death. It was held in the White House cabinet room and was the only meeting that Kennedy held on presidential politics looking forward to 1964. Of the ten or so people there, I was the only nonpolitical newcomer to the group because I was a specialist on elections. All the top Kennedy political advisors were there, including Larry O'Brien, Ken O'Donnell, Robert Kennedy, Stephen Smith and John Bailey. Vice President Johnson was not in attendance.

Everyone was upbeat in the meeting. The group was almost

euphoric in their optimism over the prospects for winning in 1964. This was in sharp contrast to the gloom-and-doom attitude of the same politicians prior to the 1960 fall campaign. The main topic on the meeting agenda was to discuss what to do about the South. The President seemed to favor an idea of John Bailey's, with which I agreed, to slowly reduce the power of the South in the national Democratic Convention in 1964. We also discussed ways to enliven the upcoming convention since there would be little drama concerning who would be the candidates. I still remember the last thing the President told us as our meeting of several hours concluded, "Gentlemen, I will see you when I get back from Dallas."

Looking back at the Kennedy years, I believe he showed great promise in his brief administration. If he had been reelected, as I believe he would have been, he likely would have been one of our great Presidents. I looked forward to his next term with high expectations. Kennedy was very smart and grasped complex ideas rapidly. He often "got the point" before the person making it was done. In his first administration he was building a sense of respect for his leadership, both in the United States and throughout the world.

I held the President in high regard both personally and professionally and deplored seeing his promising career of brightness snuffed out just as his work was reaching a point of fruition. Finally, John F. Kennedy will always be remembered as the first Roman Catholic to be elected President, thus ending one of the great taboos in presidential politics and helping to open the gateway for people of other religions and races to enter presidential politics.

Gerald R. Ford, U.S. House of Representatives
Ford later became President of the United States and is the only living member of the Warren Commission.

The death of John F. Kennedy hit me hard. We had become very good friends over the years going back to 1949 when I arrived as a new member of the House, two years after Jack's election. We had several common interests, including Navy service in World War II. I was

Courtesy of the Gerald Ford Library

Warren Commission Chairman, Chief Justice Earl Warren presents President Johnson with the Commission report; Gerald Ford, second left of Johnson, September 24, 1964.

assigned an office right across the hall from Kennedy. Another new member was also in a nearby office, Lloyd Bentsen of Texas. The three of us became comrades as together we often walked back and forth from our offices to the House floor. That four-year affable companionship in the House developed into a solid friendship that lasted until Kennedy's assassination. Over the years, Mrs. Ford had gotten to know both of the Kennedys, and they were very nice to us. On several occasions we had gotten together with the President, including dinners at the White House and trips down the river on the presidential yacht.

On November 22, 1963, Betty and I were driving back from a meeting with a son's high school guidance counselor when we heard on our car radio that the President had been shot. In a state of disbelief I rushed to my office to find out more details. Of course, I soon learned that I had lost my President and friend. We attended all the ceremonies of that tragic weekend, which still stands out as vividly as Pearl Harbor on December 7, 1941.

A few days later, I received a phone call at home from President Lyndon B. Johnson asking me to be a member of a bipartisan blue-ribbon committee to investigate the President's assassination. I was to be one of two members from the House, with Democrat Hale Boggs as the other. Chief Justice Earl Warren would serve as chairman. I told Johnson I would be honored to serve even though I was hard pressed for time.

In my service on that commission, I listened to testimony from dozens of witnesses and even flew to Dallas where we interviewed Jack Ruby, who killed Oswald. It was a very eerie feeling to study the death of a personal friend.

Today, I still adhere strongly to the commission's critical findings. First: Lee Harvey Oswald was the assassin, period. Second: the commission found no evidence of a conspiracy, foreign or domestic. All of the critics, including Oliver Stone, director of the movie, *JFK,* have not come up with one scintilla of new, credible evidence. They have hashed and rehashed commission-developed evidence and have wildly speculated based on unfounded rumors. Conclusions, such as those in *JFK,* are in my opinion misinterpretations, half-truths and fraud. I believe these efforts badly misled the American people.

Looking back at my personal contacts with Jack Kennedy, right from the outset, I liked him. He was a very attractive, friendly young man with a nice smile. As we got better acquainted as neighbors in the House Office Building, we enjoyed talking about differences on legislation as we walked to and from the House floor. His staff and my staff became very good friends and I was very impressed with the high quality of the people he had working for him. As a House member, he became a prominent member of the Education and Labor Committee. One thing I recall that was somewhat unusual was his active interest and participation on the District of Columbia Committee, not considered a very prestigious committee assignment. To my surprise, he got caught up in controversial issues, such as home rule, when clearly there was no personal benefit for him in such duty.

However, he really seemed to enjoy this work.

When Kennedy became President, I still maintained my friendship with him and was very supportive of his efforts to maintain foreign aid, particularly military aid for U.S. allies. Kennedy's Aid Program by the fall of 1961 was in real trouble, being opposed by a coalition of Democratic and Republican conservatives who wanted to reduce aid, not increase it. I had been elected to Congress in 1948 on a platform supporting Truman and the Marshall Plan and continued my support of Eisenhower's NATO policies. Because Kennedy knew my views on internationalism, he called me to give him a hand. On several occasions, I met with him in the White House to be briefed on helping him with his efforts on the Hill to continue these policies. I was able to persuade a number of moderate Republicans to join liberal Democrats in passing his Aid Bill. By the narrow margin of three votes, we succeeded.

Looking back at the brief Kennedy years, he brought a new look to Washington—cut from a much different mold than that of Eisenhower, Truman, and Roosevelt. He came from a different generation than his predecessors. He acted and talked like one of the new breed with a great personality. My impression of him as President was that he preferred the public side of the job but didn't care as much for many of the day-to-day details of the office. By the time Kennedy went to Texas, there was a growing feeling among the Republicans that he could be defeated in the reelection campaign of 1964, if the right candidate was offered. Of course, we will never know. One thing is very certain: I lost a valued and good friend with the death of John F. Kennedy and one that I still miss today.

George A. Smathers, U. S. Senator
Smathers was a close personal friend of the President for a number of years.

A short time before President Kennedy made his trip to Dallas, he vacationed in Palm Beach, Florida. On his return trip he gave me a ride back to Washington with him on *Air Force One*. While on the flight, he asked me to chat with him a while. He was bothered and told me, "God, I wish I didn't have to go to Dallas." He knew though that there was no way he could get out of it because it was a big occasion for Lyndon. He was also fretting over the protocol of meeting in Dallas with the various feuding elements in Texas Democratic politics. He was even concerned over who Jackie would ride with in the Dallas motorcade. Lyndon wanted her to ride with Lady Bird. I remember Jack saying, "I don't have a good feeling about this trip."

A few days later I was sitting in the copilot seat flying to Sea Island, Georgia, from Jacksonville in a small private airplane. The pilot was suddenly very disturbed, pulled off his radio headphones and said, "Put these on, Senator. I just heard some disturbing news." Placing the earphones on my head, I learned that President Kennedy had been shot. We immediately turned the plane around and headed back to Jacksonville while remaining glued to the radio. We soon learned the President was dead.

When I arrived at the Jacksonville airport, I found a crowd of some 200 to 300 people gathered in a lounge around a TV. Seeing and recognizing me, several people cleared a path for me to the television set. People were crying in the crowd, and I did a little bit too. I arranged a private plane to fly back to Washington and arrived there Friday evening. That night, I waited with the family and friends at Andrews Air Force base in a state of shock. Except for some sad moments involving my own family, this was the saddest moment up to that point in my life. We tried to console the family. I remember hugging Eunice Shriver, the President's sister, and commiserating with her and others. None of us really knew what to do or what to say. Of course, I attended the well-known ceremonies of that gloomy weekend.

I had the great pleasure of knowing Jack Kennedy since we both arrived in Congress together in January 1947 as new members of the House of Representatives. He was certainly an unimposing figure when I first met him. He was very thin, sickly and hardly able to walk. Of the members of that freshman class in Congress, I probably would have, at first glance, picked Jack as the least likely to succeed. Over the years we became the best of friends and remained so until his death.

One of my favorite memories of him was his lack of consciousness about money. Early on as Congressmen, we traveled together on several trips in the United States and one to Europe. I soon learned that he would frequently go on a trip without a single cent in his pocket. He really seemed unaware that somebody had to pay bills along the way. I remember often asking him if he had any money, and he would fumble in his shirt pocket but almost always failed to find anything. Once in a while, he might discover a crumpled $20 bill in his watch pocket and, if he found such money, he seemed surprised as anyone else over the discovery.

I got to know Jack's father, Joe, pretty well. He once asked me as Jack's friend to talk to him about shaping up his handling of his finances. Finally I worked out a system that, when I traveled with Jack, I would pay all the bills. Then I would show them to him and he in turn would see to it that his secretary, Evelyn Lincoln, would get my share back.

In November of 1950, I was elected to the Senate from Florida, but the big race was beating Claude Pepper in the May primary. Since Claude was considered invincible up to that point, I think my win encouraged Jack later in November to take on Cabot Lodge in Massachusetts. Lodge was very well regarded in the state and throughout the country. He would be tough to beat. Jack seemed very interested in my race, and he and his father followed it closely. Later we talked a great deal about my campaign including organizational details. Of course Jack went on to an upset win over Lodge in 1952 bucking an Eisenhower landslide nationally.

Jack and I had many great times together. I was pleased to be an usher at his wedding in 1953 to Jackie. I liked him, and I think he liked me very much as well. Even when I opposed him politically, we got along. One event of some disagreement between us was Jack's presidential race in 1960. In 1956 at the Democratic Convention held in Chicago, I made one of the two vice-presidential seconding speeches for Jack. Of course, he narrowly lost. However, by 1960, he was clearly a major candidate for President. He badly wanted me to help him get delegates in Florida, but I also was a close friend of Lyndon Johnson. For the sake of maintaining Democratic unity in Florida, I ran as a favorite son and received 29 votes in the Los Angeles Nominating Convention.

Early that year, Jack was really after me for my support for him as President. One morning, he met with me and pulled out every stop to convince me to support him, including reminders that I was his best friend and an usher at his wedding. I finally told him I was going to run and the only way for him to get Florida's votes on the first ballot was for him to beat me. He was really furious with me, and I sadly returned to my office. A little later he asked me to meet with him and at that time pulled out a big sheet of figures. It was a poll arranged by his father in Florida that showed I would have easily beaten him there. By this time he was laughing and really wasn't mad. I promised him that, after the first ballot at the Democratic Convention, I would withdraw from the race and support him.

For 16 years, Jack and I were good friends. I probably remember him best for his marvelous sense of humor and great sensitivity to others. He always seemed aware of who was happy or unhappy. I never saw him do an unkind thing, except when he intended to do it and had thought about it. Of course he was very bright and constantly growing and seeking new ideas. He always was totally realistic and never kidded himself. He was candid in his self-appraisal as anyone could be.

Looking back, I think he looked on me as just a hell of a good, loyal friend. Even today I find it difficult to talk about his death. As a guy, he was sweet and such a terrific person, not in terms as President but as a fellow human being. I will always miss him!

Ken Hechler, U.S. House of Representatives
Hechler recalls the President's good sense of humor and how well JFK was regarded in South America.

When I reflect back on my experiences with John F. Kennedy, many pleasurable images flood my memory. In particular, I always enjoyed Kennedy's terrific sense of humor. One summer day I was attending one of his frequent news conferences, which he thoroughly enjoyed. A reporter asked him in an angry tone: "Mr. President, the Republican National Committee has just passed a resolution stating that you and your administration are a complete failure. What do you have to say about that?" Now the average politician would have reacted defensively, naming his accomplishments. Kennedy just gazed very coolly at his questioner and right away shot back: "I assume it passed unanimously."

On that fateful November day in 1963, I was in Huntington, West Virginia, pounding out a speech on my typewriter I was scheduled to deliver several hours hence at a Democratic rally. I chose Kennedy as my subject. I had just typed out "He knows more about the past than most of his predecessors did, yet he keys every decision to the way it will affect the future of the nation and the world." For some strange reason, I flipped on the television set in my office, and the tragic events in Dallas were just unfolding. My speech was canceled, and I returned from West Virginia to Washington, D.C.

While teaching political science at Princeton University in 1947, I brought a group of my students to the nation's capital. Having recently read about the freshman Congressman from Massachusetts, we all thought it would be informative to interview him. Both the students and I came away with a poor impression. He seemed to take a casual and dilettantish approach to serious problems. When I next saw him at close range at the Democratic National Convention in Chicago in 1956, what struck me was the rapid growth of his intellectual powers. His gracious concession address, after losing a close race for the vice-presidential nomination, persuaded many delegates that he was clearly presidential timber for 1960.

Kennedy did a masterful job winning the 1960 presidential primary against Senator Hubert Humphrey in West Virginia. While serving in the House of Representatives, I was inspired by his leadership. My support of his program was so high that one newspaper dubbed me the "Daniel Boone of the New Frontier."

Shortly after his assassination, I was dispatched to South America

to inspect our space-tracking stations and other scientific facilities on
that continent. What impressed me were the long lines of poor peasants traveling toward their country's capital cities. In most cases, their
clothes were in tatters, and their possessions were piled high on carts
and wagons. Most of them explained to me that they were traveling to
find the American embassy, so they could sign the type of book which
funeral homes provide, to express their sympathy for President
Kennedy. "What did President Kennedy ever do for you?" I asked.
The answers were very similar: "He brought us hope for the future,
and gave us a sense of our dignity and worth."

Orville L. Freeman, U. S. Secretary of Agriculture

*Secretary Freeman relates the harrowing return flight from the
Pacific to Washington by several cabinet members after the death of the
President.*

My wife, Jane, and I were eating our breakfast on our way with
most of the President's cabinet on a flight to Tokyo from Honolulu.
On board were the Secretary of State Dean Rusk, Commerce's Luther
Hodges, Labor's Willard Wirtz, Stewart Udall of Interior, and Douglas
Dillon of the Treasury. Also with us was the presidential press secretary, Pierre Salinger, and several other officials. Our goal for the trip
was to meet with our Japanese counterparts and begin the effort to
restore America's prestige in Japan, paving the way for a later visit by
President Kennedy in 1964.

We were one hour out of Honolulu with eight hours to go when
I was asked to abruptly stop eating and come at once to see the
Secretary of State. We had only been flying an hour or so. I said, "Tell
him I will be there when I finish my breakfast." I was told to come at
once, and I couldn't imagine what could be so urgent on such a long
flight.

Dean Rusk was white as a sheet as he told me, "The President has
been shot." I asked "where" and he said, "in the head." I responded
that I had been shot in the head as a marine in combat in the Pacific
and maybe he would be all right. The news was a real "stunner." We

were all overwhelmed and perplexed as to what we should do next. We really had no information and communication beyond the initial brief news item. A little later, Dean Rusk's voice came over the plane's intercom, "The President is dead; God bless our country." We then turned back to refuel at Honolulu and returned on a long and gloomy trip to Washington.

During our trip back, my wife Jane sadly commented that she was deeply sorry for Jackie but was also "so glad I had not been chosen Vice President at the Los Angeles convention even though it was selfish of her." Later at a private moment with President Lyndon Johnson at Camp David, he asked me "Did I know who JFK would have named as Vice President if I didn't take it?" I said, "I don't know," and Johnson said, "You would have been his choice because I asked him and he told me."

Several of us during the trip scribbled notes, and I wrote, "What an incredible unbelievable tragedy." The return ride was unreal. None of us really knew what to do with ourselves. Pierre Salinger, who was probably closest to the President, organized a poker game in which several joined, but no one seemed to clearly focus upon this unhappy game. I spent some time soberly speculating with others as to what kind of President Lyndon Johnson would make. I knew him better than the rest of our group, and so my views were solicited. I reassured them that in my judgment, Johnson would be a strong leader and would carry forward the dead President's program aggressively. We were informed while on the flight that we would have a cabinet meeting the next morning at eight o'clock with the new President. We arrived in Washington around 12:30 A.M. Saturday morning, some 24 hours after our plane left from Honolulu to Tokyo. It seemed as if the trip lasted an eternity. When we arrived, Dean Rusk as ranking member of the cabinet, made a brief statement as we left the plane. Then my wife and I headed home to watch television

As I reflect back on my personal relationship with Jack Kennedy, I recall when I first met him at a 1955 Jackson Day Democratic Dinner held in Minneapolis when I was Governor of Minnesota. At that meeting, he really didn't make much of an impression on the crowd. He was very low key in speaking style and tended to understate his remarks. He seemed rather pallid compared with the dramatic oratory of Senator Hubert Humphrey who also spoke. Little did I anticipate the rapid rise to power and the growth and development of John F. Kennedy as a senator, presidential candidate, and President. I had the honor and pleasure to nominate Senator Kennedy at the 1960 Democratic Convention in Los Angeles. As I travel around the world, people everywhere, knowing my relationship with him, still ask me about him. Working under him as Secretary of Agriculture, I got to see firsthand what an outstanding leader and chief executive he became. It was impressive to see him in action, particularly when considering that he had never had any management or executive experience in his career. He inspired the whole country and the world with his unusual talents.

The President was smart, always available, knew what was going on, how to delegate and was easy to work for. He was really a joy to be with and I thought a lot of him. President Kennedy will always have a special place in the hearts of the people of our nation and the world.

Margaret Chase Smith, U. S. Senator

Most people are unaware that the late Senator Smith was seriously considering a run for the presidency when President Kennedy was assassinated. She remembered JFK with her favorite symbol, a rose.

By late November 1963, I was reaching an important crossroads in my political career. At that point, I was considering a possible candidacy for the presidency in 1964, taking on fellow Republicans, Senator Barry Goldwater and Governor Nelson Rockefeller among others.

I never felt I knew President Kennedy very well in the Senate even though we were on a committee together. This view changed in October 1963 when I accompanied him to the University of Maine where he received an honorary degree. It was after that October visit that I remarked I thought he was "getting ready to be President."

President Kennedy and Senator Margaret Chase Smith waiving as they prepare to embark on a flight on Air Force One from Maine to Washington, October 20, 1963.

At the time of the Kennedy tragedy, I was in my Senate office in the midst of a filming session with an NBC television crew. NBC had planned a program on my possible presidential candidacy in 1964. I told my staff not to interrupt us for any reason and I was not pleased initially when my executive assistant, Bill Lewis, stepped in my office. However, when he told us the terrible news about President Kennedy, I understood the urgency. We were all shocked, and the NBC crew packed up and ended the filming session at once. Bill canceled all of my public appearance commitments (the most immediate being the Air War College, NBC "Today," The Women's National Press Club, and the Jack Paar program) in deference to the President's death.

On Monday, the day of the funeral, we gathered in the Senate chamber before a full press galley prior to the eulogies to be given in the Capitol rotunda. I debated what to wear on the occasion and chose brown as a somber color. Mike Mansfield, Senator Majority Leader, spotted me and asked me where was my rose? This was the rare occasion where I chose not to wear one. He suggested that I place a rose on President Kennedy's former Senate desk. Liking the idea, I ran back to my office, got a red rose, darted back and placed the rose on his old desk in the back of the room. I then joined the rest of the Senate in participating in the funeral activities for the day.

Following these tragic events, I continued to speak out against the regrettable hatred and bigotry that was known to us and was not aimed solely at President Kennedy, but had been going on for many years and against many people. I also pledged my support to my very close friend, the new President Lyndon B. Johnson. We had both entered the Senate together in 1948 and served together on the same committees more than anyone else in Congress.

Paul B. "Red" Fay, Jr., Under Secretary of the Navy
Fay was a longtime friend, going back to his shared experiences with JFK in the Navy. He also argues that Kennedy would have not continued expanding the war in Vietnam if he had lived.

On November 22, 1963, I was visiting Bremerton Naval Shipyard near Seattle, Washington. My assignment was to convince the leader-men that they had to increase productivity if they wanted to continue receiving naval shipbuilding business. A commander came up to me and said, "Mr. Fay, I think the President has been shot." I replied, "What do you mean you think the President has been shot? You either know or you don't know." Then I heard that John Connally was in the operating room and the President was outside. I figured that if he was outside, he was probably all right. I then spoke to the shipyard leader-men. After I went over to the admiral's house, I learned the tragic news by television.

I immediately returned to my parent's home in San Francisco and then with my wife Anita and daughter Sally caught a flight to Washington. Upon arrival we went directly to the White House. We were all devastated. Sally was particularly upset and felt lost because JFK was her godfather.

Rather than dwelling on those most dreadful hours, I like to think back to all those happy and marvelous times I had with Jack Kennedy. I remember when I first met him in early November 1942. I was in naval torpedo boat officer training at Melville Center in Rhode Island. In our free time, several of us decided to play touch football. While we were playing, a skinny looking kid came up and asked if he could play. He was wearing a sweater inside out with an H showing through, which I assumed was his local high school. We told him he could play if he could locate another player to balance out the sides in the game. I really was happy to unload the kid onto the other team. I soon learned that was a mistake because the skinny kid played opposite me and gave me all the trouble I could handle. The next morning when I reported for a class in boat handling, I discovered that the same skinny kid was the instructor named John F. Kennedy. Later we became very close friends while serving together in PT boats in the South Pacific.

During the time I spent with Jack Kennedy in the service, I became convinced of his potential greatness and even believed it quite possible he would someday become President of the United States. Other close friends at the time also held this view.

When Senator Kennedy ran for President, I worked actively in his campaign and when he took office, I became Under Secretary and then Acting Secretary of the Navy. For those wonderful 1,000 days JFK was in office, our families became close friends.

I have many fond memories of Jack Kennedy as we shared numerous happy moments together. JFK was an exceptional man. He had a tremendous personality, marvelous sense of humor and was very, very bright. He had the ability to separate himself in making a decision from what was best for the country versus what was best for JFK and then would act on behalf of his country. He also had tremendous ability in getting the most out of peoples' talent. He would focus on the greatest strengths of a person and motivate them to achieve more than they ever knew was possible. He certainly did that for me. Everybody around him sensed that Kennedy really cared about people as individuals and drew the best from them. These same great qualities of Kennedy also were demonstrated worldwide. It seems people everywhere had their hopes raised by their perception that Kennedy cared for people from all walks of life in all parts of the globe.

One area of controversy that I well recall is the United States' role in Vietnam. I have no doubts that the Vietnam War would not have taken place if Kennedy had lived. I was on his yacht, the *Honey Fitz,* when he received a call from a military adviser in Vietnam wanting to get more involved in fighting. In no uncertain terms, I heard JFK tell the leaders, "For every man that gets involved in an ambush there, I will remove him and a like number. If 20 go in there, I will bring 40 out." He made it indelibly clear that we were out there as advisors and not to lead an attack.

Looking back at those wonderful days, I will always think of Jack Kennedy, my friend, as well as John F. Kennedy, my President. Young people today need to think of the triumphs of his life rather than the dark tragedy of his death.

Rowland Evans, Jr., Columnist, Author

The late Rowland Evans was a good friend and former Georgetown neighbor of JFK.

I first met John F. Kennedy when he was elected to the Senate in 1952, but I didn't get to know him well until after the Democratic Presidential Convention in 1956. I was assigned to cover the Senate for the *New York Herald Tribune.* I saw him frequently there and got to know him well, particularly after traveling with him as a reporter covering his 1960 presidential race.

I also got to know him socially during his Senate career. I lived in Georgetown. His brother-in-law, Stephen E. Smith, and sister Jean moved to a house across from mine in 1959. In 1960, the Senator was on the road most of the time campaigning for President, but when he came back to town, he often spent the evening at the Smith's plotting strategy with Kenny O'Donnell and Larry O'Brien. Some of my favorite memories of Kennedy occurred after these meetings. He would leave the Smith's late in the evening, perhaps even midnight, and yell across the street to me. There he would be, standing at the Smith's door and hollering, "Rowland! Come out of there, Rowland." I would let him in and we might have a brandy or go back in the garden to chat. When we finished talking, I would walk him home, three blocks away. My wife and I saw a good deal of him at parties and family gatherings.

The last time I was with Jack Kennedy before he became Mr. President was the day before his inauguration in January 1960. Mrs. Kennedy didn't want him around while she was loading barrels and cartons to move into the White House and more or less kicked him out. So the President-elect spent the day at the home of close Georgetown friend and neighbor, Bill Walton. As usual, he was busy with appointments throughout the day. It was blustery and snowy, and I had the good fortune of having lunch with Kennedy and Walton. Kennedy wanted me to get into the house without being seen by the crowd of reporters waiting outside on the street, so I climbed a fence around the garden. Bill decided we should toast the soon-to-be President and after scrounging around, he unearthed a nearly empty bottle of bad wine and squeezed out a half glass for each of us. It was a happy occasion.

I had a dual relationship with Kennedy, one political because I wrote about him as a reporter, the other as a friend. At times the friends could be a burden on my professionalism because he read everything I and other reporter-friends wrote about him. I sometimes had the feeling he was standing right behind me waiting to bore in!

Needless to say, I was an admirer of John F. Kennedy as a person. On November 22, 1963, after a luncheon meeting in a downtown Washington hotel with Barry Goldwater's campaign manager, I learned of the shooting in Dallas on the taxi radio. Kennedy's death was a severe loss to me personally. I participated in the events of that tragic weekend, doing a stint standing guard by the President's coffin in the White House. The entire city of Washington was numbed.

When I think back about John Kennedy, I remember him for his special appeal as a human being. He liked being with people and he had a genius for humor, irony and paradox. It was always fun to run into him. He liked to tease people and knew how to use a little needle without pain. He was witty and wry and a delight to be with. With the heavy pressures of the presidency on his shoulders, his sense of humor, like that of Abraham Lincoln, made his life tolerable. During a frenzied midnight campaign rally of supporters, Kennedy accidentally (on-purpose) maneuvered his huge audience to the edge of the press box. The surge of the crowd sent one reporter standing on a chair flying through the air. He landed on the floor with his typewriter upside down beside him and his papers scattering in all directions. Kennedy watched the reporter take his plunge with mock horror. I was the reporter, and on my way down, I watched the candidate's eyes glitter with malicious pleasure.

Kennedy is held in high regard throughout the United States and the world because he gave voice to the romantic side of the American dream, both in word, deed and appearance. He offered a vision for the future that nurtured hope in those who lacked it.

George E. Reedy, Special Assistant to the Vice-President

The late George Reedy reveals some of the bitterness toward Texas among some of Kennedy's staff. Reedy later became President Johnson's Press Secretary.

On the afternoon of November 22, 1963, I was working in my office located on the west front of the Capitol. I hadn't gone to Texas with my boss, Vice-President Lyndon Johnson, but knew he was not particularly happy over the visit there with President Kennedy. As usual the Texas political scene at that time was a complex and fierce struggle between diverse wings of the party. In particular, Governor John Connally and U.S. Senator Ralph Yarborough were greatly at odds with each other. Johnson decided to make the trip as low-key as possible and was trying to be careful not to cozy up to one feuding faction over the other.

While in my office, I received a call from a staff member in Johnson's office, Yolanda Boozer, informing me the President had been shot. From that point, I stayed by the United Press ticker in my office until I received confirmation of the President's death.

Johnson staff head, Walter Jenkins, was summoned by the White House. When he arrived there, he sent for me. I left right away riding down in Johnson's white Lincoln. When we got to the White House, we found considerable confusion as the staff was trying to grieve and function at the same time. Walter and I were asked what we thought should be done, but since neither of us were familiar with specific White House procedures, we told the Kennedy people to take charge of arrangements, which they did. One person with whom I was pretty good friends was Kennedy special assistant, historian Arthur Schlesinger, Jr., and when he saw me at the White House, he expressed his great sorrow, burst into tears and threw his arms around me.

The situation at the White House was particularly difficult for the Johnson people because of the uncertainly of the transition of power. We were now in charge as Johnson's staff, yet felt somewhat like intruders during this touchy interim period. I had a good working relationship with most of the "Irish Mafia" being of Irish descent myself, and as a former boy from east Chicago rather than Texas.

While Kennedy's body was on the way back to Washington aboard *Air Force One,* the staff at the White House hurried over to Andrews Air Force Base to greet the plane's arrival. I rode there with Jenkins and Ted Sorensen. Sorensen was bitter and said to me, "George, I wish that God-damned Texas of yours had never been invented." I kept my mouth shut, for what could one say at that point.

One other subject that I recall from those few, hectic hours was that several of the Kennedy aides were concerned over what would happen next as a result of what they considered possibly an organized plot in Dallas. I regarded the assassination as a isolated act that could have taken place anywhere.

The events of that dismal weekend are well known. I do believe the actions of President Johnson during this trying time showed him at his best. The way he acted and looked presidential as he held the country together was one of his finest performances. He had to delicately balance the need to show continuity of leadership without offending the sensibilities of the distraught family and friends of the deceased JFK. Of course LBJ, being from Texas, only made his task that much more difficult. I think he did the job brilliantly.

Reflecting back on the brief years of John F. Kennedy in office, I think he represented a sharp changing of the guard as the first President born in the 20th century just as Bill Clinton's win in 1992 brought the post-World War II age group into power. Kennedy's youth made him a contemporary President in contrast with his predecessor, Eisenhower. In addition to his youthful vigor, he and his wife Jacqueline brought class to the White House with their emphasis on talent and intellect. The President of the United States is the one unifying force politically in our country and helps set the pace for the nation. Kennedy with his focus on wit and intellect helped uplift the nation and inspired people to focus on ways to serve their nation.

Mrs. Edward R. (Janet) Murrow

The late Mrs. Murrow was the wife of the noted correspondent, Edward R. Murrow. She describes the relationship between Kennedy and her late husband and comments that her husband believed that if President Kennedy had lived, he would have "pulled out of Vietnam."

The mood of our household in November 1963 was already one of gloom since Ed had only a few weeks earlier had a lung removed because of lung cancer and was undergoing cobalt radiation treatments. During his recuperation he had to step back from his busy duties as Director of the United States Information Agency (USIA).

On November 22, 1963, we were at home together. Ed was still ill and weak from the radiation treatments. He could hardly talk and looked terrible. We were having lunch in the library and our housekeeper called me out into the corridor to tell me the President had been shot. I didn't tell Ed until we got him upstairs into bed. Ed was a hunter and very familiar with guns. He recalled the friends he had known who had been shot in shooting accidents and recovered, and he was hopeful that the President would still survive the shooting. He left the radio on, and it was soon apparent that the President had died. Of course we were very hard-hit by the news, and Ed was terribly

Courtesy of the John F. Kennedy Library

President Kennedy visits with Edward R. Murrow, wife Janet, and son Carey, as Murrow
prepares to be sworn in as the new Director of the USIA, 1961.

upset and shaken. Despite his weakened physical condition, he was
determined to pay his respects to the President. The next day, we went
to the White House where Kennedy's body had been placed in the
East Room for close friends to view. We went in the back entrance and
Ed sent me on ahead. I later learned he was barely able to climb the
stairs. A close friend found him there looking awful, on the verge of
passing out. He did make it to the East Room and sat in the corner
for a few minutes. I was in a daze that morning and went through the
motions required for the occasion. Many people were there, but Ed
stayed to himself only wanting to make it through the event without
drawing attention. In a short time, he had recovered enough to return
to work, even though he still was very weak. In January he stepped
down from his post because of his declining health.

Looking back at the Kennedy years, Ed early on had mixed emotions about the actions of the Kennedy family in public life. When
Kennedy's father, Joe, was Ambassador to Great Britain, we were stationed in London. We really didn't have a very good impression of the

Ambassador at that time. When Senator Kennedy became President, Ed was very doubtful of working for him as USIA head. When Ed, in March 1961, underwent his confirmation hearings before the Senate Foreign Relations Committee, he made it very clear what he wanted to do as head of the distribution of information about the United States to the rest of the world. Senator Capehart from Indiana suggested the job was like that of a car salesman, and therefore you only feature the good things about your product. Ed strongly opposed this approach insisting that, in telling of America's story, you presented both the good and the bad. Ed tried to carry through with this policy of honesty and brought a new look to the USIA and upgraded the status of the agency in Washington.

Arthur Schlesinger, Jr., in his 1965 book on the Kennedy administration, *A Thousand Days,* offered this comment concerning Ed's work as USIA Director:

> He revitalized USIA, imbued it with his own bravery and honesty and directed its efforts especially to the developing nations, where, instead of expounding free-enterprise ideology, it tried to explain the American role in a diverse and evolving world.[10]

Schlesinger declared, "Under Ed Murrow, the Voice of America became the voice, not of American self-righteousness, but of American democracy."

Ed often would sit in on cabinet meetings and was part of the National Security Council (NSC). As was his nature, he often hesitated to say too much in these meetings. Ironically, at his funeral held in New York in April 1965, then-Senator Robert Kennedy came up to me after the service and reminisced about Ed's participation in the Kennedy administration and said, "I wish Ed had spoken more in the NSC."

Ed was most concerned with our activities in Vietnam and the exclusion of the American press from what was happening there. He believed, however, that if Kennedy had lived, he would have pulled out of Vietnam, thus avoiding the eventual war occurring there.

Although Ed had considerable doubts over JFK when he was first elected President, he soon changed his views as he observed Kennedy in action. He felt the President was steadily growing in stature in the office, admired the Kennedy intellect, and thought he was doing a very good job. He was particularly impressed by Kennedy's ability to listen to people and grasp ideas so quickly.

I once had the pleasure of sitting by the President at a cozy White House dinner for some eight to ten people and found him attractive, charming and kind as a person. Both Ed and I deeply felt the loss of John F. Kennedy and missed him as a President and a friend.

Chapter Three

The White House Scene

While official Washington was aghast and numbed by the assassination, behind the scenes at the White House, basic activities still had to carried on in the face of overwhelming grief. Bob Foster, a Secret Service agent working at the White House shares a Kennedy farewell as the President left for Texas, the subsequent events, and happier memories from the White House. White House usher, Nelson C. Pierce, Jr., recalls that dreary weekend as "the saddest days of his 26 years working in the White House." Evelyn Lincoln, the President's personal secretary for many years, offers her recollections of the President including the final days there. Finally, James I. Robertson, who had a bird's-eye view in his office across from the White House, watched as the news of the President's death spread. He then recalls the unusual nighttime search in the Library of Congress to find the details of the Lincoln funeral.

Robert W. Foster, Secret Service, White House Detail

Probably no other Secret Service agent had closer ties to Caroline and John F. Kennedy, Jr., than Bob Foster who was assigned to oversee their protection and care. In that role he became very fond of the Kennedy children and shares some of those fond memories here.

The last words I ever heard from President John F. Kennedy were, "You take care of John for me, will you Mr. Foster?" They were spoken as Kennedy said good-bye to his son, John, at Andrews Air Force Base on Thursday, November 21, 1963. It was raining and cold. John was very upset and began to cry because his father was leaving on a trip to Texas. My job was to help guard and care for Mrs. Kennedy and her two children. I had been on the so-called "kiddie" detail in the White House for nearly three years.

Bob Foster and John F. Kennedy Jr., 1963.

The farewell comment by Kennedy to his son, given after he tousled his hair and hugged him, struck me as odd at the time, almost in retrospect as if the President had misgivings about his trip. It gave me a funny feeling. We had similar farewells, perhaps 50 times. This was the only occasion he had bothered to come back from his airplane to say goodbye. As I sat with John watching his father's plane fly away, I thought something was going to happen but quickly dismissed the idea.

Only a little over 24 hours later did I learn from a White House policeman that the President had been shot. Because of our fears for the safety of the children, we were obviously concerned. It was decided we take them and their British-born nanny, Maude Shaw, to the Georgetown home of Mrs. Hugh Auchincloss, mother of Mrs. Kennedy. Later that evening, we brought Miss Shaw and the children back to the White House arriving there around 8:00 P.M.

One incident happened shortly after that I shall never forget. A White House policeman gave me a brown paper bag and, when I looked inside, I was horrified to find a pink pillbox hat that was covered with blood and brains. I immediately located the policeman, who informed me that he thought I was Agent Clint Hill and he had given me the bag by mistake. Earlier that day I had another bad moment when I had to inform Miss Shaw that the President was dead. She made an unforgettable remark to me, "What's the matter with you American people?" She then had the terrible task of informing Caroline and John of their father's death. The next morning, we took the children for a drive from the White House and everywhere flags were flying at half-mast. Caroline asked me if this was for her "daddy" and I said, "Yes, Caroline."

The rest of that dreadful weekend was spent helping to care for the children, particularly John in my case. Several specific memories still stick in my mind of those gloomy four days. One was when the body of the President was taken to the Capitol to lie in state. I waited with the children in the office of Speaker John McCormack while a service was given for the President. While in the office, one of McCormack's aides, Martin Sweig, gave John an American flag. John then asked, "Can I have one for my daddy?" There were some 50 or so flags from UN nations around the world on the desk. John picked what I swear was the Cuban flag. I had to con John out of that one trying to convince him it wasn't very pretty. I then picked one for him, which I think was the Irish flag.

On Monday, the President was buried. During the funeral procession from the Capitol to St. Matthew's Cathedral, I walked alongside the car carrying the Kennedy children. During the doleful march, the window of the limousine rolled down and Caroline reached out to hold my hand as we proceeded together.

Another memory is well known, that of John saluting the coffin holding the body of his daddy as it left on the way to Arlington Cemetery. Everyone nearby that day must have the image of a little three-year-old boy giving a precise military salute forever etched in their mind. Because I was so close to John, I was particularly moved by his unsolicited action.

After the Mass I returned with Caroline and John to the White

House and joined Miss Shaw and two other agents for lunch with the children. While eating tomato soup and sandwiches, Caroline asked me, "Mr. Foster, Mr. Oswald killed my Daddy. He's a bad man isn't he? "I replied, "Yes, Caroline." She continued asking me, "Well Mr. Ruby killed Mr. Oswald; that makes him a good man doesn't it?" I told her, "No, Caroline, it's not proper to kill some-one." Next, she really floored me when she said, "Mr. Foster, Patrick died, and he went to heaven." Patrick was her little brother who died shortly after birth earlier in the year. "That's right," I answered. "Well, Daddy died, and he went to heaven, right?" Again I agreed with her. Then she asked, "Well, will Patrick grow up with Daddy in heaven?" Somewhat stunned by the question, I told her, "Caroline, I don't know. We'll have to ask the priest."

A few days after the funeral, the family moved out of the White House. Because of space limitations, I was given one of their dogs, a Welsh terrier named Charlie. The Kennedys loved dogs and, of course, the children adored playing with them.

I remained on the White House detail until December 1964. I will always remember the happy days I had at the White House. All the family and staff were so nice to deal with and thoughtful in their relationships with employees such as myself. It was like being part of a family. Shortly after the family departed, I received a love-ly thank-you note from ever-gracious, Mrs. Kennedy. She enclosed with it a message to me from John with her translation.

President Kennedy had a great sense of humor. When he learned that I was a Protestant Republican who had voted for Nixon instead of him in the 1960 election, he loved to needle me about my choice. Kennedy was very interested not only in his own chil-dren, but in those of others. When my son was born, his face was somewhat beat up from delivery. When JFK asked me about my new son, I told him, "It was the ugliest kid ever born." He laughed and told me, "He couldn't be any uglier than John."

When I first learned of my assignment at the White House, I was uneasy that I would really be a baby-sitter. Looking back at those years, it was great fun and a time in my life that I will always recall with fondness, except for those four dismal days in November.

Nelson C. Pierce, Jr., White House Usher

Some of the key people working to keep the White House functioning as a household are the ushers. Here, Nelson Pierce tells what it was like in the White House after the assassination from his firsthand perspective.

The weekend of November 22, 1963, will always be for me the saddest days of my 26 years working as an usher in the White House. I began my job in the White House soon after the arrival of John F. Kennedy as a new President. I was one of five ushers and soon learned in my new work that we would perform a great variety of duties. The primary purpose of the usher's office was to see that the first family got what it needed, when they needed it. The term usher is somewhat misleading as we were not really ushers but managers of the White House, including overseeing the maintenance. Working under us were the maids, butlers, electricians and carpenters. All the ushers, butlers and maids were black.

On the day President Kennedy was killed, I was on my way to the White House from a part-time job running an offset press at a nearby office. I arrived at the east gate of the White House at 1:45 P.M. and the policeman on duty said, "Pierce, hurry up and get to the office; the boss has just been shot." Well, of course my mouth dropped open and I could hardly believe what he had said. He repeated, "I'm on the level." I rushed to our office and, when I saw the news on the television, that's when it really hit me.

Within minutes all of the ushers had arrived, and we waited to find out what we should do. Many people don't understand the chemistry between the President, his family and his personal White House staff. We were in some ways like a family. Our job was to serve our President and his family the best we could. Politics were not involved in our job; and our loyalties were with our President.

Although quite different from Kennedy's death, but also a very sad occasion for me, was the departure of the Nixons from the White House. Again both Kennedy and Nixon were my Presidents and I served them to the best of my ability.

Returning to the events of November 22, 1963, we all waited for word about what we were to do. Within ten minutes after *Air Force One* left Texas, we received a message from Mrs. Kennedy that she wanted to replicate Lincoln's funeral. Everyone immediately went into action. As the afternoon usher on duty, I manned the office phone. We were flooded with calls from everywhere. I ordered the flag to be flown at half-mast. The other ushers were busy through most of the night decorating the East Room in black, replicating the resting place of the body of Lincoln there. While the Kennedys were in Texas, we had placed new carpet in the Oval Office. With the news of his death, we at once pulled the new carpet and put back the old because Mrs. Kennedy wanted everything to remain as the President had left it.

Through all of this, we were suffering from tremendous shock, and I was personally very moved because of my great liking for the President and his family. However, we were so busy, we had little time to grieve.

Early on Saturday morning, I looked out my office window into the dark and watched the hearse arrive carrying the President's body. It was very difficult to choke back my tears at that moment. Sometime later that early morning, I wanted to help get the family upstairs. I was on the elevator to make sure no one else could slip by. I still remember waiting on Mrs. Kennedy to arrive and wondering what I should say to her. When she came around the corner, I looked at her for just an instant and felt such rapport with her that words were not necessary. She was still wearing her bloodstained pink suit and was crying very hard at that point.

Some people were critical of Mrs. Kennedy for not appearing more grief-stricken in public during these events. I would like to correct those that hold such a faulty opinion. Mrs. Kennedy is the most remarkable woman I have even known. I greatly admire her tremendous composure during these hours as she took a personal hand in the arrangements. Of course she was greatly helped by her brother-in-law, Sargent Shriver. Yet she was behind the scenes, like any other wife who had lost her husband, and even more so under such tragic circumstances, suffering from such a terrific shock.

The entire weekend was one of total confusion and activity. We grabbed a few moments of sleep when we could. I finally got to bed at 5:30 A.M., Monday morning, and much to my regret I was so exhausted I missed the activities on Monday. I was very, very unhappy that no one awoke me at that point.

We continued to work closely with Mrs. Kennedy after the funeral for the next 11 days as she prepared to move on. On the day she left, all the staff in the White House was invited up to say good-bye to her. It was so wonderful to see she was able to smile again. I greatly admire Mrs. Kennedy for the little things she did and the courtesy she showed her staff. I have fond, very fond, affection for her.

After serving six Presidents during my 26-year tenure as an usher in the White House, I will never forget President Kennedy. When he smiled, you couldn't help but smile with him. He was truly a man's man. Both he and Mrs. Kennedy were wonderful to work with in a close and warm setting.

Evelyn Lincoln, Personal Secretary to the President
As the personal secretary of President for many years, the late Mrs. Lincoln had a ringside view of President Kennedy unlike anyone else.

I had the great honor and pleasure to serve as the personal secretary of John F. Kennedy from the time he took office as the new senator from Massachusetts in January 1953, until his death. I had badly wanted to work for John F. Kennedy since becoming convinced he had the leadership and drive to someday become President of the United States. At first it was a toss-up of which one I would work for: Congressmen Franklin D. Roosevelt, Jr., of New York or John Kennedy. In the end I decided on Kennedy, but I also learned he had no staff vacancies. Since he was running for the U.S. Senate against Henry Cabot Lodge, I volunteered to work in his office at night.

Courtesy of Evelyn Lincoln

Evelyn Lincoln with her boss in the White House office.

During the day I worked for a congressman from Georgia.

I still remember the first time I ever met Kennedy. I was working one evening as a volunteer in his office, and he came to my desk and thanked me for helping in his campaign. I recall thinking how young and thin he looked as he kept pushing his hair off his forehead. Then he told me, "close the door when you leave" and he left. Little did I realize that, only a few months later, I would be working closely with him for the rest of his life. However, since I didn't hear anything more from Kennedy for some time, I thought he had forgotten me. Much to my elated surprise, three days before he was to be sworn in as senator, I was asked if I would work in his office. I soon learned I was going to be his personal secretary.

I learned early on that Kennedy was a tough taskmaster, that he wanted things done expeditiously and correctly. He didn't accept the answer that you were unable to do an assignment he gave you. I learned that the end result was to do what he wanted you to do.

His handwriting was impossible. In the end I became the only one who was able to decipher his scribbling. I memorized dozens and dozens of telephone numbers so I could make calls for him immediately. I made all of his appointments, travel arrangements, and even served lunch brought in from his home to him and sometimes to guests. I also took all of his dictation, letters and speeches, as well as kept track of what was taking place on the Senate floor. I advised him when there would be a vote. I wrote all his personal checks, ordered his suits and shirts, and reminded him of holy days, birthdays and anniversaries.

I came to work early, left late at night, and never took a vacation. I was in the campaign in 1960 and in Jack Haley's Los Angeles hideout with Kennedy when he learned that he had won the nomination. I was in Hyannis Port, Massachusetts, when he learned that he had been elected to the presidency. So by the time we entered the White House, it was merely transferring our operation from one office to another, except the White House served the whole country.

My workday began at 8:00 A.M. Shortly thereafter, Kennedy would call from the mansion to find out what the agenda was for the day and the time of his first appointment. I would get ready for his arrival, making sure everything was in readiness for him. Shortly before the time for his appointment, Kennedy would appear on the veranda and walk past my office windows to the entrance of the Oval Office. Since the door to my office was open as soon as he opened his office door, he would start giving me approximately ten reminders of things he wanted done during the day. Then he would ask if there were any telephone calls or messages. I handled all of his telephone calls and kept a record of them.

I also went through his mail, which had been delivered to my office, and separated letters for him to read, which I placed on the upper left corner of my desk. I continued to take all of his dictation for speeches, letters and memos. I also continued to write his personal checks, order his suits, shirts and ties. Likewise, I continued to remind him of those special occasions, holy day, birthdays and anniversaries.

Although Ken O'Donnell was his appointment secretary, many people were given appointments by Kennedy for them to come in through my office. Dignitaries who came to see Kennedy would always be brought into my office to go to the cabinet room. Kennedy would generally take a swim in the pool before going to the mansion. My lunch was brought to me at my desk from the Navy Mess. I didn't leave my desk because Kennedy would generally call me several times during the lunch break. The afternoon was more of the same. I would stay until he finished his schedule and left for the mansion. Then I too would close shop. It was generally pretty late.

Ironically, 1963 began as a great year for President Kennedy. He and Mrs. Kennedy received worldwide adulation and acclaim in successful trips overseas, including a Berlin Wall visit and a personal return to his "roots" in Ireland. Despite great conflict over civil rights issues, progress was being made there as well.

In late summer the President's luck seemed to turn. On August 7, 1963, around 11:40 A.M., a call came from the Cape that Mrs. Kennedy had been taken to nearby Otis Air Force Base Hospital. She was pregnant at the time. As soon as the President was advised, he immediately ordered a Jet Star to take us to the base hospital. Upon arrival, we were advised that a four pound, ten-and-a-half ounce boy had been born. However, it was determined that the little boy had a respiratory problem. They moved him to the Children's Hospital in Boston. For three days it was touch and go, and then he died. That was the only time during my 12 years with John F. Kennedy that I saw him cry as tears rolled down his cheeks.

By the fall of 1963, President Kennedy was eagerly looking ahead to the next year's presidential campaign. Since Texas was such a pivotal state in his winning again, he agreed to a political swing through Texas in late November to mend fences there.

Several days prior to the trip to Dallas, my husband, Abe, who was the Liaison Officer for the White House on behalf of the Veterans Administration, was having lunch at a local restaurant. He overheard, at the table behind him, a conversation about an assassination attempt in Dallas during Kennedy's visit. Abe called me immediately at the White House and told me to tell Kennedy that he should not go to Dallas. I rushed into the Oval Office and told Kennedy what Abe had heard and also that he didn't think he should go to Dallas. Kennedy shrugged his shoulders and said "Miz Lincoln, if they want to get me, they'll get me in church." Then he thanked me for our concern.

On a beautiful day in Dallas, we got off *Air Force One* and began climbing in our cars for a motorcade through the downtown. There was a huge crowd around us as people pressed up against the President's car. Mrs. Kennedy was carrying a bouquet of red roses and everyone was smiling and friendly. As I got into my car, I looked over to the President's car that had just started to move. There he was, his right hand in the air, waving at his excited followers. It was the last time I would ever see him alive. I will always remember him that way, a handsome, young, energetic President who had grace and intellect, a man who loved every inch of his country, especially its people.

The first few hours after Kennedy's death, I felt aimless and bewildered. One of my saddest tasks was to oversee the removal of the President's effects from the White House virtually hours after his death. To pinpoint history minutely, 30 minutes after I came to my office on November 23 at 8:00 A.M., President Johnson came in and ordered me to remove everything belonging to President Kennedy out of the Oval Office, my office and the Cabinet Room by 9:00 A.M. (Robert Kennedy interceded and was able to extend the time until noon.) General Maxwell Taylor generously offered his office in the Executive Office Building across the alley from the White House for the Kennedy material to be moved. Nothing could be sadder than to see his rocking chair carried out into the rain while the President's body was lying in state in the East Room of the White House.

President Johnson had an office from which he could operate, but he didn't have the courtesy to wait until President Kennedy was buried in Arlington Cemetery on Monday, November 25 to move into the Oval Office. Later, President Johnson revised the records to make it appear that the removal took place after the funeral.

The end of a glorious era was over for me and the nation. During the entire 12 years that I had the honor to be President Kennedy's personal secretary, there was never any change in his attitude toward himself or his desire to be different in his association with other people.

He was more interested in others than promoting himself. He was humble, kind, caring and compassionate. I always felt that he had complete control of his emotions. Kennedy had an organized mind and a body that went with it. He had class and grace under pressure. He was truly a human being.

When I look back at those brief and wonderful days of the Kennedy presidency, I still recall the air of excitement he brought to our country. The winds of change were blowing in 1960. His campaign theme was to get "the country moving again." He was young; Eisenhower was old. The young people related to him, and the young men and women who became a part of the "New Frontier" brought an infectious vitality to government and politics. That vitality was felt all over the United States.

The qualities Kennedy brought to the presidency were the pursuit of excellence and a zeal of achievement. He also believed in reason. It was an exciting period of time, an imaginative time when our youth could strive and dream about doing something better. John F. Kennedy made people feel that each one of them had an important role to serve in his or her life.

James I. Robertson, Executive Director, U.S. Civil War Centennial Commission, Washington

Dr. Robertson had the unique task of searching in the dark during the late night hours of Friday, November 22, trying to locate information on the Lincoln funeral.

On November 22, 1963, I was in my Washington office on Pennsylvania Avenue and Jackson Place across from the White House. I received a call from the office of Congressman Fred Schwengle of Iowa alerting me that President Kennedy had been shot. From my desk, I turned and looked out my window at the White House. I could see cars racing to the northwest entrance and reporters dashing into the West Wing.

As the afternoon wore on, it began to rain. Indelibly etched into my mind as I gazed from my window was the sight of hundreds of

Americans slowly gathering in the park, just standing in the heavy rain and gazing at the White House. They seemed to have a sense of helplessness as if they didn't know what else to do.

I left the office early to get out of the horrendous traffic jam building up and to follow the news at home on television. Around 8:00 P.M. I received a call from the White House. As I walked to the telephone, my first reaction was that this was a sick joke. It was a White House aide who told me that Mrs. Kennedy was flying back on *Air Force One* and had expressed the wish that the East Room be decorated as it was for Abraham Lincoln's body. They asked, could I help ease the way for this decoration?

By coincidence and a macabre twist of fate, while I was in graduate school at Emory University, I had worked part time in the funeral business. As a result I had done quite a bit of research on Civil War funerals, embalming, executions and the like and was well-acquainted with the topic.

I recommended they contact my very dear friend, David C. Mearns, who was Curator of Manuscripts at the Library of Congress. Five minutes later, I received a call from David and we agreed to meet at the library to get the materials on Lincoln. By this time Pennsylvania Avenue was totally clogged with traffic. When I arrived at the library around 9:00 P.M. on Friday night, David met me at a darkened doorway. We felt we were under tremendous pressure to get the job requested by the White House done as rapidly as possible. Adding to our problem, David gave me disheartening news: all the library lights had been automatically turned off for the weekend and wouldn't go on until Monday morning. So we had to prowl through the library in pitch-black dark. Most people are unaware that the bulk of the library's holdings are underground, so we had to go into the catacomb-like bowels of the library carrying flashlights. We were fortunate in rapidly locating the E187 Civil War section we were seeking. The materials I wanted and found were issues of *Harper's Weekly* and *Frank Leslie's Illustrated Newspaper*. They were comparable to today's *U.S. News and World Report* and contained illustrations and front-page drawings of Lincoln's coffin and catafalque and several good articles on Lincoln's funeral.

I then called the White House to say that I found the materials. The guards were alerted to let me in the northwest gate. When I arrived and parked at the White House, it was really awesome to view the chaos, the sadness, the mixture of such strong emotions. I was loaded down with books in the rain trying to get into the West Executive Wing. I had to pass in front of the cameras and correspondent Sander Vanocur making an NBC news broadcast. I went into Kenneth O'Donnell's office, which soon became crowded. As we moved into the President's office at that moment, I think the first real impact of what had happened hit me. I had previously met twice with the President along with Dr. Allan Nevins to discuss the Civil War Centennial. This time, the walls had been stripped of paintings, and the shelves were devoid of bric-a-brac, but the President's rocker and two sofas were still there.

We spread the material out and then went to the East Room where there were piles of rolls of black bunting. We worked until after 3:00 A.M. decorating the room. My job was to compare the work of the aides and carpenters with what the drawings and accounts from 1865 showed. The only hang-up we had to decide was which way the President's body should lie. I left by the northeast gate, and I remember a big commotion at the gate that later I learned was the President's body returning from Dallas. My overriding memory of those tragic hours in the White House that night was one of absolute grief and chaos.

Chapter Four

The Military Role

The efforts by many people to prepare an elaborate state funeral in a very short time were Herculean in nature. Adding to the problem were the specific and unique requests made by Mrs. Kennedy. Important parts of these ceremonies were carried out by the military. Major Bert Turner shares some of the difficulties faced by the military in making these arrangements. Another participant from the military was Air Force Staff Sergeant Richard Gaudreau who served on the military burial detail during the weekend of the funeral from the first stages to the end at Arlington Cemetery. Finally, Sergeant Keith Clark describes his memorable role as the military bugler playing the last plaintive notes of taps at the funeral.

Major Albert F. Turner, Washington, D.C.

Bert Turner was a key figure in arranging the military funeral of the President. His testimony provides a close look at the feverish pace of the behind-the-scene preparation activities.

On November 22, 1963, I was Secretary of the General Staff in the Military District of Washington (MDW). My immediate boss, the Chief of Staff was in the hospital with a heart attack. At 12:40 P.M., General Wehle, the Commanding Officer for the MDW, called me from his quarters and asked: "Have you gotten anything on President Kennedy being assassinated in Dallas?" I was completely startled and said; "nothing!" General Wehle said, "I just heard a blurb on the radio." So I put him on hold and attempted to call one of the military aides at the White House, but I couldn't get through.

General Wehle then told me to schedule a meeting of commanders and staff at 1:00 P.M. in the office which I did. While the meeting was going on, one of the secretaries came in crying and sobs to me, "He's dead!" The meeting was dismissed, and we took over our conference room as the Funeral Operations Center. We had done this before in rehearsals and everyone knew their jobs.

While we were caught totally off-guard on the news of President Kennedy's death, we had already been busy throughout 1963 in planning for the possible state funerals of our three living ex-presidents, Hoover, Truman and Eisenhower as well as General Douglas MacArthur. Everything was in place for the four, including their burial location and ceremonial plans. Unfortunately no plans had been made for the President's dying while in office. This was one we had not planned for.

We badly needed information but every office and resident in the D.C. area seemed to be talking to each other and the lines were completely clogged. The entire happening resembled something lifted out of the 1963 novel, *Seven Days in May.*[11] Could this be an attempt to overthrow our government? We were eager and ready to commence operations. The key liaison officers and funeral planners were assembled, but we all asked, "what's the plan?"

We soon learned that the President's body would arrive around 6:30 P.M., then be sent to Bethesda Naval Hospital for an autopsy. Next the body would be taken to the White House and later to the Rotunda of the Capitol to lie in state.

In my opinion there was a greater love affair between John Kennedy and the military, than with any of the former Presidents I knew. Everyone wanted to do the best job possible for Kennedy. At this point, people from all over the country were asking where the religious ceremony was going to be, where he would be buried and how the family was holding up. Through the efforts of many dedicated people, we were able to put a plan into action for the next few days culminating with the burial in Arlington National Cemetery on Monday.

By Sunday everyone was living on borrowed energy after going full bore for two days. We also badly needed showers. A great deal of work still remained for the next day's events and a group of about 60 of us met in General Wehle's office early Sunday afternoon. We suddenly received a request from Secretary of Defense McNamara's office telling us Mrs. Kennedy wanted an eternal flame. We also were informed she wanted a funeral procedure used in Ireland. Someone rushed to our library to research Irish procedures. General Wehle, a man with ulcers and under unbelievable pressure, stayed calm through it all. We got a break and learned the next day that Ireland was sending over a contingent so we were off the hook on that problem. I called the chief engineer at Ft. Myer and told him we needed an eternal flame. Now it was his problem to solve.

The Air Force planned a 50 jet plane flyover of Arlington National Cemetery, one for each state. During the meeting, I told General Wehle I thought the best time for the flyover would be when the caisson with the casket was crossing the Potomac on the way to Arlington National Cemetery. Wehle asked me, "Turner, were you ever in the cavalry?" I answered, "no," since I entered West Point in 1945 and was in the first class that didn't have to learn to ride horses. Wehle told me, "I can see it now. The jets fly over at 300 feet, the horses throw their traces, and we toss the casket into the Potomac River." He directed that the flyover would be done after the casket was off the caisson at graveside.

Through all of this, we were working under great pressure. The duplicating machines broke down, the stenos were suffering, and calls poured in from all directions. Some were demands and threats from Secretary McNamara's office. We even received a call from a mother asking, "My son is coming from West Point to march in the parade. Where do I meet him?"

By around 3:00 A.M., early Monday morning, all the plans were in order including uniforms, parade routes, sequence of march, and countless other details. We were done. We arrangers, unshaven, smelling like pigs, could sit down and watch our plans unfold on television. Despite some minor glitches, everything went marvelously well, even to the final note of taps when the note that cracked expressed the grief of our entire nation and the world.

Whenever I return to Washington, I stand at the Lincoln Memorial and look down the center line of Memorial Bridge. There on the hillside in Virginia is the Custis-Lee Mansion and, at a lower elevation on that line, is the flickering of the eternal flame. To me it is a reminder of a strong woman, who helped restore the faith of an unbelieving nation and saw to it that our slain President was laid to rest in dignity. It also reminds me of the hundreds of "no names" who helped her in this sad task.

Richard E. Gaudreau, Staff Sergeant U. S. Air Force, Washington, D.C.

Gaudreau offers a detailed look at some of the problems facing the military in carrying out the funeral plans, including the specific concerns facing the bearers of the casket.

It was a pleasant November day, and things were slow in the office on that fateful Friday. I was stationed at Bolling Air Force Base, serving as part of the Air Force honor guard detachment. I was in the orderly room with music playing on the radio when suddenly I heard, "bulletin, bulletin, bulletin," followed by the announcement that the President had been shot. At once we began a recall of our ceremonial detail to be ready for further orders. I was the noncommissioned officer in charge of the Air Force casket team. With several enlisted men I went to Andrews Air Force Base by bus to await the arrival of the President's body from Texas. When we arrived, casket teams from the other service branches joined us. Lieutenant Sam Bird from Ft. Myer was in charge and soon organized a casket-bearing group consisting of servicemen from the Army, Marines, Navy, Air Force and Coast Guard. Bird picked me to be the single Air Force member. While all this was going on, traffic was piling up around the area where the President's plane would end its voyage. Everything was very confused, and no one was sure what was happening.

Air Force One arrived shortly after 6:00 P.M., Friday evening and the chaos continued. A big trucklift pulled up to the airplane as soon as it landed and General McHugh, Kennedy's Air Force aide, told us

Leaving St. Matthews Cathedral, Gaudreau second back on left, November 25, 1963.

the Secret Service would unload the casket from the plane. As they lowered the lift, I saw Mrs. Kennedy was wearing a pink outfit with much of her dress and stockings spotted with dried blood. I will never forget this scene. That is when it really hit me that the President had been killed.

When the Secret Service tried to move the casket from the trucklift to the ambulance, it was too heavy for them. Another serviceman and I helped them carry the casket to the ambulance. Our unit then was flown to the Bethesda Naval Hospital by a "Flying Banana" Army helicopter and waited outside the morgue entrance for the ambulance to arrive.

At the hospital, we took turns guarding the door to the entrance to the morgue under strict orders to admit no one without the OK of the

Secret Service. During this time a second casket was brought in to replace the damaged one as well as clothes for the President. In the middle of the night, we received an American flag, which was placed on the casket, and then the President's body was moved to the White House. At the White House, we struggled to get the casket to the East Room and then were relieved by a military "Death Watch" unit. We then went home for a couple hours of sleep.

Early on Saturday morning we were back at Ft. Myer to practice folding the flag as a unit. In the evening we went to the Tomb of the Unknown Soldier in Arlington Cemetery and trained by carrying an empty casket up and down the steps. To simulate the President's weight, we had the tomb guard get in the casket and, leaving the lid open, we carried him up and down. This went on for around two hours.

On Sunday we were in action again, carrying the casket from the White House to a caisson. We walked behind it on the procession to the Capitol. Still embedded in my mind is the sound of the muffled drumbeat as we marched along Pennsylvania Avenue. My dominant thought through all of this was to represent the Air Force with honor.

The long haul up the 36 Capitol steps to the Rotunda was extremely difficult as the coffin weighed around 1,000 pounds. It was particularly tough for those carrying it at the lower end. When done, we once again returned to Ft. Myer to practice folding the flag. We operated without any voice signals. Everything had to be done on a count with only the slightest cue by a cough or the nod of a head to signal us when to do what.

On Monday, we once again carried the casket from the Rotunda down the steps to the caisson while a band played "Hail to the Chief." We then went by bus to St. Matthew's Cathedral to await the cortege. Despite all the pressures of the time, I was well aware of the famous dignitaries I was seeing at the Cathedral, such as Haile Selassie of Ethiopia, Charles de Gaulle of France, and Prince Philip of England. Cardinal Cushing of Boston blessed the casket while we held it. We got one break in that Lieutenant Bird insisted we get a dolly to carry the casket down the aisle to the church altar.

From the Cathedral we marched to Arlington Cemetery. I was well aware of all the crying and yelling that was going on. I recall a woman in the crowds lining the streets shouting, "Don't worry John, we are with you." We kept our heads facing straight ahead, but we could feel the intense atmosphere of great emotion all around us.

At Arlington Cemetery, I had one moment of panic when I feared we were going to allow the coffin to slide into the open grave, but we managed to hang on without such a disaster occurring. Then we held the flag pulled tight above the casket for a period of time, which seemed to last a lifetime. I was really worried that I would pass out, and I wiggled my toes and flexed my knees hoping no one would notice my extreme discomfort. At this point, I was hanging on to make sure that, when we passed the flag, I did my job right. I was thinking to myself, "If you drop this flag, you're dead, you're gone." Then the nine of us stood for what seemed like forever until everybody left. Finally we were done, and I never will forget seeing the empty hillside covered with flowers. I was glad it was over and, not until a few days later, did it hit me that I was so intimately in the center of a great and historic event. I also got some hell back at my base from the other members of the Air Force casket unit who were not being chosen to participate.

Thinking back, I still remember that Friday night as a madhouse of mass confusion. Only when the young Lieutenant Sam Bird took charge, did things suddenly fall into place. He should receive great credit for his efforts. You couldn't ask for a better guy to work with. I also will always remember Mrs. Kennedy as she stepped out of the plane and our parade across the Potomac to Arlington Cemetery. I am only glad that I could make my small personal contribution to giving our President a fitting farewell.

Sergeant Keith Clark, U. S. Army Band, Washington, D.C.

Sergeant Clark will long be remembered as the bugler playing taps at the funeral of President Kennedy. He describes the breaking of a note during that rendition, a rare mistake in his career, although many observers thought he played it that way on purpose.

Looking back at the 20 years I spent serving in the U.S. Army

President Kennedy at Arlington Cemetery, Veterans Day, as taps are being sounded at the Tomb of the Unknown Soldier by bugler, Keith Clark, November 11, 1963.

Courtesy of the John F. Kennedy Library

Band, one event is indelibly etched in my mind. In November 1963, I was the first cornetist in the U.S. Army Band stationed at Ft. Myer, Virginia, located adjacent to Arlington National Cemetery. I headed a section of 22 trumpets, and by 1963, I had been in the service 17 years. As the lead solo cornetist, I also played taps for special occasions, such as when visiting heads of state laid a wreath at the Tomb of the Unknown Soldier in Arlington Cemetery and presidential wreath-laying ceremonies such as Armistice Day. I averaged playing taps about once every two weeks as this was only a special assignment beyond my regular duties in the band. The last time I ever saw President Kennedy alive was on November 11, 1963, when I played taps for his placing a wreath in Arlington Cemetery as part of an Armistice Day ceremony.

On Friday afternoon, November 22, 1963, I was at my home in Arlington helping a friend of mine do research using my private collection of books on church music. Around 3:30 P.M., my 11-year-old daughter, Sandy, yelled up the stairs, "President Kennedy has been killed." Of course we interrupted all work and were shocked by the news. I immediately realized that I might be chosen to play taps if a military funeral was to be held at Arlington Cemetery. I thought it likely that a Navy bugler would be chosen because President Kennedy had been a Navy man. Just in case, I wanted to look my best, and I went out to get my hair cut.

The next two days were a waiting game for me as I kept hearing that the President would be buried in Arlington but no one had told me if I would be participating. Not until early Monday morning was I informed that I would play taps that day. I was told to report for duty by 6:00 A.M., Monday morning. At 5:45 A.M., I arrived at the cemetery but found nobody there. After waiting around, I gave up and went back to the band studio where I was told to report at noon. I walked back to the cemetery at noon and stayed there until the funeral was completed shortly after 3:00 P.M.

My concern for this traumatic afternoon was to do my job as professionally as possible. The other buglers for Arlington Cemetery ceremonies would have an occasional mistake. I had played taps officially nearly 150 times and was fortunate in that I had never had a major flaw during all the years I played this somber piece.

My wait standing at the cemetery was long and uncomfortable. It was a cold day, and unfortunately, I hadn't eaten anything since 5:00 A.M. I was well aware at this point that the entire world would be watching all the ceremonial participants. Several obstacles were added to my assignment. To accommodate the television cameras, it was decided that I would be placed in front of the firing squad because it would make a good camera shot when I played taps after the firing squad volleys were fired. Colonel Curry, commanding officer of the band, kept telling me not to worry and said, "Son, you will do just fine." Another of the bad decisions by the news media was to place a microphone right in front of me. I knew this would create a sound problem. They did not correct the mistake until taps was started. A sound man flipped down the volume. I was standing on a slight mound so that Mrs. Kennedy could see me play even though she was some 1,000 feet away. The military had an X made from masking tape on the ground, and I had to remain on that spot. Should I play to the microphone or to Mrs. Kennedy? I opted for the latter.

While I was well aware that the world's great leaders were standing nearby, I really focused on playing to the President's widow as I always did for such sad affairs. I was to play immediately after the firing squad fired over my head. This added one more burden to my task as the extreme noise from the rifles left my ears ringing and, of course, made my job that much more difficult as I had trouble hearing myself play.

As many people know, I made the first bad note in my career in playing taps that day at 3:07 P.M. William Manchester his book, *The Death of a President*,[12] described the note like this, "It cracked; it was like a catch in your throat or a swiftly stifled sob." I finished the number without another flaw. Ironically many observers concluded I played the piece like that on purpose. One magazine article described my broken note as a "French tear." I presume many people today credit me with this distinctive touch, which was certainly not the case at all.

After the burial was completed, I walked back to Ft. Myer and hurried to get ready for a 4:00 P.M. trumpet lesson. I continued several individual lessons until 10:00 P.M. that night. This certainly seemed the longest day of my life.

Looking back over my lengthy career in music spanning some 50 years, I will always recall that cold and gloomy day in November. I had great respect for President Kennedy. I was well aware of the heavy pressures on him from the Cold War conflicts he faced. I still think of him as a sincerely excellent President and remember him with fondness and affection.

Chapter Five

The Last Days

While the White House and the military were trying frantically to arrange the funeral in accord with the wishes of Mrs. Kennedy, people nationwide were in a state of turmoil. Those in Washington and some who traveled to the funeral remember those last few days quite vividly. One that made a very long trip to be there was Tom Goodale, who flew from North Dakota. Another was college student, Terry Graham, who attended Kennedy's inauguration and, 1,000 days later, drove from his college in Delaware for the funeral. A Peace Corps worker, Ned Chalker, shares his memory of the President's last march to the cemetery. Another local resident, Carl McDaniels and his daughter were able to enter the Cemetery and to witness the ceremonies as spectators.

Thomas G. Goodale, Journalism Instructor and Sports Information Director, North Dakota State University

Tom Goodale, like many college students, was particularly hard hit by President Kennedy's death. Here he relates a poignant account of his attendance at the final days in Washington following JFK's death as well as some earlier and happier memories.

In stirring the ashes of my past, nothing moves me more emotionally than my bittersweet memories of John F. Kennedy and his brother Bob. I experienced some of the most exhilarating and happiest moments of my life working for the election of both to the presidency and, at their deaths, suffered the deepest despair I can recall.

In early 1960, I was a college student majoring in journalism at Iowa State University and became interested in working for the election of John F. Kennedy. I was contacted by Iowa State Senator Harold Hughes, later a Governor and U.S. Senator, asking me if I could be persuaded to drop out of school for the spring quarter to become a campaign worker for JFK. I did so and ended up having a wonderful time working in primary activities, which culminated in my being able to attend the Democratic Presidential Nominating Convention in Los Angeles that summer working as a page.

I returned to school in the fall but still devoted all my spare time to working for Kennedy's election. My favorite recollection was a visit by JFK during his 1960 fall campaign to the annual state fair held in Des Moines, Iowa. I was given the assignment of escorting Minnesota Governor Orville Freeman, who was accompanying Senator Kennedy at the fair.

I will never forget the visit JFK made to the hog pavilion. It was a hot and muggy day and, as could be expected, the pungent stench emanating from the hog stalls was less than desirable. I got to meet Kennedy at this point. I still recall Governor Freeman asking Kennedy if he had ever seen an Iowa hog and Kennedy laughing as he replied, "He had eaten a lot of pork but had never been close to any Iowa hogs before." The image of the immaculately dressed and elegant JFK meeting the hogs still remains with me today.

In January 1961, I attended the President's inauguration, which I greatly enjoyed despite the bitter cold. Like thousands of idealistic young people throughout the country, I was thrilled and convinced that our nation and world were entering a new era of hope and progress for all people.

In the fall of 1963, I was working at North Dakota State University and also serving as a pilot in the North Dakota National Guard. On November 22, 1963, I was attending a conference in Minneapolis and was taking a break in a nearby hotel bar when Walter Cronkite came on the air with the tragic news that our President was dead. This terrible news really tore me up and I broke into tears. When I walked outside, the street was hushed, cars were stopped, and an unusual mood seemed to hover over everyone. It was as if time had stopped.

I returned at once to Fargo where I learned I was to be the copilot

The funeral cortege proceeds to Arlington Cemetery, November 25, 1963.

on a flight taking North Dakota Governor Bill Guy to the funeral events in Washington. Because of the priority aircraft bringing in foreign dignitaries, we had some difficulties in getting a clearance to land at Andrews Air Force Base. We were running low on fuel, but finally made it in safely.

On Sunday, wearing my uniform, I was able to enter the Capitol Rotunda ahead of the line where the President's body rested in state. I still recall being bothered because I saw a spot like a big brown footprint of dirt on the catafalque below the coffin. I also vividly remember seeing the Kennedy family there and watching Mrs. Kennedy kneeling with her hand under the flag on the coffin. At this point I saluted the coffin and really lost it. I began crying and sobbing as were many others around me. Two nearby nuns gave me a linen handkerchief to clear my tears.

Wanting to make some visible symbol of my grief, I went to a department store and obtained some black piece goods that I made into a black mourning band and placed on my arm. I was soon stopped by a colonel who told me I was out of uniform. I was so annoyed I cursed him, and he walked away from me. Today, that black armband is still one of my prized possessions.

On the day of the funeral, I walked beside the funeral cortege on the way to Arlington Cemetery. As we crossed Memorial Bridge, I could see a blaze of color on the hill in front of me where the President was to be buried. One striking scene was the incongruous sight of a large and impressive figure, General Charles de Gaulle of France, walking beside the diminutive Emperor of Ethiopia, Haile Selassie. Right at a point near the middle of the bridge, the sun glanced off the long sword worn by the emperor and momentarily blinded me. It was like a spiritual experience.

Through all of the march, the constant and dismal beat of the drums echoed in my ears. I still can remember that muffled sound today. I was able to stand some 100 yards or so from the Arlington Cemetery gravesite. When Cardinal Cushing completed the last rites, he came within two feet of me. I saw tears streaming down his cheeks, and it impressed me how even a famous and veteran leader of the church could be so moved.

The death of John F. Kennedy was a terrible blow to me. It was only when I became involved in the campaign of Robert F. Kennedy that I felt a rebirth of enthusiasm and hope that we could get the nation going again. I was at that peak moment of political triumph for RFK in 1968 in the Los Angeles hotel ballroom when my jubilation was dashed into despair. With the death of Robert Kennedy, the loss of JFK was even more accentuated in my psyche. By November 1968, my spirits were at a very low ebb.

However, when I reflect back to John F. Kennedy decades after his death, I prefer to dwell on my happiest thoughts of him. There is little doubt that Kennedy was a role model for me in several ways. I greatly admired his wit and humor, his incredible charisma, and his ability to enunciate ideas with clarity and passion. His concepts have always remained with me, ideas of hope, spirit and a vision for a better world. Finally John F. Kennedy left with me the idea of courage. He greatly admired deeds of courage, whether in the military or in everyday life. I have never found again a political figure to fill the void left in my heart and mind by JFK's death. John F. Kennedy personified for me the ideas of courage, vision and hope.

Terry Graham, College Student, University of Delaware

Terry Graham was another of the many students who admired President Kennedy. He was in the inaugural parade in 1961 and returned again to Washington to be with his fallen President. He describes the long wait at the Rotunda for the last public viewing of the President's casket and related events.

Though I had heard much about JFK and had seen his picture and read news reports about him in print, I was unable to vote. But with my parents, avid followers of politics, we became mutually involved in the aura JFK held for young and old alike. Kennedy's series of primary victories and his ultimate nomination changed me from a political bystander to a political activist. JFK still remains a political hero for me today.

As a freshman at Dickinson College in Carlisle, Pennsylvania, I immediately became active in campaigning on Kennedy's behalf. My college program included my participation in their military ROTC program. I was assigned to Company C, which proudly became an outstanding marching unit. To our company's delight, even more so to my own, our unit was chosen to participate in the January 1961 inaugural parade for our and my newly elected President.

Early on a yet dark chilly morning, we gathered together in a bus bound south for D.C. The excitement was high for all as we covered icy roads passing snow-covered hills. A rather heavy snowfall and chilling temperatures from the day and evening before had nearly canceled our trip, but on we went. I remember well our arrival and getting into formation. Our wait was long with cold feet and hands, but I knew the chill I felt was more than from the day's cold. As our company and flag passed the President's reviewing stand, I stole a glimpse of my new President with what I knew then explained best my chills. Maybe I had contributed something to the future in my campaign activity. That cadence of my feet with thousands of others can still be felt. This was and remains a most memorable highlight of my life.

By the fall of 1963, I was a junior at the University of Delaware. On Friday mid afternoon, I had just completed an exam and, feeling good, I sat with some friends in the student union. Suddenly people from across the room, like a wave effect, joined each other in loud whispers calling for quiet. As silence replaced the usual garble of voices, a couple of hundred students learned from television that the President had been shot. Stillness and silence took over. Each of us stared at one and then another.

My friends and I then decided without the usual excitement to drive to our regular site where on Fridays we traditionally played touch football. As we arrived in a somewhat befuddled state, we heard on the radio that the President was dead. Another of our group had driven up, stepped out with a football, and after briefly deciding teams, we tried to play. Suddenly we were bickering, arguing, and even pushing one another around seemingly with no reason. We soon realized we were in a terrible emotional state; we mutually and quietly quit. The next day, a close friend and I decided we must go to Washington, D.C., a way of saying farewell to our President. The train station in Wilmington, Delaware, where we boarded the next train to D.C. was amazingly quiet. All who were not reading a paper or schedule were staring blankly into space. A black shoeshine man sat on his box with his head in his hands. The train ride was also uncommonly quiet; some cried softly.

We arrived in late afternoon at Union Station. To kill time we wandered around the city through the evening and night moving from one coffee shop to another. We talked and read everything we found available at newsstands on Kennedy's death. There seemed to be lots of us that night in search of something.

We knew that JFK's body was to be taken to the Capitol for viewing early on Sunday afternoon. We joined the throngs of people of every variety lining Pennsylvania Avenue, some 20 deep, and watched the procession passing by. The dismal beat of drums dominated the scene. In retrospect they almost seemed deafening. I had that same chill I'd felt in another earlier procession, that of JFK's inauguration parade. The people, even the children, were remarkably quiet. Strangers held hands as occasional softer to louder sobs were heard.

After the procession passed our view, we dashed up the square to the front of the Capitol building, discovering there too was a mammoth crowd, waiting patiently to view JFK's body lying in state. We quickly discovered there were no shortcuts or bypasses around this throng, so we settled in line with others. Our wait was nearly seven hours and, not so surprisingly, everyone was remarkably courteous and kind, even respectful of one another. There was no shoving or pushing despite the enormous crowd.

Our wait in line was a test of everyone's endurance. Some dropped out to rest; some rejoined after sitting on the side for a while. Senior citizens seemed to be having a particularly difficult time. Infants and young children held to the parent's shoulders, nodding but not waking as the crowd shuffled on. Even in the bitter cold and darkness, people amazingly were not complaining. The line slowly plodded along.

By early morning we were inside the Capitol Rotunda and were able to briefly view the flag-covered coffin. Again the chills of the inaugural parade returned. My friend's and my mission was now accomplished. We had paid our respects to our hero. We returned by train early that Monday in the wee hours of the morning.

A week later I drove to Washington, D.C., on one last and solitary pilgrimage to say my private farewell to John F. Kennedy at Arlington Cemetery. It was there by myself a short distance from his grave that I finally knew JFK was gone; his life was over, but maybe not his purpose. This visit was for me one of closure, so important in matters of death "in the family." While JFK was one no more in body, he remains with me in spirit.

Ned Chalker, Peace Corps Employee, Washington, D.C.

Ned Chalker, like people everywhere, wanted to do something to show his love and respect for President Kennedy, particularly since he had recently returned from the Peace Corps.

In the fall of 1963, I was 25 years old and had just returned from serving two years as a Peace Corps volunteer in Colombia, South America. I was working at the International Peace Corps Secretariat

(ISCP) in the Peace Corps building right across from the White House. That Friday, I was returning from lunch to my office with one of my coworkers and found peoples' radios blaring and the news reporting that the President was dead. We couldn't believe it: not our President, not President Kennedy! It can't be true! The disbelief turned into tears as we began to realize what was really happening.

My office was near the corner of the building facing Lafayette Park. Outside the window of the corner office was the flagpole for the Peace Corps building. I said to someone, "Shouldn't we be lowering the flag to half mast?" As I looked around at all the other buildings surrounding Lafayette Square, I noticed that none of the other flags had yet been lowered. I thought to myself that it was fitting and proper that the flag on the Peace Corps building should be the first to be lowered. The Peace Corps was, after all, John F. Kennedy's creation and embodied the spirit of what he stood for. After a pause, I opened the window, climbed out on the ledge and lowered the flag.

My friend Sally and I didn't know what to do. Nobody knew what to do. It was all over, the dreams and the hopes. Why would anyone want to kill President Kennedy? Our inability to understand what was going on and our confusion was so overwhelmingly great that we went to a movie and tried not to think about it for a couple of hours. It didn't help. We just cried.

The next few days in Washington were totally surreal. We wandered around in a daze. We watched television and saw Jack Ruby shoot Lee Harvey Oswald. We watched as the nation mourned and wept. On the morning of the funeral procession, I stood on the corner of 18th and I Streets and watched world leaders, who up to now had only been faces on TV, march up 18th street to pay their respects to our President and to our dreams. Konrad Adenauer and Haile Selassie slowly walked by, old men paying homage to our hero.

The clop-clop of the horses pulling the caisson and the footsteps of these world leaders seemed to signal the passing of an era. Jacqueline, veiled in black, and Caroline and John-John walked slowly behind the caisson. I can still hear those horses. Hope, what would happen to hope, to Camelot? Would Johnson be able to pick up the banner? Would there be another leader who could inspire greatness and bring out the best in people . . . all over the world? There were many fears mixed in with the tears, and those of us who were part of that time will never forget the way we felt. These few days will forever be etched in my mind. I can never forget them. What might we have become if...?

Carl O. McDaniels, Staff Member, American Personnel and Guidance Association, Washington, D.C.

Dr. McDaniels and his young daughter were long-time local residents living near Arlington Cemetery. They came in the back way over a stone wall to observe the events from a nearby knoll.

In 1963, I was living in Arlington, Virginia, working as a professional staff member of the American Personnel and Guidance Association (APGA). My interest and enthusiasm concerning John F. Kennedy grew steadily as I first watched him campaign for the presidency and later become President. From the beginning I thought he would be a marvelous President and still strongly believe he was, despite his brief time in office.

On November 22, I was working in my APGA office in Washington. Someone called us from their home to tell us of Kennedy's being shot and his subsequent death. We were in a state of shock and were dazed. Being so upset, nobody could work, so we closed the office and one by one gradually drifted away. I recall a despondent mood seemed to grip all of us, which continued with my family when I returned home to Arlington. Like others, my family and I stayed glued to the television set and were spellbound as we watched the pageantry unfolding before us, including the participation of semilegendary international figures from all parts of the world, such as the enormous Charles de Gaulle of France and small-in-stature, Emperor Haile Selassie of Ethiopia.

Being distraught over Kennedy's death and a Washington area resident, I wasn't sure how to participate in helping to honor his death. I grew up in Arlington and had a special and personal relationship with Arlington Cemetery. First, my home was only a block away and both my parents were buried there. My father was a Navy veteran from World War I. As a result of these family connections, Arlington Cemetery was a neighborhood for me as a boy. When I learned my departed President would share the same beautiful burial grounds with my parents, I was convinced that I wanted to be there to honor him in a final farewell.

I realized this was a very significant point in history, so I decided to go to Arlington for Monday's last rites. With my 10-year-old daughter, Lynn, we parked at my sister's home near the west side of the cemetery. I knew a back route that few people knew existed. With my daughter, we climbed over the Cemetery's low stone wall and walked some two miles to the burial site. On the way we passed the graves of my parents. No one asked us any questions and we ended up on a knoll, some 20 yards from the gravesite. I was very surprised at the small number of people in attendance, but few were allowed to enter through the main gates leading in from the Memorial Bridge, and people generally were unaware of other points of entry.

The sounds of that day still ring in my ears. The solemn notes of taps and the crack of the rifles of the firing squad will last forever in my mind. The most memorable moment for me of the very moving occasion was when *Air Force One* flew low over the Potomac River, came over the hillside, and tipped its wings in a salute to Kennedy. I can't imagine there was a dry eye in the entire assembly at this point. It served as the immortal last tribute to a slain President.

When the ceremonies ended, we took the long walk back across the cemetery. Somehow the bright, crisp and sunny fall day seemed to have a gray cast to it. It was during the quiet and somber walk that the finality of JFK's death really hit me. At the time I didn't think my daughter, because of her youth was greatly affected by Kennedy's death. A few years later, after graduating from the University of Virginia, she entered the Peace Corps spending two years in the country of Bahrain. I am quite sure that Lynn's lingering memory of John F. Kennedy's goals for young Americans to serve their country partially influenced her to join the Peace Corps. The long-reaching legacy of John F. Kennedy is still ongoing today for millions of Americans as evidenced by the example of President Bill Clinton, an early admirer of JFK as a high-school student.

Dignitaries, including towering Charles DeGaulle and diminutive Haile Selassie, on the way to Arlington Cemetery, November 25, 1963.

I consider John F. Kennedy to have been an outstanding President. He represented a "new generation" as he characterized it. Many of the great changes made since 1960 in American society were initiated by JFK. Some of these are still ongoing, for example, in policies concerning the retraining of workers.

The call for service by Kennedy is clearly still alive with the Peace Corp, his best symbol. Kennedy seemed fundamentally interested in the welfare of the average American, including those with very limited opportunities and without a voice in government. He demonstrated this in his support of civil rights and programs for helping the less able. Again these controversial issues are still with us today. Kennedy represented well that tradition of those coming from a background of great wealth who entered into a life of service and philanthropic activity, such as Nelson and Jay Rockefeller.

The foundations of progress over the last three decades were laid in the Kennedy years. The legacy of JFK is still alive and well today. America is now a much better place because of the legacy of John F. Kennedy. He set the path and laid the base of prototypes that are still with us at the present. John F. Kennedy still lives today in the best ideals of the American dream of life, liberty and the pursuit of happiness for all.

Chapter Six

Overseas Military Reaction

Most Americans settled down in front of their television sets after Kennedy's assassination on a Friday afternoon and stayed glued to their sets through the funeral on Monday. However, the military, greatly concerned that the attack on Kennedy was the forerunner of large-scale aggressive action by the Soviet Union or some related form of conspiracy, went on full alert. Military personnel throughout the world feared a possible strike by the Soviets. Two officers recall the responses on military bases to the news of Kennedy's death: Mike Burton, an Air Force Second Lieutenant in England, and William Landis, an Army Captain in the Pacific stationed at Okinawa near Japan. Both had the difficult task of carrying out their military responsibilities while absorbing personal shock and grief over the loss of their Commander-in-Chief.

Mike Burton, Air Force Second Lieutenant, Lakenheath, England

Mike Burton comments on the concerns of the military worldwide that Kennedy's assassination was a prelude to a possible attack by the Soviet Union on the United States.

As a recently commissioned second lieutenant in the Air Force, I had become accustomed to pulling Officer of the Day (OD) duty on weekends. I was assigned to the 48th Tactical Fighter Wing at Royal Air Force Base, Lakenheath, near Cambridge in England. The base was one of the largest in Europe, housing three fighter squadrons. In November 1963, most military duties were routine. The Cuban missile crisis was behind us, and the Cold War now seemed to exist only in the newspapers.

On that November 22 weekend, my responsibilities as OD were
to conduct flag ceremonies, check any incoming operations messages,
and watch the BBC-TV comedy shows. The day began as expected as
I assumed my duties at 5:30 P.M. (12:00 P.M. EST) on Friday,
November 22. By 9:00 P.M., I had retreated to the OD room and was
deeply absorbed in a television program when the phone rang. The
voice on the other end was laconic but adamant: a cryptographic message had been received in the command post and I was told I should
hurry over. As I drove over to the command post, I searched my memory in an attempt to remember what a "cryptographic" message was.
All I could recall was that it was classified higher than "top secret."

At the command post, a sergeant started to hand me the encod-
ed message but then withdrew it and said: "Lieutenant you do have
cryptographic clearance, don't you?" I told him I didn't think I did,
and he shook his head. "We had better get the Wing Commander.
These things usually mean war alert." My stomach turned over, and
my thoughts were that the Cuban missile crisis had not been resolved
and we might be at war with the Russians. It seemed like hours, but it
was probably only minutes when the Wing Commander arrived. He
immediately went to the decoding room with the message after telling
me to standby. A few minutes later he came out looking solemn. For
a second, he looked at each of us in the room and said, "They've assassinated the President." Then he added, "The dirty bastards."

I felt a cold chill run through me and I wondered how the
"Russians" had managed to kill the President. I was transfixed and certainly unable to say anything. The Wing Commander then took me
by the arm in a caring fashion and told me to follow him. He had
orders to put the base on "full alert."

The alert status meant we fully armed the aircraft. The United
States never confirmed we had nuclear weapons in Europe, but the
"lack of denial," it was said, implied the kind of weaponry on the aircraft. Pilots were left in the cockpits and the engines were left on auxiliary power hookups for immediate takeoff. The Commander then
ordered me to close down the Officers' and Noncommissioned
Officers' clubs and make certain all personnel reported to their duty

stations. The Officers' Club was empty when I arrived so I drove quickly to the Noncommissioned Officers' (NCO) Club, which was jam-packed. The club manager greeted me with, "Kinda early, aren't you, Lieutenant?" The OD was expected to inspect the clubs but usually not until closing several hours later.

I told the manager I was there to shut down the club at the order of the Commander. He looked at me in disbelief. "Why?" he said. "The President's been assassinated," I told him. It was the first time I had said that. My mouth was so dry the words almost stuck there. I could see he still couldn't comprehend what I had told him. I repeated the statement and added that I wasn't joking. The manager's eyes grew large. He asked me to make the announcement to the troops in the club because he was afraid they wouldn't believe him. I went to the dance floor and commandeered the bandstand microphone and announced, "The club is closed, report to your duty stations; the President of the United States has been killed." There was an eerie moment of silence as the eyes of most in the room seemed fixed on me. Then pandemonium ensured as the room ignited in noise and movement. The NCOs rushed toward the exits. One sergeant came to me and asked if this meant we were at war. When I said no, he said, "Well, we'll kick the Russians' butts anyway," he said.

As I drove back to the command post, for the first time I had a moment to think about all that had happened in the last hour. I decided this was all a mistake, that the military, as usual, had screwed up a message or that this might even be a ploy to get us into real war with the Russians, but certainly John F. Kennedy wasn't dead. I felt too close to him; I had campaigned for him when I was in college. He had sparked in me a strong sense of ownership in a set of ideals that transcended mere mortal thoughts; he just couldn't be dead. Back at the command post all hell had broken loose. It was confirmed: the President was dead; we were on alert. I spent the next few hours shuffling messages back and forth and doing errands at the Commander's direction. I hand-delivered some messages to the squadron lines where the heat of the jet engines made me shiver as I thought about their potential missions.

We stayed on alert for several more days. Personnel were being restricted to the base and we became curiosity points for the British press. I was given the responsibility of saying "no comment" to inquiries. Since the journalists were mostly interested in our single quote feelings surrounding the death of our President, not our nuclear weapons, my comment seemed out of place.

By the day of the funeral, the base was back to normal operating status, but the reality of the assassination was just beginning to be discussed. Most of us were so absorbed in the alert operations that we had not had time to assess our own thoughts, let alone those of others. At a hastily put together memorial parade on November 25, I was lined up next to another lieutenant when taps was sounded. I knew this lieutenant to be a very nonpolitical, southern conservative, who seemed perturbed to have to be in the parade that day. As those solemn notes sounded out, I looked at him to see tears streaming down his cheeks. That's when I first cried.

William M. Landis, Captain, U.S. Army, Okinawa
Bill Landis stationed on the other side of the world in Asia also comments on the prospects of war with the Soviet Union and the reaction of his fellow soldiers to the President's death.

On November 22, 1963, I was a newly promoted captain serving with a logistical and administrative headquarters on Okinawa, one of the Ryukyu Islands, located south of Japan. We supported troops in training on Okinawa and were ready for commitment anywhere in the Far East.

Okinawans generally were friendly to Americans and grateful for our help in recovering from the abject poverty and insecurity they had experienced before and during the World War II. Okinawans respected Americans as a people who had developed a high standard of living, who were strong, and who seemed both lucky and invulnerable. American soldiers were perceived by Okinawans to have an especially close, personal, and affectionate relationship with a powerful and charismatic President. It was heady indeed to be a "rich American soldier and his fortunate family" on Okinawa.

That atmosphere was destroyed forever when President Kennedy was assassinated. I was a duty officer, at home in the early morning, when I received a phone call. A telegram was read to me indicating that President Kennedy had been shot. Before that telegram was finished, another was received and read to me indicating that the President was dead. I was stunned, bewildered, and suddenly felt our isolation. My first thought was of Abraham Lincoln's assassination and the attempt on the life of a Lincoln cabinet member. Who else among Kennedy's top leadership might also be targeted? Was the killing part of a larger plan? If so, what was the plan? Much later, I had a feeling of great loss about Kennedy as a man, but right then, I had a gut reaction of controlled fear and professional commitment. I reacted as if the assassination of the President and Commander-in-Chief of the armed forces was an act of war to which we (the military) had to be ready to respond.

I immediately made a series of phone calls as required by the emergency action plan. I remember that when I called Colonel Ralph N. Huse, the Adjutant General, there was a long silence, a gasp, and then, "Oh my God!" His tone of voice is fresh in my memory.

As I finished the calls, officers were streaming out of their homes, tugging on whatever uniform came to hand, jumping into their cars, and tearing off toward their units. Later I learned that only a few had actually been ordered to report. Most had simply reacted to the news as it filtered down to them or they heard radio announcements. Later I heard from the participants that some units had gone so far in their alert countdown that the men were in combat gear and ready to load. The aircraft had their engines running before the units were ordered to stand down and return to their barracks.

There was a general feeling that the assassination might be a prelude to war. In my own office, everyone immediately reported in when they heard the news. We pulled out the emergency plans, made sure we were ready to receive and pass on casualty reports and then stood around talking in hushed tones. There was nothing to do, but we felt better in uniform at what we thought might become a wartime command post.

I recall that my office supervised the raising and lowering of the headquarters flag. For some reason, the expected telegram from Hawaii about flying the flag at half-mast was delayed. When the time came, as duty officer I ordered half-mast despite the lack of authorization. One of the most stirring sights I have ever seen was the American flag at half-mast against the sharply white clouds and intensely blue sky typical of Okinawa.

That evening at a long scheduled dinner party, attendance was very high and all were wearing somber clothes. There had been no discussion or official decision. It just happened. Later all social events were canceled but that first evening we needed to be together, dressed for the saddest of all occasions.

The commemorative parade was a "pull-out-all-the-stops" affair, including much equipment rarely seen. One oddity I remember was a donut-shaped tire, which turned out to be a towed fuel tank. One friend, a brand-new captain, was so determined to attend the parade that he went, even though he could not be in proper uniform. In the excitement he could find only one of the required pair of captain's bars. He told people the other must have fallen off his uniform; in fact, it was never there.

Afterwards, Okinawans asked us why had we allowed our President to be killed? The event shook their faith in the invincibility, the invulnerability, and the luck of Americans. From then on, Americans seemed to be ordinary people. Camelot turned out to be an illusion after all.

Chapter Seven

The Nation Reacts

John F. Kennedy was greatly admired by the American public from all walks of life. Margaret Truman Daniel recalls her early introduction to JFK and later remembers visits to the White House, including those with her father, Harry S. Truman. Cliff Robertson who portrayed Kennedy in the movie, *PT 109*, depicting the wartime exploits of Kennedy, describes his contacts with JFK concerning the film. Because Kennedy was the first Catholic President, his death was a particularly difficult loss for many Catholics. Special attention is given here to the reactions of the Catholic clergy, including the former President of Notre Dame, Rev. Theodore Hesburgh. Former President Jimmy Carter shares his perspective as well as political scientist, James MacGregor Burns, who was the earliest biographer of JFK and had a long-term relationship with him prior to Kennedy's presidency. Other Americans, ranging from teachers to blue-collar workers, offer their recollections of the President, including a poignant reminiscence of a young JFK returning from war in the Pacific by a California physician.

Margaret Truman Daniel, Author, New York City
Mrs. Daniel is the daughter of former President Harry S. Truman. She is also well-known as an author of mystery novels. She recalls the days when she knew Jack Kennedy as a young congressman and continues on to the last days after the assassination.

The death of John F. Kennedy was a great shock to both me and my father. I first learned of the President's being shot from the doorman of my New York City apartment building. At first I didn't really pay much attention to the news and thought he was out of his mind. I turned on the television to see what the doorman was talking about and soon learned of the enormity of the shooting. Both my parents had narrowly avoided assassination a decade earlier.

On Sunday, I went to Washington to be with my 79-year-old-father, who came from Independence, Missouri, to attend Kennedy's funeral. LBJ arranged for a plane to bring him to Washington and we stayed at the Blair House. We both attended the funeral at St. Matthew's as well as the graveside burial. My father was shaken by the event as he had become quite fond of Jack Kennedy.

We sat near the front during the service at St. Matthew's. An aide asked us if we minded sharing a ride with General and Mrs. Eisenhower to Arlington Cemetery. Of course we agreed and they rode with us. After the funeral, Jackie, Bobby and the family had left. Since the Eisenhowers had driven in from Gettysburg, I asked them if they would like to stop at the Blair House for sandwiches and a drink. They did and we had a pleasant talk together. Despite reports in the press that this was a major reconciliation between Eisenhower and my father, this was not true as they had been in friendly contact with each other earlier.

Reminiscing back about Jack Kennedy, I first got to know him when he was a young congressman from Massachusetts. I had the first party at the White House after World War II, a dinner-dance, and Jack and his sister Eunice were there. Eunice served as his Washington hostess before he married Jackie. I also interviewed Jack when he was a senator on my show about his book, *Profiles in Courage*.[13] I liked Jack very much and also enjoyed Bobby.

My father campaigned hard for Jack's election in 1960. One of the happiest occasions for my father after leaving the presidency was Jack's honoring him at a White House dinner on November 1, 1961. Dad, Mother, and my husband, Clifton, and I attended. In a way it was like a reunion since so many of Dad's appointees were also serving in the Kennedy administration. Kennedy remarked on the close connections between the Truman and Kennedy staffs. We all had a lovely time at the dinner despite the tough grouse served as the main course. When I heard Jack complain about the bird to Jackie, I told Bobby Kennedy, who was sitting next to me, "Those White House

Courtesy of the John F. Kennedy Library

Former President Harry Truman plays the piano at the White House while watched by the featured pianist, Eugene List, November 1, 1961.

knives never could cut butter." This line broke up Bobby and others. After dinner, we were entertained in the East Room with a piano concert played by Eugene List, who had first played for Dad when List was a staff sergeant at the Potsdam Conference. After List concluded, Dad was persuaded to play for the group. We all went upstairs to the family quarters after the dinner and concert and Jack said to Dad, "I'm going to say goodnight because I know you start out early." I told Jack, "I would rather start out with you. I don't like to get up early either." We thanked both Jack and Jackie and went to bed.

The next morning Clifton and I had an early breakfast with Mother and Dad, left the White House, and went to the Mayflower Hotel. Shortly after we arrived, I received a phone call. It was Jackie in a very small, quiet voice asking, "Margaret, where are you?" I said, "Jackie, we have left. We are at the Mayflower Hotel." Jackie said, "My goodness, you did get up early." I responded, "Don't tell me, I know

I got up early." I agreed with her but never could prove it to Dad.

Little did I know that only two years after that delightful visit to the White House, I would once again return to Washington to make a final farewell to John F. Kennedy. I was a great admirer of Kennedy and thought he was becoming a wonderful President. It was just too bad in so many ways what happened. If he had lived, it could have saved us untold amounts of misery. He really knew what he was doing and his death was a great loss to the nation.

Lucy Kroll, Literary Agent, New York City

President and Mrs. Kennedy were patrons of the arts and were highly admired by writers such as Carl Sandburg. Mrs. Kroll was a close friend and the agent of author, Carl Sandburg. She relates the association of Sandburg with the President.

I was having lunch in New York with an editor discussing an upcoming publication when we learned the terrible news of President Kennedy's death. We both were shocked by the assassination and went home. Like everyone, I spent the next few days with my son and husband glued to the television.

One of my favorite clients during this period was the 86-year-old poet, Carl Sandburg. He and his steadfast friend and wife, Paula, lived at their home in the Blue Ridge Mountains near Flat Rock, North Carolina. I became Sandburg's agent in 1958 and soon became good friends with him and his wife. In time I felt like one of the family. Since I became his agent only in the latter years of his career, I found myself serving in multiple roles, assisting not only as his agent, but also as his protector and financial mentor.

Sandburg had become a great admirer of John F. Kennedy and worked for his election in 1960 as he had done for earlier Democratic candidates, FDR and Harry Truman, even though he claimed to be politically independent. In October 1961, Sandburg came to Washington, D.C., to help open the Civil War Centennial Exhibition at the Library of Congress. As part of this celebration, Mrs. Kennedy sponsored an "Evening with Carl Sandburg," a black-tie occasion.

Courtesy of the John F. Kennedy Library

President Kennedy and Carl Sandburg share thoughts in the Oval Office.

Sandburg also visited President Kennedy in the White House and commented that "Mr. Kennedy looks as if he might become a great President."

After the meeting with President Kennedy, he gave a press conference that stirred up controversy because of his remarks about former President Eisenhower. Eisenhower had made a recent speech degrading the Peace Corps, and Sandburg accused "Ike" of putting "his foot in his mouth."

Sandburg admired Kennedy's intelligence, courage, and forthright style. He was particularly taken by his inaugural address, calling it "an American classic." Once when speaking in Orange County, California, a bastion of conservative Republicans, he began by reading all of Kennedy's inaugural address and described the phrases of the speech as "Lincolnesque."

In 1961, John W. Gardner, President of the Carnegie Corporation, asked Sandburg to write the foreword to a book of

Kennedy's speeches and writings that Gardner was editing. Sandburg did so, and in his foreword to *To Turn the Tide,* he concluded about John F. Kennedy:

> When our generation has passed away, when the tongues of praise and comment now speaking have turned to a cold dumb dust, it will be written that John F. Kennedy walked with the American people in their diversity and gave them all he had toward their moving on into new phases of their great human adventure.[14]

In 1963, my family and the Sandburgs both were devastated by the President's death. The Sandburgs asked me to share their feelings in a letter of sympathy from me to Mrs. Kennedy. The Sandburgs felt that the poem that Carl had written in 1945, *When Death Came April Twelve, 1945,* in memory of Franklin Roosevelt, was appropriate and true now, and it reflected their strong affection for President Kennedy. My letter to Mrs. Kennedy ended with the lines from the Sandburg poem: "Dreamer, sleep deep, Toiler, sleep long, Fighter, be rested now, Commander, sweet good night."

Cliff Robertson, Actor, Pacific Palisades, California

Cliff Robertson is a well-known film star and Oscar Award winner who played the role of Jack Kennedy in the film, PT 109, *that relates the story of Kennedy's wartime exploits in the Pacific theater in World War II as a PT boat commander.*

I learned that President Kennedy had been shot in a somewhat ironic fashion. That November I was shooting a movie in southern California and was temporarily living in a rented house in Pacific Palisades. On that tragic Friday, I was talking by telephone with a dear and good friend of mine, UPI reporter, Vernon Scott. We were by coincidence discussing my role in the recently released movie, *PT 109,* where I portrayed a young navy lieutenant and hero, Jack Kennedy. In the midst of our conversation, I heard bells ringing in the background from Vernon's office. He told me, "Hold on Cliff" and left. He soon came back and asked: "Are you sitting down?" I said, "Why?" He informed me, "The President has just been shot. He is in the hospital and it doesn't look good." A little later my secretary came to the door with tears in eyes and I told her to go home.

I then went out an hour or so after that in my car and the entire town seemed silent. Everything was so quiet and I don't even recall a single horn honking. This entire sequence of time seems to be wound down in some form of slow motion. It was as if the entire community had been struck down. I felt a sense of loss and shame. It was so tragic that, in such a good and democratic country as ours, we are so ridden with violence.

Reflecting back on the film, *PT 109,* I remember that my original involvement in the project was unique in my experience. In 1962, while in the midst of doing a picture with Paramount, I was called to do a film test for the movie, *PT 109.* I was told by my agent that it had all been arranged. Since neither one of us had heard about this before, this was a surprise. Nevertheless, I did the screen test and promptly forgot about it. Shortly after that I got a call from a friend in New York inquiring about my new role. He asked, "What is this about you and *PT 109?* Your picture is in the paper alongside President Kennedy and the article indicates you are being sought and the White House wants you to play the role of Kennedy in the movie." I called my agent and all of this was news to him as well as to me.

When I learned that Lewis Milestone was to be director of the film, a man of great cinematic reputation and very sound and good character, I wanted to meet Milestone, or "Millie" as he was affectionately known, to discuss the project. We met, and he convinced me that we could make this a better picture than the script indicated. Warner Brothers for years had tended to produce formula action films. We wanted to improve on the script with *PT 109* and do the best job possible to honor and serve the President.

At this point, I found out that President Kennedy had personally viewed footage of screen tests to determine who should portray him in the film. Pierre Salinger, the White House Press Secretary, was a liaison between Warner Brothers and the President on the project. Salinger told me, "On the day that your test was shown, Jack came in, sat there, and when they showed your test, he said, "That's him!" and so I was selected.

We shot the film in several locations in 1962 on a small mosquito-ridden island located off Key West, Florida, and Key Largo. We also filmed in Hollywood using a very large set. We had two PT boats in the Keys and another one in Hollywood. The Hollywood set included the entire huge bow of a Japanese destroyer built to scale.

We had considerable discord making the film due primarily to the producer Bryan "Briney" Foy, who had a reputation of being quite difficult to work with. Foy soon clashed with the director, Lewis Milestone. I also had my own misgivings about Foy. While we were shooting in the Keys, Foy replaced Milestone, who was extremely popular without exception with both the cast and crew. All we knew was that Milestone was out and a new director, Les Martinson, was suddenly selected to replace him. When the crew learned that "Millie" had been dropped, they came to me and announced they wanted to quit. I talked them out of this, arguing for the need to fulfill our professional obligations, but I did call Pierre Salinger to see if he could help out, but nothing came of this. Ironically, the new director also ended up clashing with Foy. I recall a shouting match between the two on a dock in the Keys.

In 1963, I began a picture in New York costarring with Jane Fonda in a film entitled *Sunday in New York*. I got a call from the White House asking me to come down for a visit with the President. I arranged to be off shooting for a day and went to Washington. I actually went very early, not wanting to be late. I had to kill time for a couple of hours in the National Gallery of Art. I think I was the only person who ever saw every picture in the Gallery in such a short time without really remembering seeing a thing about any of them because of my excitement over meeting the President.

In the White House, while briefly waiting a few moments outside the President's office, I noticed models of old New England sailing ships on the wall. One was of particular interest to me: a famous whaling ship. In my own collection of artifacts, I had an original harpoon that was

Courtesy of the John F. Kennedy Library

President Kennedy and Cliff Robertson discuss the film, PT 109, March 24, 1963.

used on that very same boat on the wall. To my surprise, a door behind my chair that I didn't realize was there opened, and a very friendly voice said, "Cliff, sorry I kept you waiting, come into my office." It was the President. We had a very cordial discussion, particularly sharing thoughts on our two daughters while the President sat in his famous rocking chair. He was very impressive as a man and couldn't have been nicer as a person. He was also very interested in the picture and again told me I was his personal choice to play him. One decision we made in making the film was not to have me use a Bostonian accent. We feared that the distinctive accent might detract from the role. The President was very glad we had not used this approach and was pleased we focused on the character and interior of him as an individual in a nonregional way. All in all, the White House half-hour visit was a delightful experience. I also received several presidential White House mementos for myself and my family.

Subsequently, I took the old metal harpoon in my collection and had a New England craftsman, using antique tools and original wood, add a shaft to make it as nearly authentic as possible harpoon for a gift from me to the President. The job was so well done that a check with a naval museum assured us that we had an exact replica of the original harpoon. The President received the gift while visiting his sister Pat in California and sent me a lovely note of thanks for it. All of these events in the earlier days of 1963 are among the happy recollections I have of our President.

Nearly 40 years later, I still remember President Kennedy as a man of unusual personal charm and warmth. Even more importantly, I remember him as a leader of great promise who never had the chance to carry out his potential. Even in his brief tenure in office, he lit a torch that touched the world and gave hope that he would be a leader of the West who could help lead other nations out of darkness. Over the years I have traveled all over the world in my activities for various charities. Everywhere I have gone, from Ethiopia to the Ukraine to China, people of all races and walks of life still respond to John F. Kennedy and the mere mention of his name lights up their eyes.

Sam Huff, Professional Football Player, New York

Sam Huff was an all-star professional football player with the New York Giants and had worked for Kennedy's election campaign of 1960. He recalls the dilemma facing professional athletes about playing a game in the face of a national tragedy.

I heard with unbelievable shock the news that President Kennedy was shot while I was riding in the middle of the Triborough Bridge in New York City. I was with fellow player, Don Chandler, the team punter on my way from practice to my home in Flushing, Long Island.

Thinking back, I recall my first meeting with then Senator John F. Kennedy when he was running for the presidential nomination in West Virginia. It was a rainy and cold day in April, 1960. I met

Kennedy in Clarksburg and was helping him in his campaign. We then drove to Fairmont, a small city in the heart of the coal fields near my hometown. I remember Senator Kennedy asking me what I thought he should talk about in his speech. I urged him to tackle the Catholic issue head on, which he did in a magnificent speech. As everyone knows, Senator Kennedy went on to a sweeping victory over Senator Hubert Humphrey for the West Virginia primary. This win clinched for him the Democratic Presidential nomination by demonstrating that a Catholic candidate for President could win in a overwhelmingly Protestant state.

Returning to those terrible days in November, 1963, I strongly opposed playing our game against the St. Louis Cardinals scheduled for Sunday afternoon, November 24, at Yankee Stadium. Even though I was a great admirer of Kennedy, I don't believe we should play football games if any President has been shot, or if another event of such magnitude has occurred. National Football League Commissioner Pete Rozelle's decision to play the games that day was one of the few mistakes he ever made. The American Football League canceled their four-game schedule, including the New York Jets against the Kansas City Chiefs at the Polo Grounds in New York.

Until the game that Sunday, November 24, I never had before or since regretted playing a football game in high school, college, or in the pros. In that game I didn't want to be a participant. A vital part of playing sports is to have the right mental attitude. I was not in any mood to play football that day, and our team was accurately described as playing like "sleepwalkers." Even though we were fighting for the Eastern Conference lead, our heads weren't in the game and we lost. Yet our loss seemed very insignificant when compared to that of our nation. I still remember back to that day in Fairmont, West Virginia, where John F. Kennedy stirred me with his inspirational words.

James L. Stephens, High School Social Studies Teacher, Marietta, Ohio

American history teacher Jim Stephen's angry reaction to Kennedy's death was to blame a right-wing conspiracy.

For me, looking back at that awful Friday, November 22, I remember I was in the school yearbook's darkroom, working with students when a tap came at the door. "The President's been shot!" was the breathless message brought by someone, I forget who. We were dumbstruck. Several emotions raced through my mind, fear for Kennedy's life, rage at the attacker, suspicion of who might have plotted this outrage, and, of course, deep sorrow.

Like many people my age, 38, I identified with the Kennedy presidency. We admired his vigor, ideas, leadership, humor, and his family life. I was married and the father of three young daughters. Another teacher and I had traveled to Washington in 1962 to visit the Capitol, the White House, and all the city's governmental attractions. I remember especially the happy tone of the White House under the direction of Mrs. Kennedy.

In my United States history classroom where my students had been informed of the shooting, some were crying and others asking questions. Then we received the worst news possible: he was dead. I must confess that I lost my composure and lashed out, "Just you bear in mind, I think some right-wing bunch has done this. They couldn't take all the liberal changes in the country and got rid of our President!"

I fell into a deep despair. That weekend was a nightmare. Our family never left the television set and sat there fascinated as the drama unfolded right before our eyes. Oswald's capture, the emergency room turmoil, Lyndon Johnson's swearing-in with Jackie standing there in blood-stained clothing.

Our weather was beautiful the day of the funeral. I remember watching the ceremony with the kids and young neighbors. Afterwards we took a walk and I can still see how the setting sun shone on the electric and telephone wires looping down our street toward the river. It was a slow, sad walk, we didn't have much to say.

Despite his faults, revealed years later, I still think Jack Kennedy's presidency was a breath of fresh air after eight years of Republican "do-nothingism." What kind of country would we be today if he had not been killed? Oswald did far more than just kill one man; he destroyed the spirit of idealism in America.

Rev. George F. Riley, Instructor and Priest, Villanova University, Pennsylvania

Father Riley was a young Irish-American priest from Massachusetts who recalls his earliest memories of Kennedy as a young congressman.

It was a raw, overcast November afternoon. Having been ordained a Catholic priest only two years earlier and still in relatively good athletic shape, I deemed myself to be "king of the kids on campus." I had completed my doctorate and was teaching and serving as prefect in a dormitory at Villanova University.

In reality I was perhaps, and still am, more of a kid at heart than the students. On that particular Friday afternoon, I was playing basketball with the students. I can remember with dreadful precision that we were on the south end of the university's field house court when the Sports Information Director, Ken Mugler, yelled down from the balcony where his offices were that, "They had just shot President Kennedy."

We were stunned but, in the sweat and excitement of heavy-duty athletics, we all thought that somehow everything was going to be all right. It was not until I returned an hour later to the monastery common room where I lived, that I realized the situation was graver than I had originally anticipated. A good number of the priests were glued to the television set and one was openly sobbing. The President was dead and all were very saddened, shaken and shocked beyond belief.

Like everyone else, I went through the psychological trauma that most of the country felt. "What the hell were we coming to?" We had just gone through the Cuban missile crisis that had really flabbergasted the students and brought them back "in droves" to religion, all thinking that Armageddon was at hand.

I had met President Kennedy during his first congressional race in my hometown of Lawrence, Massachusetts. A picture of the young, very thin, malaria-ridden, yellow-colored, congressional candidate taken with my uncle is displayed to this day in my office. His tragic death and the ensuing drama that followed will be forever carved into my long Irish memory.

As I concluded my sermon on the Sunday following the assassination, I used the somber words of Senator Michael Mansfield spoken in the Capitol Rotunda:

> There was a man of laughter . . . in a moment it
> was no more. There was a wit in a man, a wit full
> of old man's wisdom and young man's hopes and
> . . . in a moment, it was no more. There was a man,
> marked with scars for love of his country, an active
> body with a surge for life, far, far from being spent
> . . . an in a moment it was no more.[15]

President Kennedy in his inaugural address sounded a call to arms for a new spirit of volunteerism and a rekindling of America's pioneering tradition. His countrymen responded by joining the Peace Corps, Vista, and other cultural and service organizations. At the same time, he set in motion plans for mankind's greatest achievement: the landing of a man on the moon. In my opinion, no president since Franklin Delano Roosevelt had been able to arouse the American people to such heights of confidence, courage and compassion. Today we cling desperately to that legacy.

Jimmy Carter, Peanut Farmer, Plains, Georgia

This is the only vignette in the book drawn from an outside source. It is from a speech given by President Jimmy Carter at the dedication ceremony of the John F. Kennedy Library, October 20, 1979.

On that November day some three decades ago, a terrible moment was frozen in the lives of Americans. I remember that I was working in a field of my farm. I climbed down from the seat of my tractor, unhooked a farm trailer, and walked into my warehouse to weigh a load of grain. I was told by a group of farmers that the President had been shot. I went outside, knelt on the steps and began to pray. In a few minutes, I learned that he had not lived. It was a grievous personal loss, my President. I wept openly for the first time in more than 10 years, for the first time since the day my father died.

People wept in Boston and in Paris, in Atlanta and in Warsaw, in

San Francisco and in New Delhi. More than anyone had realized before that day, the spirit of this young American President had taken hold of the hearts and the imaginations of countless millions of people all over the world.

Sixteen years later I spoke at the dedication ceremonies for the John F. Kennedy Library in Boston. These are excerpts from the Carter remarks at that ceremony:

> I never met him, but I know that John Kennedy loved politics, he loved laughter, and when the two came together, he loved that best of all.

> President Kennedy understood the past and respected its shaping of the future. Yet he was very much a man of his own time. The first President born in this century, he embodied the ideals of a generation as few public figures have ever done in the history of the Earth. He summoned our nation out of complacency, and he set it on a path of excitement and hope.

> The accomplishments of those thousand days, as you well know, are notable, though his presidency was too short for him to finish all the tasks that he set for himself. We honor him not just for the things he completed but for the things he set in motion, the energies that he released, and the ideas and the ideals which he espoused.

> The problems are different; the solutions, none of them easy, are also different. But in this age of hard choices and scare resources, the essence of President Kennedy's message—the appeal for unselfish dedication to the common good—is more urgent than it ever was. The spirit that he evoked—the spirit of sacrifice, of patriotism, of unstinting dedication—is the same spirit that will bring us safely through the adver-

sities that we face today. The overarching purpose of this Nation remains the same - to build
a just society in a secure American living at peace
with the other nations of the world.[16]

James MacGregor Burns, Professor of Political Science, Williams College, Massachusetts

*Burns wrote the first biography of John F. Kennedy. His relationship
with Kennedy went back to the early 1950s. He was one of the first
observers to realize that Kennedy would become a serious candidate for
President.*

I was teaching a class in the basement of the First Congregational
Church in Williamstown. While I am a member of this church, the
reason was a shortage of classrooms at Williams College; the church
sits in the middle of the campus. I always have felt that there was a
symbolic importance in my having been at this place.

A student came to the door. I have been so rarely interrupted in
teaching a class at Williams that my first reaction was that there was
some crisis in my family. But the student quickly explained that
President Kennedy had been shot and wounded. The reaction of the
class and myself was interesting. We were a bit stunned but of course
did not know how serious the incident was. I also had to remember
the number of times over the years that reports such as this had been
exaggerated or just plain invented. So in a kind of distracted way, we
continued our class discussion. Then a few minutes later, the same student, as I recall, came into the classroom to say that the President had
been killed. Once again, it took a while for this to register, perhaps a
minute or two while the class and I looked at each other. Then we
realized that the class could not go on.

I walked down the street to my home, about a three-minute walk,
to find everything in chaos and consternation there. Because locally I
was considered something of a Kennedy expert, having known him
and written a biography of him and campaigned with him in 1958,
the media had turned to me for lack of anyone more prominent in the

area. So calls were flooding in, two or three television vans were parked in the driveway, and the house was full of bedlam. We were all grieving, but still too stunned and shocked to vent our emotions. In a way the turmoil probably helped us get through the first hours, simply because we had to cope with phone calls and visits.

Reflecting back to 1958, I was then the Democratic candidate for Congress in the westernmost district of Massachusetts. During the campaign I maintained a friendly working relationship with Senator Kennedy, who was a candidate for reelection. I had earlier been a backer of his in his dramatic upset victory over the incumbent, Senator Henry Cabot Lodge in 1952.

Senator Kennedy was reelected and I was defeated. He offered me a responsible position in his office. I declined because I felt that, despite my affection and admiration for him, I did not know enough about his presidential qualifications to make the complete commitment that such a job required. It was very clear to me at that time he aspired to the presidency.

Late in 1958, Harcourt, Brace suggested that I write a biography of the senator. I did so for two reasons. It would satisfy my own curiosity about his presidential potential and, more importantly, it would give me a chance to write about a man before the voters might have to pass judgment on him. As a result of my decision, I wrote in 1959 the first biography of John F. Kennedy, *John F. Kennedy: A Political Profile.*[17]

One urgent question bothered me greatly with the book. Could I get full authentic information on a candidate running for high office? I put this question to President Kennedy late in 1958 and asked for complete and unrestricted access to his official and personal files. To all this he agreed, and with such an understanding, I proceeded.

After accumulating a considerable amount of information on Kennedy, it became clear to me in 1959 that he must be taken with the utmost seriousness as a presidential candidate. I concluded he had far more intellectual depth and steadfastness than many supposed. I discovered him to be far different from the image many held of him,

that of a sunny, gregarious type who liked nothing more than stumping the country, or as a glamorous matinee idol who would be a
Hollywood star if he were not a Washington politician. Actually I
found him to be a serious, driven man, about as casual as a cash register, who enjoyed the organizational, technical part of politics but not
the stumping, which he considered simply grinding hard work. One
word stood out to describe Kennedy more exactly than any other: self-
possession. He had never been seen, even by his mother, in raging
anger or uncontrollable tears.

In the last few pages of my book, I speculated on what sort of a
President Kennedy would make. I concluded he would probably create a no-nonsense type of administration, run by men young, dedicated, tough-minded, hard-working, informed, alert and passionless.
I predicted the administration would be unusually sensitive to criticism and there would be a never-ending process of self-appraisal. The
sharpest immediate shift from the Eisenhower years would likely come
in federal social-welfare policies, but there would not be abrupt breaks
with the outgoing administration. In foreign policy, new actions
toward Africa, India and Latin America would probably be undertak-
en. However, Kennedy believed that foreign policy was based on our
strength at home in areas such as education and productivity of the
economy.

The concerns I raised for Kennedy were in the area of leadership
and depended on the demands of the 1960s. I found considerable
resemblance in the Kennedy potential with that of FDR. Both were
pragmatic and could stand up under tremendous pressure, but I perceived differences in the two as well. I was concerned that Kennedy
lacked Roosevelt's humor and joyousness, his superb acting ability, his
magnetism with crowds, his power of oral expression. I wondered if
Kennedy would show similar imagination and daring under critical
conditions.

Looking back to the brief Kennedy presidency decades later, I will
leave it to others to decide the accuracy of my 1959 speculations. I will
remember President Kennedy as a terribly bright man with a great
mind. In less than three years he had a psychological impact on the

world unlike any other figure in modern history. Pictures of him are still found in homes all over the world. His active accomplishments were limited in his few years in office, yet his image transcends his limitations and subsequent critics. I will remember him as one of the finest persons I have ever known: enjoying, intellectually responsive, simple, direct, remarkable frank, and always very human.

Bob Wright, U.S. Marine Corps, Great Lakes Naval Training Station

President Kennedy was particularly popular among members of the various branches of the military as illustrated by the observations of Bob Wright.

I was a 21-year-old bugler in the U.S. Marines in November 1963 at the Great Lakes Naval Training Station. I was in Field Music, a drum and bugle corps. Each Marine barracks had two Field Musics. I will never forget that Friday. It was a routine day, and I had just returned to the third floor of my barracks from the chow hall. When I reached the squad room and found a bunch of Marines gathered around the radio, one told me the President had just been shot. I then received a call on our pay telephone from my wife, who just had seen the news on television. For the next 20 minutes I continued talking to my wife who relayed the news from television to me and I, in turn, kept yelling out the news to others gathered outside the telephone booth. Nobody could really believe it. We all were devastated. Everybody then headed to our recreation room where we had a television and stayed there watching the news. By 3:30 P.M. nearly everyone had cleared out.

Very early Saturday morning I was notified that I was to be the bugler for a flag-lowering ceremony to be held that morning. It was 8:00 A.M. on a chilly, gray and overcast day on the edge of Lake Michigan. Under dull skies, a group of some 50 military personnel with around 500 to 600 spectators, including the press, watched the carrying out of our solemn military ceremony. We had both a Marine and Navy color guard.

The emotional setting for the event was one I never will forget. As a bugler, I always tried to give my playing of taps my best shot. The last thing anyone will remember from military ceremony such as this are the plaintive notes from my bugle. In a way I provided the final farewell for the person being honored. If I brought tears to the eyes of the audience with my rendition, I thought I had done my job well.

The brief 15-minute ceremony involved my playing "To the Colors," and the flag was raised to full mast. Then there was a three-shot volley by the firing squads followed by the lowering of the flag to half-mast as I played taps. My adrenaline was really flowing, and I desperately wanted to do a perfect job. We had no speakers. The simple but moving event ended leaving many in tears, and I was really choked up. We then all marched off. In my eight and one-half years as a Marine, I took part in some 300 funeral ceremonies; none were close to the emotional setting of the one I participated in for President Kennedy that Saturday.

Thinking back about President Kennedy, I still regard him as a great leader and a man who cared for all the people. He never seemed above others. He was extremely popular with the Marines including myself. One concern that Marines shared was that Oswald was a former Marine and we felt a little guilt over the association. I still believe President Kennedy to be one of our better Presidents and greatly liked him and miss him even today.

Kathleen O'Connell, O. P., Principal, Edgewood High School, Madison, Wisconsin

For the late Sister O'Connell, her most haunting memory of this event was that of a young student praying and sobbing at the back of the chapel.

Instinctively, I shrink from looking back to the November weekend that marked an end to the hopes and dreams of so many Americans. "Where was I when I heard the news? What was I doing? What images of that weekend stand out most clearly?" As I struggle to answer these questions, I am overwhelmed by the remembrance of disbelief, of grief, of numbness.

In 1963, I was principal of a coeducational Catholic high school in Madison, Wisconsin. On November 22, I was on my way out of my office to supervise a late lunch period when the phone rang. To this day I do not remember who the caller was. I only remember standing with the phone in my hand and hearing someone say, "The President has been shot. He has been taken to a hospital in Dallas. He probably won't make it." In shock, I put down the phone and moved toward the public address system to relate the message to teachers and students. I stopped midway thinking, "This cannot be true! I should check the information before I make an announcement." I turned the radio on and received a confirmation of the startling news.

Moments later the school community came together to hope and pray for a miracle. Soon word of Kennedy's death ended all hope. Students left the building in stunned silence. One image of that tragic afternoon haunts me and transcends all others. It is the image of a high-school boy, kneeling in the back pew of the chapel long after the others had left. His head was buried in his arms and he was sobbing his heart out. I knew that in pre-election days this young man had haunted local Kennedy campaign headquarters and had worked tirelessly preparing mailings and distributing campaign literature. I knew, too, that Kennedy was his hero. How I agonized for him! For me, the image of that young man has always symbolized the grief of the nation.

In the days that immediately followed Kennedy's death I, like many Americans, experienced a sensation of unreality, a feeling that life was suspended, that time had stopped. Many images of those days crowd into my mind. All of them are vivid, never-to-be forgotten memories of a time of tragedy. My remembrance of Oswald's murder is especially strong. I can recall exactly where I stood watching the television when that fatal shot was fired. I can still hear the involuntary gasp of disbelief with which my cowatchers and I responded. This image, as well as Kennedy's assassination has become, for me, a precursor and a symbol of the violence that has increasingly dominated our society.

In the years since Kennedy's death, "What if's" often appear in reflections about his presidency. "Would America be different if he had lived?" "Would he have continued to be a hero to thousands of young people?" "Would he have been a truly effective president?"

We have no valid answers to these questions. We do know that we have learned little from the violence of that November weekend. Much of our world still believes that problems are best solved by force, by violence. Not only nations, but many individuals live by this belief.

There are, however, glimmerings of hope. Voices for a peaceful society are being raised. The United Nations is becoming more active in the cause of peace. A number of world leaders are growing in the realization that the resolution of conflict by force is seldom permanent. Even more significant is the fact that in many lands individuals and groups of individuals are working tirelessly to remove the injustices that breed violence.

If Kennedy were alive today, where would he be in all this? I believe he would be a voice for the poor, the oppressed, the dispossessed, that he would still be providing hope and vision for the future of this country. I believe he would be a voice for peace. Of course, I can never be certain about this. I do know that, when I look back through the years since 1963, I grieve, not only for the loss of what was, but also for the loss of what might have been.

Darrel Clowes, High School English Teacher, Turin, New York

Just as after the tragic bombing of the World Trade Center in New York, the first inclination of many Americans was to fly the American flag. Such was the case here.

At first it was just a whisper, a wave of unease that seemed to seep into the room from the empty corridors. The class period had ended about 15 minutes ago, and I had settled down to use my free period to prepare for the last two classes of the day. Fridays were always difficult. Senior English classes on Friday always competed with the students' weekend social agenda. There was usually an undertone of excitement in the air and it would intensify as the afternoon wore on. However, this was different. There was a low murmuring outside my room. Students whispered to one another, something was wrong, something more than being in the hall during a class period. Then they scurried swiftly but quietly down the hall and away.

The door opened and a face appeared, my friend the social studies teacher, now white-faced and anxious. Had I heard? Was it true? He brought the first hint of something seriously wrong. We went through the now empty and quiet halls to see if anyone else had heard. The teachers' room was empty. We walked downstairs and toward the administrative area. Still no noise in the halls, still the hum of activities behind closed classroom doors. We went into the principal's office, past a silent secretary, into his office. The Vice-Principal was silent, but tears were streaming down his face. The principal was on the phone, his voice husky, his face sad. It was true, the President was dead. Shot in Dallas!

No one said anything more. The Principal cleared his throat and waited. "I'll have to announce it soon," he said. He didn't want to do it. My friend and I didn't want to stay, didn't want to hear, but we too felt a need to do something. Then we looked outside. We had to look away, from that closed room to the light and the fresh clear sky and the clear autumn world of upstate New York. Then we saw the flag bright and full against the sky, and we knew what we could do to mark our sorrow and to share our sorrow. We turned and, without a word, we walked out the door and toward the flagpole. Our military service was years behind us, but automatically we fell into step. We reached the flagpole and stopped. We saluted the flag and held the salute. Then we lowered the flag, folded it, saluted again, and brought the flag inside. We hadn't talked, hadn't planned anything. It just felt right and we needed to do something.

It was well into the following week when we had returned to school after the shared ordeal of the funeral. We were told that our act had coincided with the Principal's announcement. The flag-lowering had been observed by many students and faculty and had been met with tears and silence as we had conducted it in tears and silence. For me and perhaps others, it represented a participation in a tragic loss too large to contain and only manageable if shared.

James Nightingale, Welder, Fram Corporation, Providence, Rhode Island

John F. Kennedy served in the Navy during World War II. Many veterans such as Jim Nightingale shared a special affinity with him because of their common experiences.

From 1942 to 1962, I served in the Navy as a rigger on landing craft and pulled combat duty in both the European and Pacific theaters of operation. After retiring from the Navy, I got a job as a spot welder at the Fram Filter Corporation in Providence, Rhode Island. My wife also worked there as a press operator.

On Friday, November 22, 1963, I was driving along Rt. 95 on my way to the second shift of work when I heard the news on the radio that President Kennedy had been shot. I was so upset over the news, I had to pull over to the side of the road to recover. I then went on to work. My shift had around 250 workers on duty, and everyone was in a somber mood of disbelief. Some were very angry and were sounding off who had been responsible for the killing. Many could not believe this could happen here in the United States. We stopped for an hour of silence and after that everyone seemed to have lost their energy. The entire time it seemed as if we were in a daze. No one showed any joy over the death.

That weekend there were several special services for the President. As a Navy veteran I attended services at the Naval Air Station and the Naval War College. We had a tremendous but also very mournful turnout for both events.

President Kennedy was extremely popular in the Providence area. Most of the people really loved him, although of course, there were some who didn't. He brought a new look and energy to the presidency. In my eyes he was a hero in his own right for his PT 109 actions in the Pacific. He had a keen concern for people and showed an interest in the working class and those downtrodden people who needed help. Italian friends of mine used to affectionately call him, "my piz-zano."

Even today I am still in mourning for his death. His passing only showed me the hatred, and jealousy in our nation related to race and religion, which we still have with us. I will always miss him and what he stood for. He brought a fresh uplifting of spirit for our country.

Rev. Theodore M. Hesburgh, C. S. C., President, University of Notre Dame, South Bend, Indiana

Father Hesburgh was a good friend of the Kennedy family. He has been associated with social reform and civil rights issues. An early and controversial decision he had to make was whether or not to play the Notre Dame football game that weekend.

On November 22, 1963, I was in Boulder, Colorado, as a member of the National Science Board. That morning we were on a plateau atop a snow-covered mountain overlooking Boulder inspecting a possible site for a new atmospheric research laboratory. We came down the mountain to the house of the University of Colorado's President, Joe Smiley for lunch. When we got out of our Volkswagen van, we were told, "the President has been shot." We went into the house. Half of us went into the front room to hear the radio, and the rest of us into the kitchen to also listen to the radio. We suffered through that terrible half-hour wait until we learned the President was dead.

I had to do some quick praying for him at lunch. We weren't really thinking clearly at that point. The 24 of us went downtown to the hotel where we were staying to continue our meeting. We sat down at the table with our materials around us and, after some five minutes, I said, "this is insane," I picked up all my books, waved good-bye to everyone and walked out. I went to the airport in Denver and got a flight back to Chicago. By the time I arrived, it was 9:00 P.M. and it was too late to get a flight to South Bend, so I stayed in Chicago.

The first thing I did when I got into my room was to call Iowa because the Notre Dame football team was playing the University of Iowa the next afternoon. I talked to our Executive Vice President and

head of our Faculty Board for Athletics, Father Joyce, and asked
"What is the plan out there for tomorrow?" He said, "Well, they want
to play and have a service at halftime." I said, "That's insane because
the President of the United States is lying dead somewhere. I think
they are not going to play the game because we are not going to play."
He said, "They are going to be as mad as the dickens." I responded,
"I can't help that." He asked, "What about all the tickets that have
been sold?" I responded, "Just tell them to cash in their tickets if they
want." I didn't think many would do so, but as a matter of fact some
$90,000 worth of tickets were refunded. Joyce concluded, "They are
really going to be unhappy" and I answered, "That's tough. Just put
the team on the plane Saturday morning, and if we are not there we
can't play." So he did what I told him and the team came back to
school and the game was canceled.

The next morning I returned to South Bend and learned that our
former Notre Dame President, John Cavanaugh, had gone by a plane
sent from Washington to be with the Kennedy family when the
President's body arrived from Dallas. Father Cavanaugh said a Mass
on Saturday morning with the family in the East Room of the White
House where the President's body was resting. He later went to
Hyannis Port where he stayed with Joe Kennedy, a great friend of his,
through the funeral on Monday.

I then talked with Ethel Kennedy, and she wanted me to come to
the funeral. So I came to Washington and stayed at the Mayflower
Hotel. On Sunday, the Secret Service put a gold Metropolitan Police
Badge on me and took me up a back way through a secret entrance
into the Rotunda where the President's body rested in state. I blessed
the body, and later I joined Ethel's brother and other family members
for dinner that evening.

On Monday, Father Fitzgerald, a cousin of the family and I were
in attendance at the funeral a few feet from the family. In fact, we were
really the only two "simple" priests at the sanctuary that day. The Mass
was performed by Cardinal Cushing of Boston, and the sermon was
given by the Auxiliary Bishop of Washington, Philip Hannan. I was
particularly impressed by the tender treatment given by Cardinal

Cushing to the Kennedy family. At the end of the services, he gave Jackie and Mrs. Rose Kennedy a big hug and a kiss, adding a personal air of familiarity to a solemn ceremony.

At this point, I left the cathedral and returned to South Bend. In the midst of all this tragic setting, one spark of humor comes to mind. I recall while we were waiting for the cortege to arrive at St. Matthew's, little John-John's fidgeting all over the place. To keep him occupied, one of the Secret Service men brought him a stack of pamphlets to play with. This didn't last very long but fortunately his wait wasn't very long.

When I returned to campus, I wrote a tribute to President Kennedy that was published in an "extra" edition of Notre Dame's student weekly, *The Scholastic*. In the opening of the eulogy entitled, "The Road," I recalled my first meeting with John F. Kennedy in 1950 when, as a fledgling congressman, only 33 years old, he came to Notre Dame to deliver the January commencement address and receive an honorary degree. I was Executive Vice-President at the time. He came up to the President's office after he was done, and I helped him and his sister, Eunice, get back to the Midway airport in Chicago. When he died in 1963, Kennedy had been the only man to receive all three of the highest awards that Notre Dame bestows: the Laetare Medal, an honorary doctorate, and the Patriot of the Year award of the senior class.

A brief excerpt from "The Road" that I wrote in November 26, 1963, very well summarizes the legacy that the John F. Kennedy left to our country and the world:

> One can speak of memorials and medals for them,
> but what greater memorial can Americans, young
> and old, construct for their heroes than to take up
> the torch of light that slips from their mortal
> hands, and to continue the immortal work to
> which their lives, all too brief, were dedicated?[18]

Reflecting back over the brief Kennedy 1,000 days in office, I think the greatest contribution John F. Kennedy made was to charge up the young people of our nation to get out there and do something.

The Peace Corps best symbolized this spirit. Many young people were inspired by Kennedy in the early 1960s to join the Peace Corps and get involved in politics and public service in general. Many of those 130,000 young people, who have served in the Peace Corps since it was formed in 1961, are going strong today. Those I have known and worked with are a spectacular group of people.

Dr. Graham Gilmer, Jr., Physician, Orange, California
Dr. Gilmer shares a touching account of a Christmas held far away from home. He shared that Christmas as a chaplain with a young serviceman returning from the war in the Pacific, John F. Kennedy.

My wife and I were on our way to visit our son at Stanford University and attend the Stanford versus University of California football game, the big clash of the year. We stopped at a gas station and learned that the President had been assassinated. Like everyone, we were shocked and saddened. We continued to Palo Alto for the weekend, which we spent with our children. Of course the game was canceled.

I often express my feelings through writing. As soon as we returned home I wrote my parents in Lynchburg, Virginia, and shared with them a story from President Kennedy's life known only to a few people including myself. During World War II, I served as a chaplain in the Navy and became a medical doctor after the war. Below is the letter I sent to my parents in late November 1963. It offers a brief glimpse of a young John F. Kennedy at an earlier stage in his life when I knew him for a few brief weeks. His tragic death motivated me to share this memory with loved ones.

> November 25, 1963
> My dear Father and Mother:
>   The night is dark—and the darkness seems very deeper in this world. Twenty years ago at about this date, a young naval officer came aboard my ship—THE BRETON—wounded and for transportation back to the States. He boarded at

Espiritu Santo in the New Hebrides. As chaplain of
the ship, I knew that our orders would probably
cause us to be underway on Christmas Day. So a
few days before we weighed anchor, the doctor and
I went ashore and gathered palm fronds to 'make a
Christmas tree.'

In due time the Christmas tree was finished
—a marvel of engineering—being made of a
wooden pole with holes drilled for the palm fronds.
Since we were traveling without planes, the hangar
deck made an ideal place to put the tree. And there
on Christmas morn, 1943, our ship's personnel
and passengers exchanged and opened our meager
gifts before a tree that was probably much more
like the trees about Bethlehem that first Christmas
morn so long ago. This young naval officer circu-
lated among the more seriously wounded from
Bougainville Island, lending cheer and the
Christmas spirit throughout the day. He also was
present at the ship's Christmas Party later in the
day as we crossed the international date line. And
for this reason, the next day was Christmas all over
again. For this second Christmas we had no special
celebration. But who cared? We were heading
home from the holocaust of war and in a real sense
every day was Christmas.

Particularly apropos to the Christmas spirit
of 'Peace on Earth—Good Will unto all Men' was
this extra Christmas to the young naval officer of
whom I speak. For he had been tried in the caul-
dron of war and had 'quitted himself as a man.'
And during the days at sea he read extensively from
our ship's library—and on the various occasions I
talked with him, he spoke of his dream of a peaceful world.

Courtesy of Graham Gilmer

The Christmas tree on board ship, December 25, 1943.

God did not allot to him the consumation of his vision of worldwide peace in his time, but he did grant to him an extra Christmas day in life. And thus John F. Kennedy lived in his 46 years through 47 Christmases—for it was of him that I was speaking about.

Looking back nearly 50 years later, I still fondly remember that Christmas in 1943 and the young naval officer who loved to read and dream of a world in peace.

Chapter Eight

Students Are Devastated

President Kennedy enjoyed great popularity among the young people of the country, partly because of his vigorous and youthful appearance. Young Americans had never experienced a major national tragedy, and so Kennedy's assassination was shocking to them as a unique and terrible event in their lives.

The vignettes in this section recall memories from students of all ages, from kindergarten through graduate school. Yvonne Snyder-Farley shares her diary account. Tommy O'Neill, son of Congressman and later Speaker of the House, "Tip" O'Neill, and Rich Daley, son of the late Mayor Daley of Chicago, were in college at the time. Melody Miller recalls the joy of her visit to the President and her melancholy farewell at his gravesite.

No college campus was harder hit by the President's death than that of his alma mater, Harvard, where Kennedy received his B.A. degree cum laude in 1940. For four days the campus was in mourning. Faculty and students alike were stunned. Along Massachusetts Avenue, people clustered by car windows listening to the radio. Students everywhere were listening to transistor radios and they greeted each other in low voices, "He's dead." Many students were at New Haven preparing for the annual gala weekend that included the Harvard-Yale football game. Two former Harvard students, Rob Lucas and Paul Guzzi share their recollections of JFK and that tragic weekend.

On other college campuses the mood was similar as demonstrated by recollections from students around the nation. At public and private schools alike, the news was difficult for younger students to accept.

Rich Daley, College Student, DePaul University, Illinois

Daley, the son of the late Mayor Richard Daley of Chicago, later himself became the Mayor of Chicago.

It was a typical early Friday afternoon and, like college students all over the United States, I was looking forward to the weekend. I was a junior at DePaul University, an urban Catholic school located on the north side of Chicago. While in a class of some 20 students listening to a lecture, someone burst into the room with the devastating news that President Kennedy had been shot and had died. No one could believe it. Class was immediately stopped and, along with many other students, I hurried to the school cafeteria where television sets were located to make sure the news was not a cruel hoax. I remember thinking, "They must be kidding; he can't be dead."

At this point I decided I wanted to be with my family, so I hopped on the El and went home. A little later my father, who was then mayor of Chicago, came home from the office, and with my father, mother, brothers and sisters, I stayed glued to the television set. That weekend my parents went to Washington to attend funeral services and I stayed at home with the rest of my family and friends as we watched events unfold on the television screen

I was a great admirer of President Kennedy as was my father who was an important figure in helping Kennedy gain the Democratic nomination and subsequently to be elected President in the fall of 1960. I first met then-Senator Kennedy when he attended a Cook County Democratic dinner. I also had the pleasure of seeing him on a trip with my father to Washington. One of my favorite memories as a teenager was attending the second game of the 1959 World Series between the Chicago White Sox and the Los Angeles Dodgers. I not only got to see the game in Comisky Park watching from the third base box seats, but also sat behind Senator Jack Kennedy, a presidential candidate at that time. The only bad feature of the day was that the Sox lost, 4-3. Kennedy was a friendly and warm person and I felt comfortable in his presence as a teenager.

Looking back to 1963, the assassination of President Kennedy changed the course of America. Unfortunately this new course was downhill. We were further damaged by the later killings of Martin Luther King, Jr., and Bobby Kennedy. I believe that, if President Kennedy had lived, he would have changed the course of history for our country for the good. John F. Kennedy had real confidence in himself and more importantly in the United States. He believed we could do better and seemed to have convinced the American public of this goal as well. He also was the first political leader to really use television media to communicate to the public, and he did it very well. Since his death, the United States has seemed to have gone in a decline as a nation. I have found no one since his death to replace him as a true national leader, although some have tried and met with limited success.

Yvonne Snyder-Farley, High School Sophomore, St. Marys, West Virginia

Snyder-Farley in her diary account demonstrates an example of the depth of feeling held by many students at the death of the President.

When I was 14 years old, John F. Kennedy came to West Virginia in 1960 to run in the West Virginia Democratic presidential primary. I became involved and remember hanging around at the county Democratic headquarters during that time. After he was elected, our high school band traveled to Washington to march in the presidential inaugural parade. We were warned by our band director to not look at the President as we passed the reviewing stand. When we marched by the reviewing stand playing "God of Our Fathers," I looked anyway and caught a glimpse of whom I think was the President. The weather was freezing. I ate Chinese food for the first time in my life at a Washington, D.C., restaurant.

On November 22, 1963, I was a 16-year-old sophomore at St. Marys High School in St. Marys, West Virginia, a small town located by the Ohio River. This is what I wrote in my diary that evening when I came home from school and in subsequent days:

> President Kennedy is dead. I shall never forget that
> moment on the steps coming from Latin II when

a boy said, 'The President's been shot.' I thought it was a joke. But when Karen and I stepped into the hall, we knew that it was true. I went on to speech class and he died while I gave my debate. It is late evening and I still can't believe it. There are no words to describe the horror of the situation. The man in whose inauguration parade we marched, the idol of millions, now belongs to history.

    Every time I hear the phrase, 'former President Kennedy,' it gives me a sickening sensation. He was so young. Roddy and I were talking about the Lincoln assassination this morning. But, how could something like this happen in these times? Everything is ghostly and sickening. Today I have been a nameless person. I've spent the day like a sleepwalker, not knowing what to do. Once I prayed but it was insincere. I know now that he is dead. It is the first tragedy in my life. To think, I was saving my Kennedy campaign hat for 1964. How could this happen in the United States? To me, President Kennedy seemed indestructible. I loved the president. Talking does no good. The tragedy of his death speaks for itself. Oh God, what has happened?

My parents remember that I was glued, more so than the rest of the family who took time out to eat or do chores, to the television set watching the subsequent days and the funeral. The rest of the diary reflects that obsession with the death. As my teenage activities returned to normal, there was still interspersed between the usual gossip and angst, mention of things like, "Mrs. Kennedy will move out of the White House Friday." Getting the debate grade back with the date, "Nov. 22, 1963," on the paper threw me into a tailspin.

On December 19, 1963, I wrote, "I have cried until my eyes were swollen. I feel that I must do something. But what? I could

Courtesy of Dan B. Fleming, Jr.

St. Marys High School Band at the Inauguration parade, January 20, 1961.

join the Peace Corps or go into politics. I am thinking seriously about the Peace Corps. In a small way, it might help." I was angry with a local car dealer for not closing for the funeral and predicted that someday "they'll be sorry when they see that he was great." And, I decided to read *Profiles in Courage.*[19]

I never did join the Peace Corps. Instead, I became, like many of my generation, active in the antiwar movement during college. For a time I forgot about any idea of serving my country and became very cynical about the government.

However, I realized that to live up to the ideals of President Kennedy, I needed to make my own contribution to society. In my life I have maintained commitments to various social welfare concerns and began to write political columns for the *Charleston Gazette.* I would say that the glamour of that presidential primary and of Kennedy got me involved at an early age. His death remains a personal emotional experience, and represents in my life, the beginning of political commitment as well as loss of innocence that I never recaptured.

John Burton, College Student, University of North Carolina, Chapel Hill, North Carolina

Burton relates the tolling of the bells on his campus as similar bells were ringing throughout the nation.

On the day John Kennedy was assassinated, I was a 17-year-old freshman at the University of North Carolina at Chapel Hill. The Kennedy election had been the first that really drew my attention. Although the vote would not come to 18-year-old citizens until Nixon's presidency, the idea that leadership had passed to a new generation (although Kennedy still seemed terribly old) was exciting. All things seemed possible. The President was asking all of us to work to solve problems. The feeling on our campus was that, despite their difficulty, they could be solved.

When I heard the news of the President's death, I was helping a friend of mine deliver laundry. Someone suddenly began yelling that the President was dead, that he had been shot in Dallas. Shortly we were all huddled around television sets and radios trying to figure out what had happened.

On the UNC campus, the bell in the Old South Building began tolling almost immediately after Kennedy's death. On the other side of campus, the Memorial Bell Tower echoed the same mournful sound. The Air Force ROTC band was dressed for a parade for an upcoming big football traditional battle between UNC and Duke. This group walked slowly across the ivy-covered campus playing a gloomy dirge. The campus was deadly silent except for the ringing of the bells. All the evening pep rallies, parades and fireworks, a traditional prelude to the Duke-UNC game, were canceled as was the game for which nearly 48,000 tickets had been sold.

Ironically, only two years before, the bells also rang for a visit by President John F. Kennedy, who spoke on University Day. Kennedy also received an honorary degree at that event. Within 200 yards of the spot where the President addressed the crowd in 1961, a bugler on Friday, November 22, played the doleful notes of taps. On another hilltop nearby, a second bugle echoed the first, while many students watched in sorrow.

All of this was very difficult to take. Later that Friday evening we went to Raleigh to watch the North Carolina State vs. Wake Forest game. I don't remember if we had planned to do this earlier or not. State had a group nicknamed the Mafia: four Italian backs featuring Roman Gabriel and John Scarpatti. Wake Forest had Brian Piccolo. There were a couple of brief eulogies to President Kennedy at half-time by the two university presidents. State crushed Wake. The crowd, even the winning State fans, was mostly quiet. The game was eerie. Later I realized that, after the game we had not stayed for a beer, discussed it, or, for my part, even thought of it. For us, that bordered on the unbelievable. I think the bottom line was that we were all so shocked, sad, and perhaps scared, that for once having fun didn't seem appropriate.

Rob Lucas, College Student, Harvard University, Cambridge, Massachusetts

Harvard as the alma mater of Kennedy was particularly hard hit by his death. Rob Lucas, a photographer for the school paper, recalls the time when he photographed JFK making his last visit to his old school prior to his death as he attended a Harvard-Columbia football game.

In the fall of 1963, I was a 20-year-old student at Harvard. At that stage of my life, my burning interest was being photographic chairman for *The Harvard Crimson,* the university's daily student newspaper. I later told my children that I majored in the *Crimson* at Harvard. In fact, my experience there would have been much less than what it was without the many unique experiences afforded me as a campus photographer.

One of my favorite photographic subjects had been President John F. Kennedy. On Friday, November 22, 1963, I was heading to Bradford Junior College to pick up a date and from there we were on our way to New Haven for the annual big weekend culminating in the Harvard-Yale football game. I was stunned to learn on my car radio of the President's death, and when I arrived at Bradford, I

Courtesy of G. Robert Lucas

Senate Ed Muskie, President Kennedy, and Lawrence O'Brien at the Harvard-Columbia football game, October, 1963.

found the girls there equally in a state of shock and crying. My date and I headed to New Haven and then learned the weekend events had been canceled. I met my parents there anyway since they had flown in for the game and, like those in the rest of the country, we watched the events unfold in a state of dejection.

Even though I came from a Republican background, I admired President Kennedy and felt a kinship with him as a fellow Harvard student and a temporary resident living in the Boston area. Kennedy was generally viewed on campus as a leader of a new generation that would change things for the better. His death was a devastating blow to the student body.

It was hard for me to accept his death because, only a few weeks earlier, I had my own personal experience with JFK. On the weekend of October 19, I learned through my roommate that Kennedy was coming to the Harvard-Columbia football game at Harvard. My roommate, as manager for the Harvard band, was notified to be prepared to play "Hail to the Chief." My thoughts were focused on getting a photo for the school paper of this event, the only time that JFK came to a Harvard home game while President. His arrival was kept secret and his arrival at the game was to be announced by the band playing, "Hail to the Chief." It was a balmy Saturday afternoon, and the band had a lookout posted on top the stadium to spot the President's motorcade. When he was spotted, I ran to where I thought he was going to sit and waited for his arrival. I was fortunate in anticipating the right location and, by crouching at the end of his row, shot a series of pictures of him. He was seated with Senator Ed Muskie of Maine and his aide, Larry O'Brien. I remember one thing that surprised me at the time was how little security he seemed to have and how easy it was for me to take my pictures.

JFK looked tan and relaxed and seemed to enjoy himself during the game. He smoked a small cigar and chewed his sunglasses while he chatted with friends. He only stood once to cheer as each team scored only three points each in the first half. After he viewed the halftime show in which both bands slightly razzed him playing, "Hit the Road Jack," he unknowingly made his last farewell to his alma mater as he left Harvard to visit the grave of his son Patrick, who had died only a few months earlier and was buried in a nearby Brookline cemetery.

I was fortunate while at Harvard to photograph many other famous people such as Lyndon B. Johnson, Willy Brandt, Martin Luther King, Jr., and poet Robert Frost. All these photographs serve as a kaleidoscope of memories of this exciting time in my life. Perhaps none is sadder to view in retrospect today than that of Harvard's favorite son, John F. Kennedy. It is difficult to believe that nearly four decades have passed since I photographed a smiling JFK surrounded by his friends and admirers.

After 1965, I never went near a darkroom again as I entered law school and later commenced my career as an attorney. Still the photographs now tucked away in my attic include forever one happy snapshot for me of a gone, but not forgotten, John F. Kennedy.

Jeffrey R. Stewart, Graduate Student, New York University

The brief glimpse below of the scene in New York City expresses the incredulity with which the news of Kennedy's death was greeted.

The New York City taxi driver sat motionless in his yellow cab in the middle of a city side street. His head rested on the steering wheel. His eyes were closed. I hurried across the street and approached his open window. I remember that his radio was on as I spoke.

"What's wrong?" "They shot my President," he answered quietly, still leaning forward at the wheel so he could hear every word of the news report.

My quick conclusion was that the president of the cab company had been murdered. "Oh, I'm sorry—where?" was my awkward reply. "Down in Dallas, Texas." He finally opened his eyes and looked at me. "They shot my President in Dallas.

It's difficult now to understand why it took me so long to comprehend what had happened. On November 22 1963, I was a doctoral student at New York University on my way home for Thanksgiving. I had been very busy the few days before. I was unaware that President Kennedy had been in Dallas. I was hurrying to catch a train to Washington, D.C.

"What?"

"They shot President Kennedy in Dallas!"

"How is he?"

"They don't know. It happened just a few minutes ago."

I leaned in the window as we listened to the radio. They had just switched back to regular programming. I left the driver to catch my train. I knew that President Kennedy was going to be okay.

Thomas M. Sherman, College Student, University of Notre Dame, Indiana

Another campus where Kennedy was popular was Notre Dame. Tom Sherman found that even years later the President was also held in high regard in several countries of the Middle East.

In 1963 I was senior majoring in history at Notre Dame. Several of my friends and I had thought of ourselves as Kennedy people because his election took place during our freshman year. We had already begun talking about the '64 election and debating what we perceived as several Senator Goldwater fanatics.

I remember November 22 as a bright, warm, and sunny fall day. A friend and I had decided to go to downtown South Bend to get a haircut. As we drove by a bus stop at the campus entrance, I was shouting playfully to people waiting for the bus. A friend waiting there ran up to the car and said the President had been shot in Dallas. We both thought it was a joke and drove way. Then my friend recalled that Kennedy was in Dallas, and we began fooling frantically and unsuccessfully with the radio in his old car trying to get some news. We finally got confirmation as we both were getting our haircuts when the barber turned on a radio.

For the next few days it seemed like time was suspended. Most people I knew searched for a TV to watch as the gloomy events unfolded. But life did go on. I worked in the dining hall and it was there I learned Oswald had been shot. Another friend commented that, "The same doctors who attended Kennedy were trying to remove the bullet from Oswald with a pitchfork!"

Because my roommate and I had one of the few TVs in our hall, we had a large crowd in our room the whole time of the presidential transition and funeral. None of the supposedly worldly wise, cynical college seniors gathered there could believe their eyes when young John-John saluted his father.

Three years later, I really came to understand the impact Kennedy had on other parts of the world. I was traveling in Iraq on vacation from the Peace Corps in Afghanistan. Somewhere near Baghdad, a man came up to me on the street to express sorrow. Because I hadn't seen a newspaper for days, I had no idea what he meant until he showed me an Arabic newspaper with a picture of the three astronauts killed at Cape Kennedy the day before. He spoke little English and I spoke no Arabic; but he had tears in his eyes as he said, "Kennedy." I think he was expressing condolence to me for my country's having to bear another tragedy.

Later in Damascus, Syria, then in Beirut, Lebanon, and again in Cairo, Egypt, when local people found out I was from the United

States, they would ask about Kennedy and why we would murder him. It was somewhat astounding that Kennedy still seemed to be an enormously popular figure in the Middle East even three years after his death. Despite the fact that the United States was not in favor at that time in the region. In the eyes of people I met there, it seemed that, as an American, I bore at least some responsibility for Kennedy's assassination. I've never really shaken a sense of guilt and loss for what seemed to be an unfulfilled promised we made to the world!

Mario Rivas, High School Ninth Grader, Washington, D.C.

A D.C. area high school student who was stunned by the President's death and could not believe it had happened.

Anything interrupting algebra I had to be a blessing, a gift from the Creator! To a 13-year-old freshman at all-male Catholic Archbishop Carroll High School, nothing could be worse than math after lunch. Thirty years later, it all seems like a bad dream, the day my political innocence died, the day America became a truly United States.

The first Roman Catholic President, Jack Kennedy, was not an abstract figure seen on television. He was that tanned, smiling guy in the baby blue Pontiac convertible (or was it a Buick, but definitely a GMC product), who waved at us as we all left Mass at St. Matthew's Cathedral, practically a "homeboy" in today's parlance. That initial sighting occurred quite accidentally on the D.C. streets where I was growing up.

My status as a slightly bored know-it-all ninth grader that day was one of displeasure at the idea of algebra class after lunch. Living with my mom and dad and a little sister and brother in a suburban Maryland "dream home" insulated me from much of the real world. On that Friday, there was a "break-in-the-action" as we were addressed over the loudspeaker at around 1:45 by the Rector of the school (an unusual occurrence in itself) and told not to start classes and wait for an important announcement. Instinctively, the brother who was our teacher decided to lead our class in prayer. Why and for whom were unknowns, but a somber mood immediately descended upon us. Once we found out our President had been shot while in Dallas and was in serious condition, we all stopped normal academic activities. Our Rector decided we should pray and soon told us all extracurricular activities and athletic practices were cancelled.

My immediate reaction was one of disbelief. This was the "stuff" that happened in developing third world nations, in Cold War spy novels and in war simulation games of the war colleges. This could not happen in our United States! As a matter of fact, this wasn't really happening at all.

Reflecting now on the Warren Commission Report, the assassination theorists, right versus left wing conspiracies, CIA, mob, and, militarist plots all serve to distract from what did occur: the horror of the act, the mourning, witnessing historic events on television live (who didn't see Jack Ruby shoot Lee Harvey Oswald?) and the shock that hit us from the death of Camelot? All led to a national loss of innocence.

I remember the "neatness" and the "orderliness" of life at that time and how afterward chaos seemed to reign: the Cold War fears and nuclear bomb drills and the priests and nuns devoutly praying for world peace. What's changed? For me, our charismatic Jack wasn't there to calmly and smilingly lead the way. Hindsight is always at least 20-20, if not 20-15. What if, what if?

Susan Burho-Hensley, High School Senior, Fairfax, Virginia

Another D.C. area student had the misfortune to have her birthday on the day after the President was shot. Ever since that day she has associated her birthday with the tragic event.

I will never forget my 17th birthday. On November 23, 1963, the day after President Kennedy was shot, I turned 17. I can see those days vividly. I was living in Fairfax County, a suburb of the District of Columbia.

On November 22, our entire student body assembled in the Edison High School auditorium to hear the chorale sing "Down in the Valley." I love music and was looking forward to hearing them. A couple of rows ahead of me filing in, however, was the "class clown." He had a pocket radio—strictly forbidden. Suddenly, the clown turned around and told everyone within ear shot, "The President's been shot!" Of course, none of us believed him and calmly took our seats.

The musical began. After the second song, the curtain was pulled shut. Our principal, Mr. Robinson, and the female soloist, Pam Nagle, came out onto the stage. She was shaking. Our principal made the announcement that caused us to all freeze in our seats. "Students, President Kennedy has been assassinated. Out of respect, we will all return to our homerooms."

Some girls broke down sobbing hysterically, but most of us walked, zombie-like, back to homeroom. My American history teacher, who was usually very eloquent, said nothing. She let us listen to her radio. The line between student and teacher was erased that day. That day we were all shocked, frightened, dazed Americans who could not begin to understand what had happened. How could this happen in *our* country???!!

It rained for three solid days. At home, we watched our small square black and white television. We, like millions of other Americans, stayed glued to our seats. Even after the shock and numbness wore off, our world seemed black and white like our TV. No matter how many times we watched the film of the assassination or the funeral, it didn't seem real. Not even to the adults.

A couple of days later, my class had to go to Washington, D.C., to see *Macbeth*. No one felt like going, but the tickets were all paid. Strangely enough, I felt better after seeing *Macbeth*. It was as if we had all been to a grieving ritual.

Even though it's been decades since Kennedy was shot, I still think about it every year on my birthday. The memory of sadness and loss during those days in November 1963 is forever etched in my mind in black and white. I stop each year as I grow older and remember. Out of respect, I pause, I bow my head in prayer, Please, Lord—never again.

Melody Miller, College Freshman, Penn State University

Melody Miller recalls her never to be forgotten meeting as a high school student with President Kennedy. In a letter to a friend, she offers a poignant description of her visit to his grave at Arlington Cemetery.

One of the great memories of my life that I still deeply cherish was the brief visit I had with President John F. Kennedy in the White House Cabinet Room, May 3, 1963. The reason for my chat with the President was a clay sculpture bust of JFK I made in my junior year at Wakefield High School in Arlington, Virginia. I, of course, was a great admirer of the President when I created the bust. *The Washington Post* wrote an article about my sculpture. Several friends, including a congressman I had worked for in the summer, sent a copy of the article and a letter to the President's secretary, Mrs. Evelyn Lincoln, asking her to send an autographed picture of the President to me.

Shortly thereafter, I was shocked and elated to receive a call while I was in my high school journalism class that the President wanted to meet me in person. I was certainly excited over the visit, and when I met him in his office, I took the bust along. The President patted my creation on the head and gave it a warm compliment it didn't really deserve. We had a wonderful chat, and along with giving me a PT 109 bracelet and having our picture taken, he signed my copy of *Profiles in Courage,* which I treasure to this day.[20]

My cherished experience was written up in my school paper, another example of his supportive outreach to young people. The meeting with the President only further fueled my enthusiasm not only for JFK, but also for the entire Kennedy family.

In the fall of 1963 I enrolled at Penn State as a political science major. I noticed that, after the President's death, there seemed to be a new interest and awareness among the students about the world around them and their roles in the future. I attribute these changed attitudes to the impact of President Kennedy on our lives.

Six months later I was still grieving for the loss of my President. I wrote a letter to Mrs. Kennedy expressing my sympathy for her loss and admiration for her courage and strength during those four tragic

Courtesy of the John F. Kennedy Library

Melody Miller and her mother meet President Kennedy, May 3, 1963.

days. I also accompanied my letter to Mrs. Kennedy with a letter I had written a friend earlier in the year.

In the letter to her friend, Janet, Melody was extremely frustrated that she could not attend Kennedy's funeral, but she eagerly looked forward to her personal pilgrimage to his gravesite in Arlington Cemetery. This excerpt from her letter describes that visit, one that would be made by millions of Americans over the next several decades:

> I arrived Thursday night and was at the cemetery with a single red rose (his favorite) Friday morning at eight o'clock. It was a gray misty morning, and my heels sank a bit in the soft earth. I shivered as I walked alone down the road to the site for my black topcoat and black sheath were not really warm enough for December. There were only a few people about; thousands would come later in the

afternoon. I wondered what my reaction would be as I neared the white picket enclosure, but after watching Mrs. Kennedy, I knew I couldn't cry. The two guards stood at each corner and, from time to time, advanced to the next corner. I stood beside the fence and at first just shook, but then a calm came over me and I felt nothing of the cold. My eyes and mind tried to take in the magnitude of what I saw in that first instant and imprinted it indelibly on my memory.

The 'Eternal Flame' flickered gently with the breeze. Below it on the pile of evergreens, soldiers had placed their hats. Around the enclosure were scattered wreaths of flowers, one a replica of the presidential seal, and small bouquets snuggled up to the base of green boughs. I gave a guard my rose and he went in and tucked it in the front of the greens so that it gently bent toward the head of the grave. I remember thinking that my little rose could have no more honored spot. On the left side was little Patrick's headstone and on the right was a small cross inscribed, 'Baby Girl Kennedy' and on the base was 'suffer little children to come unto me.'

I just stood at all points around the fence and looked. As hard as I tried, I couldn't visualize him there under the green turf. It was when I gazed out over the city that I realized that he could never by confined to such a small spot, for in my beloved city of Washington, I could see him everywhere. The site couldn't be more perfect if God himself had picked it. A dogwood tree on the hill will be a flowering backdrop in the spring and the flag billows majestically overhead. At night, one can see the blue and white light from the vantage points in the city. It has become the Mecca of the nation.

Although the papers don't often print it, people still
come every day by the thousands, and the flowers
never stop.

To read my letter again after all of these years is to feel anew the
searing pain of a wound that will never fully heal. I can close my eyes
and still see his incandescent entrance into the Cabinet Room,
remember the warmth of his smile and the interest he expressed in my
future. As with so many millions of others, he changed the whole
direction of my life.

The path of public service has led to an entire adult career
serendipitously spent on the staffs of Mrs. John F. Kennedy, Senator
Robert F. Kennedy and Senator Edward M. Kennedy, where I am an
official spokesperson. Also I oversee matters regarding the legacy of
John and Robert Kennedy. It has been my privilege to see firsthand
the extraordinary contributions the Kennedy family has made, and
continues to make, to our country. Now it is to my desk that the letters come from young people who have just discovered, and are newly
inspired by, President Kennedy. And when they come to visit, I can see
in their eyes: he still lives on.

Paul H. Guzzi, College Student, Harvard University, Massachusetts

*Guzzi was a football player at Harvard. He still has the game ball
from the Harvard-Yale game he played on the day the President was shot.
Guzzi was influenced by the Kennedy call to service and later served in
the Massachusetts legislature and as Massachusetts Secretary of State.*

Friday afternoon, November 22, 1963, I was a junior at Harvard
University, playing in the Harvard-Yale junior varsity football game. I
was a defensive back. This early afternoon game was our biggest event
of the year, a traditional grudge match. This was the Harvard-Yale
weekend when many activities were held. During the half-time we
heard a rumor that President Kennedy had been shot, but no one really took the story seriously in the intensity of the occasion. Only after
the game did we learn that the President was dead.

The team's bus ride back to Cambridge from New Haven after the game was one I will never forget. We rode back in deadening silence in a state of total disbelief. The rest of that weekend was typical for everyone as a number of us gathered around the television and watched events unfold. In my housing complex, I had suitemates from various parts of the country. Two were strong Republicans from Oklahoma. We had often argued about Kennedy policies. Another suitemate was from California. Regardless of their political or geographic preferences, all seemed devastated by the President's death as we banded together for mutual comfort in sharing our grief.

On Sunday, I attended a crowded Sunday service at St. Paul's Catholic Church in Cambridge where Harvard students normally worshiped. Father Collins, the Harvard chaplain, who headed our campus Newman Club, was involved in the eulogies focusing on Kennedy's death.

The game ball from the November 22, 1963, contest was given to me. I still have it today and have the date of the game written on the ball in black. The following year, I was fortunate enough again to be given the Harvard-Yale varsity game ball as well. On this ball I have the date written in white in a positive contrast to the tragic memory of 1963.

President Kennedy had a special relationship with Harvard University. He was a graduate and frequent visitor to the institution. In addition, he drew a number of appointments in his administration from the Harvard faculty. My father was very excited one time when he sat a couple of rows behind the President at a Harvard football game. My family had been political backers of Kennedy for many years, and I had the opportunity to see and meet him on occasion, even though I had no personal relationship with him.

President Kennedy provided inspiration to my entire generation and to me personally to enter public service including politics. He convinced many of us that public service was a noble calling. He made it appealing, practical, exciting, important and a worthwhile endeavor. His impact on me helped influence me to make the 1970s my decade of public service. Many of the people whom I served with in

the Massachusetts legislature and in state government were products
of that generation and were inspired by Kennedy.

Jeanne Howard-Roper, Graduate Student,
Florida State University

*Jeanne, as a very pregnant doctoral candidate almost went into labor
immediately after learning of Kennedy's death while her husband thought
the shooting was the work of the John Birch society.*

In the fall of 1963, I was living in Tallahassee, Florida, with my
husband in the graduate student housing project at Florida State
alumni village. We were both doctoral students and I was very pregnant with our first child. Possibly I was the first pregnant doctoral student in FSU history. On November 22, I fixed lunch for us, and our
plan for the early afternoon was to go first to the FSU infirmary for
immunization shots against whatever flu was going around, and then
to the library to study.

As we were leaving our apartment for the infirmary, we passed by
our next-door neighbor's front door. We heard our neighbor suddenly shout loudly to his year-old baby: "Shut up! Shut up! I have to hear
this!" Tom and I exchanged glances, meant to say "What could be so
important that you would shout at a baby that way?" and "When we
have OUR child, we certainly won't behave in such an unpleasant
way." We headed for the infirmary.

We checked in at the desk, sat down to wait; everyone appeared
to be normal. After about ten minutes a radio was switched on, and I
heard, "the President," "assassination," "shots fired," and "death"
among the spoken words. My immediate assumption was that a president somewhere in Central America or some other volatile spot had
been shot, and that this wouldn't have particular impact on us. After
a few moments I went to the desk and asked, "What president's been
shot?" The receptionist, in a perfectly cheerful and pleasant voice,
said, "Oh, didn't you know? Kennedy's been shot. He's dead."

I was stunned. As a native of Boston, transplanted to north
Florida, I had a sense of pride that a Bostonian was in the White

House. My first vote (on my 21st birthday) had been for Kennedy. I was stunned that an assassination had happened in the United States, supposedly a place where these things didn't happen. But more than anything else, I was astonished by the perky cheerfulness of the receptionist, who went on about her greeting and registering of new arrivals as if nothing had happened, while the news from the radio spun on.

A doctor emerged from somewhere and told my equally shaken husband that this was not a good time for a very pregnant woman to have a flu shot and that he should take me home. I didn't want to go home; I wanted to go downtown and find out what was going on. Tallahassee at that time was something of a hotbed of right-wing sentiment. A John Birch Society "American Opinion Bookstore" had opened on the main street, Monroe Street, and was doing good business. We reasonable assumed that the assassination had come from the rightwing lunatic fringe.

The afternoon edition of the *Tallahassee Democrat* was just appearing on the sales racks. The paper had intended to run a front-page story on turkey-farming, and the photograph on page one was of a farmer in front of his flock of 10,000 turkeys ready to meet their fate. Above the picture were the hastily substituted words, "PRESIDENT IS DEAD."

My husband, a very intense young person, snatched a copy of the paper, and I saw him run the few blocks down Monroe Street to the John Birch Society bookstore. He returned a few minutes later. "What did you do?" I asked. He said he'd run into the bookstore, shown them the deadline and said, "You did this!" "What did they say?" I asked. They said, "We've got our flag at half-mast."

Somehow we were back home in the apartment. I remember every detail of the evening. We had a simple supper, French-Canadian pea soup that I'd prepared the day before. I remember I was wearing, a pink blouse and dark red maternity jumper. I also remember frighteningly, the contractions that began suddenly and would have meant the very premature birth of our baby if they hadn't diminished. Following a call to my doctor, he advised, "Lie down and stay down!"

We did not own a television set at the time. As aspiring young intellectuals, we didn't think we should own one; we thought it would be a bad influence on our future children; and we couldn't afford one anyway. So the radio was our source of news as was the case for many students at the time. But Florida State made arrangements to bring television sets into the main campus auditorium so students could view the funeral ceremonies on November 25. With the nation and fellow students, we saw the procession of national leaders behind the caisson and the riderless horse. The discomforts of pregnancy took over before the end of the ceremonies, and we heard the description of the last rites and burial at Arlington Cemetery on the radio in our kitchen. "Well—that's that," we said as the newscast ended; we turned our heads away from one another (doctoral students don't express emotion) and both wept.

The next week Tom bought a television set. It was being said that the assassination and funeral had forged us into a newly national community, with television as its voice and interpreter. Not having a set meant being left out of the community. We watched a lot of soap operas that winter. I wonder how many other sets were bought that year?

Mary Ross, High School Junior, Parkersburg High School, West Virginia

Mary Ross describes how she got a treasured artifact that she never will relinquish.

I was on my way to my sixth period drama class in a hallway crowded by a river of students when my friend, Diane, spotted me and told me that the President had been shot. I entered class and found everyone in the room absolutely still and transfixed by the news. For a while, the teacher let us talk about John F. Kennedy and then we went home for a weekend of total despair.

I was devastated by the President's assassination as I thought back to my own personal contact with him nearly four years earlier when then-Senator Kennedy was campaigning in the presidential primary in West Virginia. It was cold and blowing that April day in 1960 when Senator Kennedy came to my hometown of Parkersburg located along the Ohio River. I had a cold and my mother didn't think I should be out in the chilly weather, but nothing would keep me from seeing John F. Kennedy.

I was thirteen then, and with a couple of girlfriends, I went to the city park to see the man we hoped would be our next President. There were several thousand people crowded everywhere to see him and no seats were available around the bandstand where he would speak. We settled down on the damp ground, right up front, until he came. When we saw his car pull up behind the bandstand, we ran around to the back to watch him get out of the car. I waved at him, and I was so excited when he waved back, just like he knew me!

I was disappointed that Mrs. Kennedy wasn't there, but the Senator's sister, Eunice Shriver, was there along with his brother, Teddy. Mr. Kennedy's throat was so sore that he could barely speak over a whisper, so Teddy spoke for him. What a wonderful speech it was! The reception from the large crowd was tremendous.

There was a platform set up to the left of the bandstand. When I saw that the Senator and his party were going over there to receive people individually, I edged over through the throng. When Senator Kennedy got on the platform, I was right behind him. I don't know where I got the nerve, but before I knew it, I was standing beside him in the receiving line, talking with him just like I belonged.

He handed me a Coke cup, and all the rest of that afternoon I held it for him. He'd sip it every now and then between handshakes and photographs. One man brought him a picture of Jackie that he had painted. I will never forget the look in Kennedy's eyes as he gazed at the painting. He seemed such a humble man to me, and I felt right at home.

Around 5:00 P.M., Teddy announced that it was time for the candidate and his party to leave to catch a plane. I was standing there by the Senator with his unfinished Coke in my hand. I asked him if he wanted to finish it, and he laughed and told me I could have it. I was careful not to spill the coke from its red and white paper container. I kept that Coke in our home freezer for a long time. Our friends came over to see it and it. It was affectionately called, "Kennedy's Coke." One day my mother defrosted the freezer and forgot about the Coke. It melted of course, but even today I have saved the cup. I wouldn't take anything for the cup and will treasure it the rest of my life.

After the President's death, I would still drive past the bandstand in the park and remember my afternoon with Mr. Kennedy. I can still see it all: the crowds, the banners, the cheers, and the wonderful man who was so kind to a young girl. It still makes me feel good to know that I was there and a part of it all.

Today President Kennedy is still my hero. I remember him for his upbeat tempo, his positive attitude that we could get things done, and his youthful enthusiasm that gave everyone help. I believed in him more than any other leader since his death.

Thomas P. (Tommy) O'Neill, III, College Student, Boston College

Tommy O'Neill was the son of Thomas P. "Tip" O'Neill, II" who held Kennedy's former congressional seat in Boston and later became the Speaker of the U.S. House of Representatives. Tommy, inspired partly by the Kennedy call to service, later served as the Lieutenant Governor of Massachusetts.

In November 1963, I was a freshman at Boston College. On Friday, November 22, I was sitting in the student sports center chatting with several other students about homecoming. Someone ran into the room and told us about the shooting of the President in Dallas.

Although there were hundreds of people in the center, an eerie and hushed quiet fell over all within earshot. Without exception from all directions students began walking to St. Mary's campus chapel. As you looked around, you could see people heading toward a common site seeking comfort. It was really a mystical experience. Whether people

Courtesy of Thomas P. O'Neill III

Tommy O'Neill, front center, and family meet Senator Kennedy on their arrival in Washington, "Tip" O'Neill to left of Kennedy, January, 1953.

were religious or not, there seemed to be a common desire to kneel in the chapel to offer a prayer for our President and wish him well.

The rest of that day and into the next, friends and family stayed glued to the television accounts of the tragedy. My father, "Tip" O'Neill, and my mother, longtime friends of the Kennedys, headed for Washington. My father had taken over Jack's congressional seat in Boston when Kennedy was elected to the U.S. Senate in 1952.

Because of my extreme personal distress at not being able to say farewell to a man I so greatly admired as President Kennedy, a friend and I thumbed a ride to Washington. Some 20 hours later we arrived and my parents were amazed to see me.

On Sunday morning, wearing borrowed clothes, I went to Capitol Hill to view the body lying in state. I remember going with my father to speaker John McCormack's office and meeting the Speaker of the House and U. N. Ambassador Adlai Stevenson there. I fully participated in all the funeral proceedings including walking down Pennsylvania Avenue and on to Arlington Cemetery. I still can hear the broken note from the bugler playing taps adding even a more plaintive air to the already melancholy ceremony.

This weekend greatly impacted my life. I was determined then and there to become an active participant in American politics and serve my country as Kennedy had urged all young people to do. Of course, I would do this as a Democrat, which I am sure JFK would have relished with a grin.

Because of my father's long years of activity in Boston politics, I had become familiar with the Kennedys dating back many years. I first remember Jack Kennedy as a newly elected Senator on the old Senate subway in 1953 when I was seven years old.

One of my favorite teachers in high school, Sister Agatha, also reinforced my interest in John F. Kennedy. In 1960, she kept focusing the attention of our class on the political scene, particularly on the progress of a young Irish Catholic Senator from Boston. She also enthusiastically supported newly elected President Kennedy's call for Americans to serve their country.

One of my favorite memories of JFK occurred without my really being in close contact with him. The very last rally held by Senator Kennedy before the November 1960 presidential election was held in Boston Garden, better known as the home of the Boston Celtics. The site was on the old North End where lanterns were once hung with the message, "one if by land and two by sea," on the night of Paul Revere's famous ride. As a high school sophomore, I was thrilled to be in the audience. After ten minutes or so of thundering ovation welcoming the next president, a hush fell over the crowd. At that point, I yelled as loud as I could, "Jack, we really love you." This reignited the crowd once again. After the rally, my father, who had been on the speaker's stand with Jack asked, "Was that you, Tommy?" He gave me a big smile when I confessed to my action. Another happy remembrance I have is attending the Inaugural Ball in Washington in January 1961 and, specifically, dancing with my mother side by side with President and Mrs. Kennedy.

I did follow through with my desired goal decided upon in November 1963, that is, to continue to be actively involved in politics. I did so in different roles up to the present. I believe my motivation came from my parents, John F. Kennedy, and not to be overlooked, Sister Agatha. Looking back, I think Kennedy had such a great attraction for me because he brought a fresh new look to politics, particularly for young Americans. I felt a certain kinship with Kennedy as this whole period of the 1960s and early 1970s of wonderful and progressive activism motivated countless numbers of people to enter public service. I look back at the selflessness of that era with great admiration and hope we can regain it once again. I only hope that my own children will follow in the footsteps of the best of the Kennedy ideals in some form of public service.

Chapter Nine

Civil Rights Community Reaction

No segment of the American public had greater regard for President Kennedy than the civil rights community. In this chapter, black and white civil rights leaders share their views of JFK. Reverend John Crowell sets the stage for the controversy related to Kennedy in the south over civil rights. Vivian Malone-Jones, one of two black students attempting to enter the University of Alabama when Governor George Wallace made his infamous doorway act of defiance, says about JFK, "I will always remember him as a person who made a great difference in my life and one who all Americans should be grateful to for helping fulfill the American dream of equality." Mrs. Medgar Evers-Williams describes him as "...our young bright hope, our star for the future of a better life for all Americans." James Farmer, director of the civil rights organization, CORE, was critical of Kennedy for not moving faster concerning civil rights, but cites as Kennedy's great contribution, "giving people hope in the world," This included people in both the United States and Africa. Entertainer Lena Horne expresses her dismay over violence in the United States, and Bernestine Williams recalls the assassination while illustrating some of the problems faced by African-Americans living in the south at the time.

John Crowell, Presbyterian Minister, Mobile, Alabama

While Kennedy was popular with the African-American population, he also had white support in the South for his civil rights policies. One such leader who risked the public ire because of his belief in racial equality, describes the hostile mood of many whites in Alabama in 1963.

Alabama was a place of great tension and discontent in 1963. Blacks were demanding from the President greater action in ending segregation practices, and many Southerners were equally adamant in opposing any changes. Birmingham was a particular point of dispute; it was named by the Rev. Martin Luther King as "the most thoroughly segregated city in the U.S." In the spring of 1963 clashes began in serious with civil rights demonstrators and the Birmingham Police Chief and candidate for mayor, Eugene "Bull" Connor. Many still can remember pictures of police dogs jumping at Negro demonstrators, even small children.

Another issue that Alabama faced was that it was the only state with a segregated state university. Governor George Wallace is still remembered for his defiant stand in the doorway of the University of Alabama's building when two black students attempted to register. After June 1963, the federal government, led by President Kennedy, opened up a full-scale effort to end racial discrimination.

In Mobile, we had similar problems to those in other parts of the state. I had participated along with other ministers in efforts to bring about desegregation of facilities such as local buses. At one point, I was under such heavy criticism by opponents of desegregation, I moved my family out of town for their personal safety. I was pastor of the Central Presbyterian Church at the time, a congregation of some 1200 members. Alabama in 1963 was a powder keg almost ready to explode. I believe if President Kennedy had pushed any harder or faster, we would have had bloodshed in the streets of our state.

President Kennedy in November of 1963 was disliked by many in Alabama, but was greatly admired by many others, both black and white including my family. On Friday afternoon, I was riding in my car with my six year old daughter, Lyn, on our way to the beauty parlor to pick up my wife. We heard that the President had been shot, and it was like a blow to my solar plexus. My daughter was equally devastated because she put President Kennedy almost next to God. When we arrived at the beauty parlor, those inside were in a similar state of shock. For the next few days, those I had contact with seemed awestruck. I was deeply affected, not only because I liked the

President, but also because of what had happened to our country.

On Saturday, I decided to change the sermon already scheduled for Sunday and do a special eulogy concerning our fallen President. Much of my day was spent in my study writing the new sermon. On Sunday, before a crowded and somber congregation, I delivered the sermon using the title "American Mourns." Some of those who passed me at the door as they left that morning had tears in the eyes. Several thanked me for expressing their thoughts in my remarks. During the sermon, I reminded my audience that:

> He [Kennedy] was a great man, for he was the President of these United States, the greatest nation of free people in the world. Disagree with him as you may have done on policies and decisions unpopular with many in the South, he was *OUR* President. Our flags now fly throughout our land at half-mast, as are even our hearts for this *OUR* President is dead. And we, the people of these United States of America mourn.

It was overall a period of universal sorrow not only in Mobile, but throughout the deep South. Despite the bitter struggle over race, people lamented the untimely death of their youthful President. I think the young people I had contact with were particularly hard hit by the tragedy. There may have been a few old diehards that were not unhappy over the assassination, but they were the exception to the rule.

Some 40 years later, I still hold in high regard the inspiration and vision President Kennedy gave to the youth of our country. I can't recall any President before or since who provided such motivation for people to help others. He had a great grasp of language and conveyed a sense of honesty. If he made a mistake, he admitted it in very clear words. During the Cuban missile crisis, I realized the courage it took for the President to make a decision with the fate of so much of the world riding in the balance. I still recall what appeared to be the inner anguish on his face during this trying period. From civil rights and foreign policy to inspiring our nation, President Kennedy was already doing well and learning and growing all the time. My family and I still miss him today.

Vivian J. Malone-Jones, College Student, University of Alabama at Tuscaloosa

Vivian J. Malone-Jones went on to graduate from the University of Alabama. In an ironic twist of fate in 1996, she was the first recipient of the Lurleen B. Wallace Award of Courage in the presence of her former nemesis, former Governor George Wallace. She continues to work in civil rights activities.

I became aware of John F. Kennedy for the first time when I watched him on television speaking at the 1960 Democratic party's presidential nominating convention held in Los Angeles. What caught my attention was that I had never heard any political leader address the civil rights issues facing the nation the way that he did. I was impressed with his forthrightness and felt that I would like for him to become President of the United States. Little did I know then that our lives would converge together for a brief moment of time in 1963.

I graduated from Central High School in Mobile, Alabama, in 1960. I wanted to attend a public college within the state of Alabama. I applied to the University of Alabama's Mobile Extension Center and was rejected. Then I enrolled at Alabama A & M in Huntsville, in January 1961, majoring in business education. I remained at A & M through the spring semester of 1963. My career goal was to become a certified public accountant, but none of the predominantly black state schools offered a major in accounting.

Because I was not majoring in the area that I wanted to pursue, I decided to forward my application to the University of Alabama because of its much broader curriculum in business. Also, since all of the white southern state universities had been integrated, I expected that my matriculation at the University of Alabama would be relatively uneventful.

In the spring of 1963, I was notified that I had been accepted at Alabama. Therefore, I decided to enter during the summer session because Alabama A & M had recently lost accreditation. In addition, I would begin my studies in business administration as soon as possible.

My parents were extremely supportive throughout the entire ordeal. They felt, that if my entering the University of Alabama would benefit me (and they both agreed that it should be integrated), they said, "Do it!" Unfortunately, the Governor of Alabama, George C. Wallace, decided to make a dramatic stand against the admission of black students to the university.

Prior to my and James A. Hood's (another prospective student) arrival on campus, the Governor challenged our admission but was overruled by a federal district judge. Later, Wallace announced he would personally "bar the entrance of any Negro who attempts to enroll." President Kennedy then ordered Wallace not to stop the integration of the school. This clash of wills was heavily covered in the news media and by the morning of June 11, 1963, the nation and world were watching to see what would happen. My earlier and naive hope of not being noticed really went down the drain on a very hot Tuesday morning. James A. Hood and I were escorted to the Alabama campus in a three-car motorcade accompanied by federal officials. We had been briefed on what to expect by several people, particularly John Doar from the Justice Department. When we entered the campus, there was a warlike atmosphere surrounding us as hundreds of steel-helmeted state troopers and other officials were there supporting Governor Wallace, while large numbers of students and news reporters watched nearby. We waited in the car while Deputy Attorney General, Nicholas Katzenbach, marched up to the doorway of Foster Hall, the red brick, white pillared registration building. There he was met by Governor Wallace who, while protesting the President's actions, retreated when Kennedy federalized the Alabama National Guard to carry out the President's integration order. Wallace called it a "bitter pill" for the state National Guard to enforce an order he opposed and left as white students cheered his actions.

Early that afternoon we paid our fees and registered for summer classes. Later I went to my dormitory room in Mary Burke Hall and was assigned a self-contained room. I was surprised, however, to have been greeted at the dorm by a small committee of students who were friendly to me on my arrival. That evening, I watched President

Kennedy address the nation by television on the events of the day in Alabama. I really had a sense of awe as I heard the President of the United States give an eloquent statement on behalf of the rights of blacks and Americans of all races and color. It felt like he was talking directly to me. Here I was, a poor little kid out of Mobile, and the President of the United States had stood up for my individual rights. A few students in the lounge walked out on the President's speech.

Although I had been apprehensive and concerned over what might happen to me when I entered the university, I really wasn't that frightened. I just saw it as something that had to be done. When I arose the next morning, I learned that Medgar Evers had been shot to death in Mississippi the previous night. That made me realize how vulnerable I was, but I still thought I had to proceed. I was glad the admission battle was over because all I wanted to do was to attend classes in pursuit of my education. It was generally a lonely time as white students usually avoided me in all aspects of campus life.

In November, 1963, I received another shock that once again pointed out my precarious position. I was alone in my dorm room listening to the radio when I heard that President Kennedy had been shot. I couldn't believe what I heard. I was stunned and hurt and followed the events of that sad weekend on television. I also talked to friends and family by telephone sharing my grief with them. I thought after Kennedy was killed, "My God, if the President can be shot, there is no protection for anyone. No matter what protection is provided, if someone wants to kill you they can." I still refused to be fearful for my life because there was little I could do about it anyway.

President Kennedy will always remain for me the President who gave hope to black people after so many years of hopelessness. He brought a new sense of self-worth to our lives and provided a fresh beginning in our country for many. I was also delighted and somewhat surprised by the legislation passed under the leadership of President Johnson. I was pleased to be included in the White House signing of the Voting Rights Act in 1965.

Although I never had the pleasure of personally meeting John F. Kennedy, I will always remember him as a person who made a great

difference in my life and one to whom all Americans should be grateful for helping fulfill the American dream of equality. As he stated in
his speech of June 11, 1963, "It ought to be possible for every
American to enjoy the privilege of being American without regard to
his race or color." He not only stated those words, he made a great step
in carrying them out. I know—I was there!

Mrs. Medgar (Myrlie) Evers-Williams, Housewife, Jackson, Mississippi

Mrs. Evers-Williams, following in the footsteps of her late husband, became a leader in the civil rights movement, including serving as chair-woman of the NAACP. She also was the first woman to head the Board of Public Works in Los Angeles.

Reflecting back on my darkest memories of the events of the
1960s, it is now very clear that the lives of four great men were inex-
tricably linked in those turbulent times: Medgar Evers, John F.
Kennedy, Martin Luther King, Jr., and Robert F. Kennedy. All were
leaders in the fight for human rights and all became fallen heroes in
the cause of justice.

At no time did all of my memories of those days converge more
vividly for me than when I first met Mrs. Jacqueline Kennedy in
Atlanta in April 1968. The sad occasion was the funeral service for
Martin Luther King, Jr., held at the Ebenezer Baptist Church. There
I happened to come face to face with Mrs. Kennedy, and I introduced
myself to her. Her reaction was one of startled surprise and as she
raised her hand to her face, she gasped, "Oh, my God!" I felt a special
kinship with Mrs. Kennedy as we both had suffered the grievous loss
of our husbands at the hand of assassins. In that split second, as we
gazed at one another, I believe similar and equally terrifying images
flashed through our minds.

Shortly after the service, I was joined by Robert and Ethel
Kennedy, who were both very kind to me and my daughter, Reena. As
we walked together from the church, Ethel said to me, "You women
are so brave. I don't see how you do it." None of us could know on

that emotional day under a blazing sun in Atlanta that Mrs. Robert Kennedy would soon join the ranks of the three other widows at the funeral.

June 11, 1963, was a memorable day for the civil rights movement as two black students enrolled at the University of Alabama, despite the defiant stand in the registrar's doorway by Alabama Governor, George Wallace. For the Evers family, living in Jackson, Mississippi, it was a time of great apprehension and fear for our lives. Medgar was in a virtual state of exhaustion because of his incessant work as a civil rights leader. He seemed to have aged 10 years in a few months. The state of Mississippi was a powder keg ready to explode, and Medgar and I were only too aware of who would be the likely targets of any violence. We both sensed that his time was near.

On that final day, Medgar was particularly touching in saying goodbye to me and the children, embracing us, and speaking of his love for us. Later in the day he called and again was unusually preoccupied with expressing his love for us. He also urged me to watch President Kennedy's speech on civil rights to be broadcast on television that evening.

That night, the children and I viewed President Kennedy on television in my bedroom. His speech was very moving as he made a direct and urgent appeal for racial justice. I was sure that Medgar, who was somewhere watching the speech, would be overjoyed and thrilled to hear our President speak the words that Medgar had voiced in similar terms in his own televised speech only three weeks earlier.

Listening to President Kennedy was as if he were speaking directly to me about all the efforts we had been making in Mississippi on behalf of civil rights. It made me feel very close to him and gave me hope. Never in my lifetime had I ever heard a President of the United States make such a poignant and eloquent speech on behalf of the civil rights of black Americans.

We expected Medgar home late that evening and, when I heard his car arrive, I looked forward to hearing his reaction to the President's speech. It was at this point that a shot rang out, and the children fell to the floor as they had been trained. I rushed to the door fearful of what I would find. I turned on the light and found Medgar lying down by the door covered with blood. Another shot was fired and I saw he wasn't moving. Neighbors took Medgar to the hospital and we soon learned he had died. Those next few hours and days were a nightmare for our family.

Because Medgar was a veteran and a newly elected member of the national board of the American Veterans Committee, a burial in Arlington National Cemetery was suggested to me. I was convinced by friends that his burial there would be fitting for him, and it would allow all Americans a better chance to visit his grave.

Very moving services were held for Medgar in both Jackson and Washington, D.C. In Washington, 25,000 people passed his casket at the John Wesley A.M.E. church. At the Arlington Cemetery burial, many hundreds were there as well. At the end I was thankful that Medgar was buried near our nation's Capital. It was the first time in my life I had a sense of being a real American, not a second-class citizen.

The next morning, my son, Darrell, daughter, Reena, brother-in-law, Charles Evers, and I visited with President Kennedy in the White House. My youngest son, Van had stayed at home. The President was very gracious and kind to us. He told me, "You're a brave woman." He also told the children how proud they should be of their father and of their heritage and gave each small gifts. I still treasure what he gave to me: an autographed copy of the Civil Rights Bill. He also arranged a tour of the White House for us, and I was particularly pleased to visit the Lincoln Room. As we watched through a window, I will never forget the President outside on the lawn leaving by helicopter as John-John waved goodbye to him. I almost broke down as I thought that my children would never again get the opportunity to wave goodbye to their father. While I was very pleased by the warmth and gentleness of the President's reception, I feel it was not a privilege, but rather a symbol of respect that was long overdue for all black Americans. We returned home and tried to go on with our lives.

Our entire family was devastated by Medgar's death, but perhaps Darrell as a nine-year-old was the hardest hit of all. He idolized his

Courtesy of the John F. Kennedy Library

Mrs. Medgar Evers, daughter Reena, son Darrell and Medgar's brother Charles meet with Kennedy shortly after Medgar's funeral, June 21, 1963.

father and became withdrawn, seemed unhappy, and didn't even eat well. By the fall we had regained some semblance of order in our lives when tragic news hit us once again.

On November 22, 1963, I was at my hairdresser's, also a good friend of mine. Reena was at home watching television. I had a copy of *Look* magazine and my friend and I were admiring the cover on which was a picture of President Kennedy and John-John. When the phone rang, it was Reena telling us the President had been shot. I went to pieces over the news, and when I regained my composure, I hurried home. When Walter Cronkite announced the President had been shot. I was gripped by a tremendous sense of despair. A friend brought Darrell home from school. He went silently to his room where he just sat and cried. He couldn't even eat supper that night.

Later that weekend, I overheard a woman say, "Mrs. Kennedy didn't have to worry, she had plenty of money." I almost resorted to physical violence at that point; I was so incensed at her statement. I called her "heartless," and in no uncertain terms, I let her know that for a wife and children losing their husband and father by assassination, their problems had nothing to do with money.

The death of President Kennedy had a great impact on our family. More than anything else, he had brought a sense of hope to people where there had been none before. We saw him as a light to lead us out of darkness. Kennedy was a youthful and vigorous President, who was also an astute politician. We thought he would get the job done for us. Unfortunately I also had concern that if Medgar Evers could be assassinated, so could President Kennedy.

For that time in my memory, we had a courageous President who stood up and took a stand for the benefit of my people, unheard of in my generation. My common sense told me that, if someone was as brave as President Kennedy to take such a stand, his life would be in danger, particularly if he continued on that path.

When I heard the President was assassinated, somewhere in the recesses of my mind, I remember thinking, I knew it! I knew it! Someone like John F. Kennedy could not be allowed to exist and continue for any length of time. His death left me very angry and at age 30 I was naive in many ways, but not in this area. I felt as though all of my hopes and dreams and those of my children and other children had been completely dashed and broken against rocks. I thought there never would be a new day. It was absolutely devastating.

John F. Kennedy was our young, bright hope, our star for the future of a better life for all American. He was a man who took our country and turned it in the right direction in the area of human rights, civil rights, rights for everyone. Those of us who were deprived began to believe a new day was coming, one that would give us our legitimate place in American society.

Kennedy's time was short, but I think he did more within that short span of being President than others have done in two full terms. It is quite possible he did more with his death than if he had lived, but that we will never know. John F. Kennedy's hopes and dreams and words will never be erased. His legacy is still with us everywhere today. He helped shape America and the world into being a better place.

I compare Kennedy's death and Medgar's, and I will always be profoundly touched by President Kennedy's life, but I do believe both did more in death than in life. The quality of accomplishment in life is not measured in time. I believe that both Medgar and John F. Kennedy will go down through the annals of American history as two of our nation's heroes.

Charlene Freeman-Coker, Office Worker, Wingdale State Hospital, New York

Not only African-Americans living in the south were distressed by the death of Kennedy as described below.

In November 1963, I was working in the medical records office of Wingdale State Hospital, a hospital for the mentally ill located in southeastern New York. I had gone there like many other blacks from the south to get a better job than I could find at home. My sister was my link to the job and assisted me in locating the job; she lived there as well. I was earning money to help me through my studies as a college student at Norfolk State College in Virginia.

On Friday, November 22, I had taken a late lunch break and was in the recreation area in an open ward of the hospital. I was trying to learn how to play pool, a sport closed to women in the south and one that was a male-only activity. I thought it would be fun to learn how to play.

I was in the open recreation room along with some 15 or so mental patients, mostly male, and a couple of hospital aides. We had a radio on the shelf above us playing music and a television operating in another part of the room. Suddenly we heard on the radio that President Kennedy had been shot. Over the next few minutes the patients in the entire dayroom became unglued. Some were screaming and moaning and others were cursing and crying. I remember one man shouting, "The only good man we have had in the White House and he has been shot." Someone yelled that the news was "just a hoax" and several people seemed in a state of denial and even when they heard the reports of his death, they refused to accept the news.

New aides coming on duty were also in a state of shock, and one was crying. All in all it was a very emotional and traumatic scene. The staff, including myself, while greatly upset by Kennedy's death, was also very worried that some of the patients might get out of control and some form of a riot might occur.

Most of the hospital staff was black working in more menial tasks. Most, like myself, had migrated north from states like Alabama and North Carolina looking for work. I happened to be the only black worker in my office section. A feeling of helplessness seemed to be shared by most of us. If Kennedy could be killed with such ease, what choice did powerless blacks have in our nation? Many of my fellow workers saw his death as part of a hideous conspiracy to halt the civil rights movement.

Because of the unsettled state of mind of the patients and the concern by hospital administrators for some outbreak by the black patients to the assassination, we were told to stay nearby for the weekend and to stay inside and off the grounds. I lived in housing provided for staff on the grounds, separate but near to where the patients were housed. The patients were kept under close security during this period, and I do not recall any incidents taking place.

Looking back at the death of President Kennedy 30 years later, I still feel a sense of great loss. As a young black woman in 1963, I had high hopes for the future as a result of the President's civil rights speeches and proposed legislation. I believed he would do what was right and wouldn't sell out. He was very popular in the black community and seemed to have a global view of what was needed for the future for blacks and whites alike.

James Farmer, National Director, Congress of Racial Equality (CORE), New York City

The late James Farmer later became Assistant Secretary of the Department of Health, Education, and Welfare.

In November 1963, I was living in New York City where I served as the head of a civil rights organization, the Congress of Racial Equality (CORE). Prior to this post, I was program director for the NAACP. I did not have a particularly friendly relationship with the

Courtesy of James Farmer

James Farmer to left of Martin Luther King, Jr., as they prepare for the march at Selma, Alabama, 1965.

President or his brother, the Attorney General, Robert Kennedy. We did not see eye to eye over the pace of action by the President in ending racial discrimination in several areas, particularly that of federally financed housing. In fact, the civil rights leadership in general was disappointed over the lack of progress during the first two and one-half years of Kennedy's administration concerning civil rights legislation and executive orders. Despite our misgivings, President Kennedy was very popular with rank-in-file blacks throughout the country. I had clashed with Bobby Kennedy when I refused to stop the "freedom rides" in the South and have a "cooling-off" period as he requested. He was furious and so was Jack. My view was that we had waited 350 years and had been "cooling off" all that time, and further waiting might put us in a deep freeze. Despite my differences with the President, I still respected him and thought highly of his position on many of the things he was doing.

On November 22, I was in Cleveland attending a conference of the Cleveland CORE. It was on my way down in a hotel elevator that I learned that the President had been shot. I overheard two businessmen wearing badges, apparently attending a conference, talking to each other in the elevator. One of them said, "Naw, they got the wrong damn Kennedy." I then looked up. The other man responded, "Yeah, they should have shot that little Bobby son of a bitch." I immediately wanted off that elevator before I lost my nonviolence attitude and committed mayhem on the two businessmen exalting over the President's being shot. I also badly wanted to learn more about the President's status. It was truly terrible to hear people like those on the elevator appearing to be happy that the President had been shot.

We had our meeting that afternoon, but it was really *pro forma* with no one concentrating, and nothing being accomplished as everyone was in a state of shock. When I returned to my New York office, our entire office staff went around for days in a zombielike state.

On the Sunday after the assassination, I received a surprising call at my home. When I picked up the telephone, someone with a southern voice told me, the President was on the telephone. I asked, "President of what?" It was the new President, Lyndon B. Johnson. We had worked together on projects when he was Vice-President. I had proposed to him an employment policy which I called compensatory preferential treatment. Johnson liked the concept, but not the name. He preferred a more positive name calling it "affirmative" action. He told me in his telephone call, "We would have to pick up the ball (referring to civil rights) and run with it. I hope I'll have your help in the days, weeks, months and maybe years ahead." I assured him he would have my full support and cooperation.

Looking back at the Kennedy's brief tenure in office, I believe his great contribution was that he gave people in the world hope, including black people in the United States and in Africa as well. I have visited many African homes where I have seen photographs of Kennedy on the wall. He had the image of youthful vigor to get the nation on the move again. People who had been downtrodden and had hopes for a better life saw him as a bright young leader who could help solve their problems. Each group had its own different perspective as to what they thought the President would achieve for them. They saw him from their own eyes. In fact, I believe the President would have been shocked if he had known what some were thinking. The civil rights movement got a new burst of speed from the rhetoric of Jack Kennedy during the 1960 campaign and afterward.

As a final reflection, it was not until 1966, when I had a long private conversation with then U. S. Senator Robert Kennedy, that we came to a new relationship of mutual respect. He seemed to understand why I needed to push so hard in the early 1960s. I, of course, was well aware of the difficult political pressures President Kennedy faced concerning civil rights during his stay in office. But my role was to push for progress as hard as I knew how, which I had done. By 1966, Senator Kennedy seemed to fully grasp what we had been attempting to achieve.

Lena Horne, Entertainer, New York City

Ms. Horne had barely returned from a visit with the President in the White House when she learned of his untimely death. She accurately points out that his death had one positive outcome: it led to the passage of civil rights legislation under the administration of President Johnson. Most political experts believe that the proposed civil rights legislation would never have passed except for Kennedy's death. Because there was a new desire in the nation and the Congress to do what many considered the right thing in honor of Kennedy, major strides were made in civil rights.

The third week in November 1963 is one that I will never forget. On Wednesday morning, November 20, along with several other entertainers, I had a short visit with President Kennedy in the White House. We were there to discuss our possible role in the 1964 presidential race. We were greeted warmly by the President, whom I had met before on several occasions. It was not my first trip to the White House as I had made earlier visits, including one with Mrs. Eleanor Roosevelt.

On Friday afternoon, along with my daughter, Gail, and a few friends, we were in my apartment making last-minute preparations for Gail's wedding to be held on Sunday. We were addressing

Lena Horne, third from left visits the White House, November 20, 1963.

envelopes when we learned of the President's death. Shocked and saddened as I was, daughter Gail was even harder hit. She was an ardent Kennedy backer and had worked for him in his 1958 reelection campaign to the Senate in Boston when she was a student at Radcliffe. We all felt somewhat guilty to continue the wedding. Yet, life had to go on. The entire weekend was one of great difficulty as Gail married movie director, Sidney Lumet, in a small ceremony. I wore black as did several others. It was a sad setting for what should have been a joyous occasion.

I was personally defeated by Kennedy's death and frankly thought it was an inevitable happening. I remembered this earlier that year in June when I had met with Medgar Evers and worked with him at an NAACP rally in Jackson, Mississippi. It was a couple of days after that rally that he was assassinated. So Kennedy's death was no surprise to me because Medgar had already been murdered. Those two events created a climate in this country that allowed brutal assassinations of people fighting for their rights. I also believed Jack's brother, Bobby, and others were in danger.

1963 became a turning-point year for me as I considered what I could do to help in the civil rights movement. From that year on, I became more active in these issues.

Of course, events got even worse later with the death of other civil rights leaders, including Malcom X, Martin Luther King, Jr., and Robert Kennedy.

As I think back about President Kennedy I greatly admired his youth, energy and efforts to bring positive changes for black Americans and all Americans. Yet, I had little hope that the majority of Americans would allow the passage of the civil rights legislation advocated by President Kennedy. Ironically his death seemed to open the way for Lyndon Johnson to get this legislation put into law.

Bernestine F. Williams, College Student and Part-time Worker, University of Arkansas at Pine Bluff

Ms. Williams reveals the status of many black workers in the south and her difficulty in learning about the death of President Kennedy.

In 1963, I was a 20-year-old college student at the University of Arkansas. At the time of the assassination, I was working at a part-time job in the kitchen of a hotel in Pine Bluff. On Friday afternoon of November 22, I was making sandwiches. In front of me was a window connecting with the hotel dining room. I could look through the window and see the restaurant's customers, but being black, I was not allowed in the restaurant, even as a waitress. We were only allowed in the dining room to clean up after the customers were gone. Our kitchen staff was nearly all black except for the chef in charge, who was white.

That afternoon, I looked through the window into the dining room and noticed a lot of commotion. I cracked the window to see if I could hear what was going on. A waitress told me that President Kennedy had been shot. I had a knife in my hand, and I remember I was so angry I stabbed hard right into the meat I was slicing at the time.

It was very frustrating because we could see customers in the dining room basically glued to the television set, but we in the kitchen weren't able to hear what was going on outside. In the kitchen, all of us stopped what we were doing, but the chef in charge got upset and told us to "get busy, we have food to get out there." We ignored him and no one moved. Since I was one of the most educated of our group, I decided to speak up. I told everyone to go to the back of the kitchen and there together we said the "Lord's Prayer." When we returned to our work stations, the chef wanted to know what we talked about and what we were going to do. I told him, "We didn't talk about it, we prayed about it; that's our way of dealing with big problems." We stayed silent while we worked the rest of the day. I think we all felt that in some way President Kennedy was there to help us, that he listened to us when no other leader would. We were angry because this link to our hopes for change had been broken. He really did listen.

Pine Bluff was located about 40 miles from Little Rock, the site of an integration crisis in 1957. Riots had broken out there when President Eisenhower used federal troops to permit black students to enter the Little Rock Central High School. Six years later, whites still seemed fearful of what blacks might do because of the still hostile tension between blacks and whites in Arkansas. I guess they thought we might do something violent. For days after the assassination there seemed to be fear in the eyes of many whites whom I guess, feared that the black community would explode in some way.

All that weekend I prayed along with my entire family for our departed President. We felt that blacks had to stick together. I was one of five children, four girls and one boy, reared by our grandmother since our parents were deceased. She always taught us that prayer changes everything. Therefore in our home, we had a prayer every morning when we arose and one every evening before going to bed. In our Methodist Church that weekend, our congregation prayed about what we could do that was nonviolent as stressed by Martin Luther King, Jr. When President Kennedy died, it was not only a very sad day for blacks in Arkansas, but also for blacks all over the South.

Chapter Ten

Space Program Community Reaction

One of the programs most associated with President Kennedy was the effort to go to the moon. The United States had lost considerable prestige when the Russians launched "Sputnik" beating us to the punch in the space race. Kennedy realized the great propaganda values of being perceived as the world's leader in technology and the military implications of controlling space. Although he did not live to see his goals reach fruition, those who worked with him on the space program considered him a pivotal figure in developing the space program.

Three vignettes in this chapter offer different perspectives of Kennedy and the space arena. First, Homer Hickam, Jr., recalls that he may have been the first person to tell the President that "we should go to the moon." He shares his contribution as a college student in keeping the Kennedy memory alive. Former astronaut, John Glenn, describes why Kennedy was so valued by his friends and his legacy to the nation. Finally, Chris Kraft, former flight director of the Manned Spacecraft Center in Houston offers his experiences with Kennedy related to the space program.

Homer H. Hickam, Jr., College Student, Virginia Tech
Homer Hickam is the author of several book including Rocket Boys[21]
in 1998 that was later made into the popular movie, October Sky.
He shares the advice he gave to a prospective President and describes the unique memorial named after Kennedy that he helped create. JFK as an ardent football fan would undoubtedly have enjoyed the name and thundering boom of "Skipper."

When John Kennedy was waging a tough political battle in the West Virginia presidential primary in the spring of 1960, I was a high school senior and just winding up my career as a rocket builder in Coalwood, West Virginia. Inspired by the sight of Sputnik, the world's first man-made satellite, and after three years of hard work, five other coal miners' sons and I had managed to learn how to build sophisticated rockets and send them miles into the sky. We had already won the county and state science fairs and were on our way to the National Science Fair to show them what West Virginia boys could do. The story of how and why we boys built our rockets is told in my book, *Rocket Boys*,[22] which later was adapted into the movie, *October Sky*.

The first time I ever saw then-Senator Kennedy was in April 1960 when I came across him standing on top of a Cadillac in Welch. I was there to buy a suit to wear to the National Science Fair. The suit I had picked was a bright orange, all the better I figured to stand out at the fair. I was so proud of my choice. I'd put my new suit on to show it off and worked my way to the front of the crowd listening to Senator Kennedy giving a speech to a knot of coal miners. It seemed to me his back was hurting him. He kept rubbing the small of it with his fist, and when he did, his eyes would squint in pain. The miners standing around listening were pretty listless. Being a boy of the hills, I immediately recognized what his problem was, at least as far as his speech was concerned. The audience wanted a little entertainment. Why else would they come to hear a politician after a hard day's work in the mines?

I decided to ask Senator Kennedy a question. For some reason, as soon as I raised my hand, he took note of me. "What do you think the United States ought to do in space?" I asked a man who'd just talked himself hoarse about unemployment and welfare and food stamps and the raw deal that coal mining was in general.

Surprised, John Kennedy looked at me for what seemed a year and then turned my question back on me. From his automobile perch, he demanded, "Well young man, what do you think we should do in space?" He had managed to corner me. The truth was, I hadn't given it all that much thought so I improvised. Lately, I'd been looking at the moon a lot through a telescope we Rocket Boys had set atop one of Coalwood's buildings. "We should go to the moon!" I said with such vigor that I got applause and cheers from everybody still standing around.

The clapping and cheering seemed to surprise Senator Kennedy. He straightened a little, surveyed the crowd and their grinning faces, and then, as if he had a sudden inspiration, he said maybe I was right, that what we needed to do was to get the country moving again, and if going to the moon could help that, maybe it was just the thing. Then he asked me what we should do on the moon when we got there, and I said we should find out what it was made of and go ahead and mine the blamed thing. That idea, too, just popped into my head. The miners responded with more whoops and hollers and cries that West Virginians could go and "mine that old moon good!" I got a benevolent smile from the Senator before Emily Sue Buckberry, a friend of mine, dragged me off to the men's store to exchange my beautiful orange suit for something drab and awful.

After that, I went on to win the gold and silver medals for propulsion in the National Science Fair, and Senator Kennedy had gone on to win his election in the state and the entire country, too. He'd done it by proposing to get the nation moving again, not only around the world but also in space. To make good on this promise, he stood up before Congress and announced: "I believe this nation should commit itself, before this decade is out, to landing a man on the moon and returning him safely to the earth." That speech officially began the race to the moon, but I like to think my question to John Kennedy in McDowell County one sunny day in the spring of 1960 started the whole thing.

Immediately following my years as a rocket boy, I went to engineering school at Virginia Tech. They were exciting years for me and for the country. While I was learning how to be an engineer, projects *Mercury* and *Gemini* forged ahead, sending Americans into space to learn how to go to the moon. It was also a dangerous time for the United States. We went through the Cuban missile crisis, coming as close to nuclear warfare with the Russians as we ever did during the

Cold War. I was proud of how President Kennedy handled everything and agreed with nearly all that he did, at least as much as I could keep up with the news, considering my college studies.

I also got involved in a project, the building of a Civil War-style cannon for the cadet corps, so that we might have a suitably loud method to celebrate special occasions, such as the scoring of touchdowns during football games. In the fall of 1963, after much work, several other cadets and I managed to get the cannon cast. It was a grand cannon built of brass from my father's coal mine. We were so proud of it, we thought it should have a special name. We argued about its name quite a lot, but nobody could come up with a good one. All we knew for sure was that our fine new cannon was going to be introduced during the annual Thanksgiving Day football game with our arch-rivals, the Virginia Military Institute. The week before the game, President Kennedy was assassinated, a cruel blow to everyone in the country.

I had an idea and took it to "Butch" Harper, the cadet who'd led the cannon-building program and suggested that our cannon be named after the President. Butch agreed, and we decided to name it the "Skipper," because John Kennedy had once been a commander of a PT boat during World War II. Our cannon was fired for the first time on that sad Thanksgiving after President Kennedy died. The "Skipper" erupted with a wondrous thunder, as befitted the man who launched our country on its greatest adventure, one that took us all the way to the moon.

John Glenn, Astronaut, Houston, Texas

Later, John Glenn served several terms as a U. S. Senator from Ohio. Glenn shares some of his favorite recollections of Kennedy that reveal some of JFK's best personal qualities and why he was so highly regarded by those who knew him best.

By coincidence I was in Dallas when I heard the news of the President's death on my car radio. When I learned that America had lost a President, I knew that I also had lost a friend. I first met

President Kennedy and John Glenn visit with Russian cosmonaut, Gherman Titov, February 20, 1962.

President Kennedy at the White House on February 5, 1962. It was a very cordial meeting. He just wanted to talk about my upcoming orbital flight on *Friendship*, including some of the details about what I expected to experience during the flight.

After my successful orbital mission on February 20, 1962, the President flew to Cape Canaveral for the ceremonies held after my flight. There were several thousand people attending the event and the crowd control wasn't very good that day. When Kennedy came down from *Air Force One*, I joined him. The confusion caused by the crowd milling around made it difficult to proceed. At this point, I was given a personal insight into the sensitivity the President had for individuals and institutions. The band, near *Air Force One*, began playing the "Marine Hymn." The President picked up on this and asked me, "What do you normally do when they play the 'Marine Hymn?'" "Well, as a loyal Marine, I normally stand at attention." The President said, "That's what I thought," and he stopped and stood at attention and I stood beside him. The throng mingling around us had no idea what we were doing. This was a good example of those little human things that you appreciate very much. It showed the type of consideration and thoughtfulness Kennedy had for other people.

After that day, I met the President and his family on several occasions, including visits to the presidential compound at Hyannis, Massachusetts. The President was extremely interested in the entire space program. While at first he only seemed to regard it as a competitive thing with the Russians, I think his attitude changed as time went on and he saw the exploration of space as the worthwhile program that it was for a variety of reasons. Kennedy also saw the value of having the astronauts as an inspiration to young people to enter fields related to science and technology. Of course, as a practical politician, he also saw the political virtue of gaining support for the space program from the public's liking of the astronauts.

President Kennedy loved good stories. One of his favorites from me was an experience I had as the host for the United States visit by the Russian cosmonaut, Gherman Titov. The President met with Titov at the White House. The Titovs had been invited to our home for one of the evenings they were here, but declined the offer. My wife Annie and I were attending a reception at the Russian Embassy for the Titovs and, as we came to the end of the receiving line, one of the people from our State Department asked if I knew that the Titovs had just accepted a dinner invitation to our home that night. It was then 6:30 P.M. and they were planning to leave for our home at 7:00 P.M. Well, needless to say, we dashed to our home in Arlington to get things ready for the dinner party now only minutes away. We were joined by Al and Louise Shepard. The Arlington police sent a special detail for security and we sent the police off to buy frozen peas and other dinner accessories. Meanwhile, Annie canvassed the neighborhood for frozen steaks that we could grill.

I started the fire in two charcoal grills and turned on two fans to speed up the process of starting the charcoal. Within minutes, I had a fire going that was like a village smithy's forge. I could just about melt steel in that fire. We thawed the steaks in the oven and I threw them on the grill. I left for a moment, and when I returned, there were flames three feet high. I threw water on them and the resulting smoke filled up our little covered back porch. I dragged the grills out onto the carport and by now the smoke pouring out looked as though our house was on fire. At this point, one of the grills broke and dumped a load of steaks on the coals. This made even more smoke and confusion. In the midst of this turmoil, big black limousines pulled up and our Russian visitors came up our driveway.

I met them and told them of our dilemma and said that, if they expected to get anything to eat, they'd have to pitch in and help. Titov took off his coat and joined in to help. His wife, Tamara, went into the house. The next time I saw her, she had her shoes off and was helping Annie and Louise with the salad.

It turned out we had a very enjoyable evening. I told them we had probably set the course of diplomatic relations back about 50 years but they disagreed and seemed to enjoy the visit. I recounted the details of the evening to the President and he laughed heartily over the scene and really got a big kick out of the story. I think every time I saw him after the grilling incident, he would ask me if I had had any barbecues recently. The last time I saw President Kennedy was during a brief stop I made to say hello some two months before his death.

I attended the funeral services for the President and rode in the funeral procession as a representative of the space program. If there is one characteristic that impressed me most about President Kennedy, it was his enormous curiosity. The President was curious about virtually everything, but especially about those things that were out of his fields of expertise or with which he had little personal experience. When I returned from my orbital flight, for instance, the President asked me a multitude of questions, and the answers I gave led to still more questions, many of them quite detailed. Frankly, this sense of curiosity, of wanting to learn as much as one can about as many things as possible, is a common quality or characteristic I have seen in all the people I've met whom the world has called "great." That it would also be a quality possessed by President Kennedy is perhaps not surprising, particularly since the byword of his Administration was "the New Frontier." New frontiers, whether individual or collective, can only be confronted and conquered through exploration and the acquisition of new knowledge. The foundation for both is curiosity, and that is the characteristic I remember best about President Kennedy.

Perhaps President Kennedy's most enduring legacy is the idea that great national purposes can be achieved only through a shared commitment on the part of the citizenry, and that all citizens have an obligation to try to make a difference for our nation. The space program, the Peace Corps, Vista and countless other activities were all expressions of that idea. Although the ideals and idealism of "Camelot" were tarnished by Vietnam, Watergate, and excessive materialism in recent decades, President Kennedy's appeal to our better natures and to high national purpose still burns as his brightest legacy, and continues to motivate thousands of people in each new generation.

Chris Kraft, Flight Director, NASA Manned Spacecraft Center, Houston, Texas

Kraft was closely associated for years as a key figure in the space program. He offers his views on the role John F. Kennedy played in the success of the program.

The death of President Kennedy, the political father of America's space program, was a deep personal loss for me and those many people associated with the space effort. On November 22, 1963, I had just returned from lunch to my downtown Houston office and learned the tragic news. Shocked and saddened as were those around me, I left work for my home in nearby Friendswood and spent the next few days watching events unfold on television as did most Americans.

Through my NASA work with the *Mercury* project, I was closely associated with the "Mercury Seven" astronauts and was flight director for several well- known space launchings, including Alan Shepard in 1961 and John Glenn in 1962. President Kennedy was the single person most responsible for the acceleration of the space program as a result of his dramatic challenge to the entire space community and the nation to land a man on the moon by the end of the decade. Kennedy

Courtesy of Christopher Kraft

Chris Kraft and John Glenn explain the function of the Mercury Control at Cape Canaveral to President Kennedy, February, 1962.

threw down the space gauntlet to the Soviet Union on May 25, 1961, asking Congress to spend several billion dollars on the effort. He declared in his address to Congress, "We go into space because whatever mankind must undertake, free men must fully share." He went on to state, "It will not be one man going to the moon—if we make this judgment affirmatively, it will be an entire nation. For all of us must work to put him there. I believe we should go to the moon." At that point many insiders in the program were doubtful that such a goal could be achieved in only nine years and feared that this was too big a step to undertake. However, the Kennedy challenge got us all going and we achieved our goal with five months to spare. In retrospect, we were really lucky to complete the job in the time allowed.

I had the pleasure of meeting the President on several occasions, including attendance at a White House dinner accompanied by my wife, Betty. My first personal contact with the President was on February 23, 1962, three days after John Glenn's successful orbital mission piloting the *Friendship* spacecraft. It was the United States, first manned orbital mission and was launched from Cape Canaveral, (renamed Cape Kennedy) Florida and later renamed Cape Canaveral.

The President decided to visit our Cape Mission Control Center, and I was selected by NASA officials to greet him and give him a guided tour of the Center. Our entire staff assumed the same work stations that they had during the Glenn mission and when the President arrived, I suddenly realized that this was a very strikingly handsome man. I don't really exactly know what unique quality he had, but there was something about him that seemed divinely inspired. I have been personally acquainted with our presidents from Eisenhower through Bush, but none had Kennedy's distinct qualities. He looked you right in the eye when he talked to you and, when I met Kennedy, I was in virtual awe of him, as were the others at the Center.

When the President arrived at the Control Center in February 1962, he was escorted by John Glenn. It was the first time I had seen John since his successful flight. I had a dilemma over which man to shake hands with first and I decided to congratulate John on his great work, which I did, while the President watched us smiling. I think he understood my choice. For Kennedy's visit, the center was packed with people including the press who were having a virtual war with each other shoving and pushing to get the best camera angle. While the President ignored their actions, it really bothered me.

Later that year in September, I again had the pleasure of briefing the President, this time on the *Apollo* program. The President was visiting Houston to give an address at Rice University and, before he left, he stopped by our Houston Center for a briefing. It was a very hot day and the President was wringing wet from perspiration when he arrived. He had several others with him including 83-year-old Representative Clarence Cannon, Democrat of Missouri. Cannon was one of the most powerful leaders in the House, serving as Chairman of the Appropriations Committee. Kennedy sat down, took off his coat and tie, loosened his collar and said, "Go ahead."

I began my presentation using several charts, and I noticed Congressman Cannon had fallen asleep. When I was about halfway through my briefing the Congressman suddenly awoke, looked at me and said, "Son, do you really believe all this stuff you are telling us about going to the moon?" Well, the President began laughing so hard at his question, he nearly fell out of his chair. Kennedy seemed very enthusiastic over what he heard and was quite animated as he asked us several excellent questions on the *Apollo* program.

Only a year later the President was dead, but his challenge to put a man on the moon continued under the leadership of President Lyndon Johnson. Yet without Kennedy's commitment, the project would never have continued. JFK was the space program's leader and champion. In fact, since his death I don't think we have had a successor with his inspirational qualities. Somehow with President Kennedy's death, a glitch seemed to take place in our national psyche, one from which we perhaps have not yet recovered. Under JFK, our nation seemed to be finding a new sense of direction that has been lost since his death.

The finest moment for the space program and, indirectly the person most responsible for the moment, was on June 20, 1969, when the first man walked on the moon. While the world and nation were jubilantly celebrating this exciting event in space exploration, I heard that a small bouquet of flowers and a simple note were placed on John F. Kennedy's grave in Arlington Cemetery. The note read, "Mr. President, the Eagle has landed." President Kennedy has been sorely missed by me, my colleagues in the space program, and our nation.

Chapter Eleven

Kennedy's Children Remember

No new program initiated by President Kennedy better symbolized his administration's ideals than the Peace Corps, known also as "Kennedy's children." Former volunteer accounts include memories drawn from letters and diaries kept by Peace Corps workers in overseas locations in remote places such as Nepal and Cameroon. Repeatedly we learn of the popularity of President Kennedy around the world. We hear from Alan Guskin, who was there as a student when Kennedy first spoke out on the idea of the Peace Corps at the University of Michigan in 1960. Guskin also was a prominent spokesperson in the celebration of the 25th anniversary of the Peace Corps in 1986.

Kennedy says goodbye to Peace Corps volunteers going to Africa, August, 1963.

A vignette by Tom Scanlon, a former Peace Corps volunteer and a student at Columbia University, is included because he was cited by JFK as an example of the best of the Peace Corps in action. Scanlon represented the Peace Corps in the funeral motorcade on Monday, November 25, 1963.

A sketch by James Bausch, a Peace Corps trainer in Washington, D.C., presents the impact of Kennedy's death on Peace Corps trainees. Peace Crops volunteers from different parts of the world describe the reaction to Kennedy's death in the country where they were stationed.

Peter A. Weng, Peace Corps Volunteer, Indonesia

Peter Weng and his fellow Peace Corps volunteers were thrilled to meet President Kennedy in the White House Rose Garden in early November, 1963. Little did they know that only a few days later, all this would change.

By November 1963, the first group of 17 Peace Corps volunteers for Indonesia, of which I was a part, had completed six months of service. For many of us it was a very difficult period, not so much from the transition to Indonesia life or the adjustment of being away from home, but because of the very volatile political environment. Anti-American feeling had been running very high during this period in Indonesia.

The fact of the matter was our presence in Indonesia was certainly nothing short of amazing and could primarily be attributable to President Kennedy's personal stature and his tremendous power of persuasion. This was in spite of the fact that Indonesia had one of the largest Communist parties outside a non-communist country. The third world nations of southeast Asia were exercising their sovereignty and independence from the west. It was not a good time for the Peace Corps to be in Indonesia. Nonetheless, President Sukarno and the Indonesian people as a whole held President Kennedy in very high esteem. Kennedy was viewed as a true champion of the people, a guardian of the little guy, the knight in shining armor.

It was late November when we gathered in the capital, Djakarta, to discuss our experiences, revitalize ourselves and taste some good "ole" American food. We had been dispersed throughout Indonesia, and some of us had not spoken or heard a word of English in those six months. We were attending a reception hosted by the American ambassador when news of the assassination was received. The immediate reaction was one of disbelief and hope that it was all a horrible mistake. Initial reports were sketchy and first indications were that he may have survived the attempt. However, subsequent reports confirmed his death. The reaction of the Peace Corps volunteers was one of shock and horror as many of us wept openly.

As I rode back to my quarters, I was overcome by an intense feeling of emptiness and uncertainly as to the future as I had been almost totally consumed by this man called John F. Kennedy. My thoughts flashed back to the gathering of our Peace Corps group in the Rose Garden at the White House shortly before departing for Indonesia where we met and were entertained that afternoon by the President. Being in his presence, speaking with him, shaking his hand, the whole experience was so overwhelming, it almost appeared to have mystical overtones. In the days following the news of the assassination, it appeared that the whole of Indonesia was in mourning. Expressions of sorrow were received from every corner of the country. One would have thought it was the Indonesian President who had been assassinated. However, the most difficult part of this for myself and the other volunteers was not to be home to share the grief and sorrow with our fellow Americans and particularly the first family.

To say JFK had a tremendous impact on my life would be an understatement. His speech, "Ask not what your country can do for you, but what you can do for your country," certainly inspired me to join the Peace Corps. In addition it set the tone for my heavy involvement in social issues after my Peace Corps service ended. I believe JFK's greatest contribution was his ability to stimulate the American conscience.

Dick Weber, Peace Corps Volunteer, Cameroon, West Africa
Dick Weber shares a sad letter he sent to his parents relating his reaction to Kennedy's death.

On November 22, 1963, I was a 22-year-old Peace Corps volunteer in my 16th month of service as a teacher at a teacher training college in Cameroon, West Africa. The time was 8:05 P.M. My three fellow Peace Corpsmen and I were preparing to host a gathering of Peace Corps volunteers from a 30 to 40 mile radius of our campus. I turned on the Voice of America prior to everyone's arrival. The letter below to my parents describes our reaction to the terrible news:

11/24/63
Dear Folks:
    Words can't describe the condition I have been in since Friday evening at 8:05 when we heard of the death of the President. I have never experienced such a feeling of loss as if my brother or closest relative had died and has left a huge void in my life. Friday evening I walked to the radio to listen to some music and the first words I got were the President of the United States has been shot while riding through the streets of Dallas in an open car. This was about 12:05 your time and it had just happened. We all gathered round and continued to listen till they finally announced that he never regained consciousness and was dead. For a few minutes the four of us sat around in stony silence so shocked and dismayed that such a terrible thing could happen in our country in 1963.
    We listened for hours into the night as the messages of sympathy poured into the White House and into the offices of the new President. Slowly our Peace Corps friends began to gather at our house and we sat around until 1 A.M. listening to our radio reports with blank looks. The feeling of shock and sorrow in the room was oh so evident. We went to bed that evening with indeed heavy hearts still not comprehending what had actually happened in the

land of the free and the home of the brave but feeling that something terrible had befallen our nation and indeed the world. That evening I dreamt about the event and awoke the next morning with thoughts of Mrs. Kennedy and the responsibilities and problems President Lyndon B. Johnson now faced.

The Catholic mission at Small Soppo is having a Requiem High Mass on Monday at 5 o'clock and they have invited all Americans to come for the service. We are all hoping to be able to attend as they have a special section in the Mass where they want us to sing our national anthem. The service will be attended by the Prime Minister and all high government officials in West Cameroon. The Prime Minister has sent his messages of condolence to the U.S. Ambassador and to the Director of the Peace Corps in West Cameroon. He has declared Monday a national day of mourning and asked that no Peace Corps Volunteer teach on that day.

In the ceremony the students from Small Soppo sang a few Protestant hymns such as 'Nearer My God to Thee.' Then following the message or eulogy given by the Vicar-General, all of the Americans stood and sang 'God Bless America,' and it never sounded better to me than at this time. Then following the ceremony we came home about 6:30 that evening and listened to the requiem high mass in Washington and the services at the graveside.

The death of John F. Kennedy impacts my life yet today. For many years, I have hung one of a small number of charcoal sketches of President Kennedy on the wall opposite my desk. He was a youthful, dynamic leader whose memory continues to bring me inspiration, as I search for meaningful ways in which to serve my fellow man. My lifelong interests have been mental health and the arts, both of which were influenced by the example of John F. Kennedy and the Kennedy family.

Jerry David, Peace Corps Volunteer, Morocco
Jerry David, a young Jewish volunteer from the Bronx in a Muslim nation offers his account of when Kennedy died.

In November, 1963, I was a 22-year-old idealistic Peace Corps volunteer living in the little known town of Larache, Morocco. The sky had just turned from dusk to semidark and I was walking slowly in the Spanish way, promenading aimlessly up and down the street, nodding and saying *Adios* to the recognizable Spanish people, some of whom I knew and others I didn't. Mustafa, my Moroccan co-worker, had come up to me and started casually talking when suddenly another Moroccan came over and asked me if I had heard about what had happened to President Kennedy. I said no. Then Mustafa started talking wildly how President Kennedy was shot in the back. It's funny when I think about it now. He never mentioned anything about President Kennedy until someone else came over and started talking to me about what had happened. Anyway, he began motioning with his arms and demonstrating where President Kennedy was shot and intermingling his words with Arabic as if he was trying to give me an Arabic lesson at the same time. I told him he must be crazy; no one would shoot the President of the United States and especially President Kennedy. I used more descriptive language but felt a gnawing need to get home and listen to the radio. I remember thinking to myself that if it were a Kennedy who had shot, maybe it was Bobby or Ted and they got the name wrong. It was inconceivable to me that this could happen to President Kennedy.

I started walking, then jogging and finally running the mile or so back to my little apartment. I grabbed the radio and tuned to the Armed Forces station. The ears listened but the mind could not comprehend the words being spoken. I was shocked by what I heard; I was in total disbelief. Kennedy's charisma was one of the main reasons why this Jewish boy from the Bronx was in Morocco. It is very hard to describe my feelings. To this day I can't watch anything on TV about JFK without a lump forming in my throat.

At the time, I was sharing the tiny apartment with Robert Spencer, a young black volunteer from Texas. He had gone to *Imam* (bathhouse) for the evening. I had just heard the news, when, no more then five minutes later, Bob came charging into the apartment. He stood at the doorway to the room looking at me. My eyes started to fill with tears. Robert seemed almost afraid to speak, but he blurted out "Is it true?" I could tell he knew the answer already and the look on my face confirmed his question. I could see his expression change immediately. Although only a second had gone by, this was in slow motion: the feelings, the friendship, the thoughts were all moving together. I finally answered his question by only nodding. He threw his towel down and said, "God damn it!" The rest of that evening was kind of a blur as we continued listening to the broadcast. It was a very sad time.

The next morning we both went to work at *Les Eau et Floret* (The Department of Water and Forest). Interestingly enough, all of our coworkers came over and offered their condolences. Our office was comprised of an international community: two young Spanish girls, one old Frenchman from the old regime, three Moroccans from the Spanish zone, some people from the Rif country. One Berber, one Moroccan Jew, and one Moroccan from the old French zone. The Moroccan Jew had tears in his eyes. Bar none, they all came over to sincerely give their support and sympathy. Some of these people were friends and others were not, but their condolences, I felt, were genuine. I never heard one unsympathetic remark from any host country national during this whole unfortunate situation.

Bob and I received permission to leave the compound early to be with other Peace Corps volunteers. It was Friday, November 23. We always spent the weekends in Tangier, some 60 miles away. We arrived at Ann Lynn's apartment at noon or so. Other volunteers were also arriving and feelings ran very deep that weekend. We all tried to console each other, not really knowing what to say or what to do. All of the volunteers went to a high Mass at a Catholic Church on Sunday. The whole experience was devastating!

Romeo M. Massey, Peace Corps Volunteer, Colombia

Massey relates the reaction in Colombia that reveals the feeling there about President Kennedy. He shares an amusing anecdote over a letter he received.

I entered the Peace Corps October 14, 1962. During training, we watched apprehensively as President Kennedy forced the Soviet Union to remove its missiles from Cuba. In December, Bill Moyers, then Deputy Director of the Peace Corps, came to our graduation to tell us that the Alliance for Progress was in full swing. Democratic governments were struggling in Latin America, and there was a "revolution of rising expectations" among the poor of the region. Each of us, he said, "...should feel proud to serve as volunteers and represent our country" and we were.

My assignment was to teach English at an engineering university in Colombia, South America. The city, Pereira, is located 100 miles west of Bogota in the central chain of the Andes at an altitude of about 4,500 feet. The campus was on the outskirts of what had been a sleepy little coffee town of 20,000 people in 1948. By January 1963 when I arrived, Pereira had grown sevenfold, overrun by a flood of 120,000 peasants fleeing the vicious civil war between liberals and conservatives.

The second week in November 1963, I received a letter on White House stationary at the university. I jokingly told the excited messenger to toss it in with my other mail. When the Vice-Rector brought the letter back to me, I had to open it. It was a short typed letter "signed" by the President, congratulating me for completing my first year as a Peace Corps volunteer. Sargent Shriver sent a green and white lapel pin.

On Friday, November 22, I had taught two morning classes and had gone home for lunch and a 2:00 P.M. meeting with a group organizing the city's first evening high school. Around 1:15 P.M. our housekeeper shouted to me that Kennedy had been shot. I turned on the Voice of America and it soon confirmed that he was dead. The five or six young organizers arrived grim and shaken by the news. We sat in a circle in the front room, not saying much of anything. One or two of them cried. I suggested that we go on with the meeting, that President Kennedy would have wanted it that way. They agreed, as if he were their leader too.

When they left, I tuned in a radio station from Texas. It was giving an account of the assassination. As the afternoon passed into night, the information shifted from the murder and hospital to descriptions of the in-flight swearing-in ceremony and the biography of Lyndon B. Johnson. I realized that the media were letting the world know of the transition, that the United Stated was in good hands, that all was under control. Between 2:00 A.M. or 3:00 A.M. in the morning, I turned the radio off. I felt a profound sense of outrage at the stupid senseless killing. What, if anything, had the killer accomplished? I had no sense of what impact Kennedy's death would have on the course of our nation.

Saturday, November 23, seemed to be somehow unreal and dreamlike in its normalcy. When I finally went outside around noon, I noticed that all of the local radio stations were playing requiem dirges, which sounded out of place blaring from the coffeehouses and bars. Stores had placed black-draped pictures of Kennedy in their front windows. The flag at city hall was flying at half-mast. The government proclaimed three days of national mourning. Strangers stopped me to express their condolences. They called him "*nuestro Presidente Kennedy*," our President Kennedy. Two people said that he was more their president than the President of Colombia.

On Monday, November 25, I arrived at the university to find that classes had been suspended for the day. The three Peace Corps volunteers and the four other Americans in Pereira were invited to attend a Mass at the Cathedral on the main plaza. The church was packed. When we entered, the crowd parted and we were led to the front pew.

A coffin, draped in a large American flag (which came from who knows where), was in front of the main altar on a bier. Civic, military, and church officials, together with many common people, sat through a solemn high Requiem Mass. The eulogies were somewhat theatrical, but it impressed me as an honest outpouring of grief for a leader they felt cared for them. I had never known how deeply Kennedy had touched their lives. When I dream about Colombia, that church and plaza are somehow always in the dream.

About a week later, a delegation of faculty members, led by the dignified University Rector, arrived at my office. They said that they knew it was a great deal to ask, but wanted to know if they could have the letter I had received from President Kennedy to put in the university archives. They didn't realize that it was a form letter signed by a machine or a clerk. To avoid their future embarrassment about the letter, I told them that I was sorry, but I had sent the letter home to my family. They said that they understood. I still keep the letter, even if it wasn't John Kennedy's real signature.

Thomas J. Scanlon, Former Peace Corps Volunteer and Graduate Student, Columbia University, New York City

Scanlon was the Peace Corps volunteer often cited as the typical volunteer by President Kennedy. Scanlon represented the Peace Corps at the President's funeral procession to Arlington Cemetery. Scanlon's 1997 book, The Waiting for the Snow[23] *is a memoir of his early Peace Corps days working in villages in Chile.*

In July 1963, I returned to the United States after a two-year stint in the Peace Corps in Chile and entered graduate school at Columbia University. On Friday, November 22, I was in the library reading room when a friend broke the staggering news that President Kennedy had been shot. Much of what happened after that is a blur as I was destroyed by the news. I took a bus to Scranton to be with my parents and watched television like everyone else.

On Saturday, I received a call from Pat Kennedy, a Peace Corps official in Washington, asking me if I could come to Washington to be the symbolic representative for all the Peace Corps volunteers in the funeral motorcade on Monday. Separate agencies were to designate a representative to be in the procession. I flew down that night and on Monday, I waited at St. Matthew's Cathedral. After the service I rode with John Glenn, who represented the space program, to Arlington Cemetery for the burial services. I remember being overwhelmed by all the dignitaries at both the church and burial services, such as President Charles de Gaulle of France, but still watched all of the pageantry through a veil of numbness and pain.

Thinking back to why I was chosen as the Peace Corps designee for the services, I recalled the day I heard President Kennedy call for Peace Corps volunteers. That day I offered my services as his message filled a void that existed in my life at the time. I was also greatly influenced by Dr. Tom Dooley's work in southeast Asia, and the Peace Corps seemed the perfect vehicle for me to be of service to others.

I originally planned to join the first group of volunteers going to Ghana, but Father Hesburgh, President of Notre Dame, where I had graduated in 1960, asked me to join a group that he was helping organize to go to Chile. So that is the group I joined. I served there from 1961-1963. Father Hesburgh later brought some of my activities in Chile to the attention of Sargent Shriver, the Peace Corps Director. He in turn relayed accounts of my activities to President Kennedy who, in a speech in 1962, cited my work as an example of the best of the Peace Corps. I later wrote President Kennedy thanking him for the honor he had given me, but assured him that it was undeserved as there were countless other examples that he could have cited as well.

I was also privileged to pay tribute to President Kennedy on the 20th anniversary of his death at a ceremony at the Kennedy Center for the Performing Arts on November 22, 1983. I think that the public should know how absolutely President Kennedy was loved and respected in the developing world. One story from my time in Chile illustrates this point. I was stationed in a small village and one day I first drove three hours in a jeep and then rode three hours on horseback to a remote village. I was feeling very proud of myself thinking certainly no other American had even been there before me. Perhaps, they had never even heard of the United States. After a cup of tea in a small hut with my Indian host, she said to me, "Did you know that yesterday was President Kennedy's birthday?" He was a hero even in this remote part of the world.

The Peace Corps symbolized John Kennedy's commitment to the free world and peace. In 1961 we were losing the war of ideas to Communism in many parts of the third world. The Peace Corps reflected Kennedy's vision of America and brought a sense of idealism and participation that represented the best of the United States. The people in the developing world saw us as the direct expression of President Kennedy's interest in them. "Children of Kennedy," we were called in many parts of Latin America.

Today, I still am a great admirer of John F. Kennedy. His ideas directed me to my life's work and took me from the halls of academe to the world of action working with developing nations. Historians must judge him not only by what he was able to accomplish in 1,000 days, but also by what he did to inspire all of us to volunteer—in the broadest sense—to do for our country.

Robert Steiner, Director of the Afghanistan Peace Corps Volunteers, Kabul, Afghanistan

Steiner describes the sympathetic reaction of his Afghan hosts to the President's death and repeats a theme shared by other Peace Corps volunteers, a sense of shame that the President had been killed.

We were abed that 23rd day of November 1963, and awoke to a brisk, bright Afghan morning. After a leisurely breakfast, we were enjoying the warming late autumn sun on our front porch. Suddenly, a pained yell came from over the high mud wall that separated us from an American neighbor. Dashing out our gate, I learned the awful news of President Kennedy's assassination as reported by BBC, Britain's reliable short-wave radio service.

The rest of Saturday and Sunday is a blur. There was a stunned shuffling between American homes and the embassy to get the latest news or rumor, to commiserate to speculate. Hushed gatherings witnessed tears, anger, frustration, shame. The American Embassy was closed in mourning on Monday, but I chose to continue with my plans to visit Peace Corps volunteers in an isolated area near the city of Jalalabad, where, three decades later, there would be desperate fighting between the Afghan *Mojahedeen* and the Moscow-backed government in Kabul.

I was in Afghanistan because Sargent Shriver had asked me to start a Peace Corps program there. He had lured me from my Vermont chicken farm, to which I had fled from a Washington, D.C., bureaucracy only three years earlier. "Sarge" had been told that I spoke Farsi (the language of Iran and much of Afghanistan), learned as a child of educational missionaries in Iran. He was swayed by the thought of having a Persian-speaking chicken farmer from Vermont as the Director of the American Peace Corps in Afghanistan!

But back to that Monday morning, November 25, 1963. I left Kabul for the two-hour drive to Jalalabad, and thence along a narrow, very dusty and bumpy dirt road up the narrowing Laghman Valley to a remote village guarding the approach to Nuristan, a beautiful, but mostly ungovernable region of the Hindu Kush. Speaking a language related to no other in Asia, Nuristanis are believed by some to have linguistic ties to the Basques of Spain.

Two volunteers were teaching English in that village. Without radio or other frequent outside communication links, they had not yet heard of Kennedy's assassination. They listened with disbelief, dismay, and in silence as I told them as much of the tragedy as I knew. It is hard to peer back through the cynical haze of the 1990s to the idealism and passion that fueled the early 1960s. These early volunteers had answered Kennedy's siren call—"Ask not what your country can do for you, but what you can do for your country," with awesome enthusiasm and sincerity. To learn of his assassination was for them like "The wound is mortal and is mine" (Huxley).

Conversation during the rest of the afternoon was desultory, listless. We were to have dinner that evening at the home of the school principal. It was dark when we arrived, but the principal welcomed us with the traditional graciousness of an Afghan host. After the usual exchange of greetings, he asked us to sit on the floor of his small room illuminated by an oil lamp and a couple of flickering candles. His next words went something like this: "On behalf of our teachers and students, the mayor and people of this village, please accept my deepest sympathy for the death of your great President; all Afghans loved and admired him and mourn his passing; the world will find his chair very empty."

Why had this kind man in this isolated corner of the world been so moved by a very distant assassination? What had Kennedy done to make such an impression on this tiny village, on a people who knew few Americans, on a country that most Americans had never heard of? Only the deep shadows in that small room hid the swelling tears of the three American guests. Barely able to control their voices, each expressed gratitude for his expression of sympathy. After the meal, we departed, humbled by a very moving experience, proud that we were Americans in Afghanistan, ashamed for what our country had done to its own leader, but convinced that we had been right to answer the call.

Jim Bausch, Peace Corps Trainer, Washington, D.C.

Jim Bausch defines what Kennedy meant to Peace Corps volunteers and how he served as an inspiration to others, such as himself, to continue life in roles to help others. Bausch later became President and CEO of the Save the Children program.

In the summer of 1961, inspired by, and in response to, President Kennedy, I left my doctoral dissertation and university teaching post to join the Peace Corps. I spent two years in Bangladesh (then East Pakistan) in an experience that changed and directed my future. What I expected to be an interruption in an academic career became a life-long focus, and I never returned to academia. Instead, in the late summer of 1963, I returned to the United States to train new Peace Corps volunteers.

In the early afternoon on November 22, 1963, our training site maintenance supervisor stuck his head into my office and told me that

President Kennedy had been shot. I stared at him for a moment and turned on the radio to learn that the President was seriously wounded and might be dead. I had to get out of my office. I walked out of the building over the grassy knoll with tears in my eyes, praying that he would pull through. When I returned, I learned that he had died.

The Peace Corps trainees were in a lecture in the great oak-paneled drawing room of the old mansion that served as the training site. I slid back the heavy pocket door and entered the class. The visiting professor gave me a strange look that I later learned was partly for interrupting him at a critical point in his presentation and partly in reaction to the way I looked. I then made the worst announcement I ever made, telling the terrible news to 30 bright and eager people who, up to that very second, had been so full of commitment and hope. I watched their faces take on a sadness that I thought might never leave them.

We adjourned classes to huddle around the radio and the lone TV set. A few of the youngest trainees were particularly shaken and I tried to console them, realizing that it was probably helping me to cope more than it was comforting them. Two days later, saturated with listening to newscasters and others and trying to come to grips with the impact of JFK's death, the Peace Corps trainees conducted a memorial service. A few spoke of why President Kennedy had been so important in their decision to join the Peace Corps. Many pledged to continue in memory of what he stood for: promise of a better future, justice for those who had not gotten it, compassion for those who had received life's harshest blows, and renewed commitment to try and change things.

Three trainees then took turns reading from Walt Whitman's reflections on the death of Lincoln. The words "When lilacs late in the door yard bloom," will always be associated with John Kennedy by everyone who was in that room, and will stay with us as long as we live. To this day, I cannot see lilacs without thinking of him. After the service, many of us wanted to be alone and think by ourselves, instead of trying to make some sense out of such a senseless and terrible event. I again headed out across the knoll and was joined by another staff member, a young man who was between college and graduate school and for whom President Kennedy's death obviously meant very little. He was smiling and shaking his head in disbelief He said. "Everybody is overreacting! It's stupid! Nobody here really knew Kennedy. People die all the time!" I was at first startled and then surprisingly and intensely angry. I told him he was an ass. Calming down, I added "You're wrong. Lots of us here really knew him. And he knew the best parts of us."

My errant colleague was right about one thing. People do die all the time. A little piece of many of us died on November 22, 1963. We were never the same again. But the influence of the ideas of John F. Kennedy and the Peace Corps never left me. After years spent working with the Peace Corps, the Ford Foundation's international development programs and the Population Council, I became President and CEO of the Save the Children program. My personal and professional journey of commitment began with, and has been sustained by, my acceptance of President Kennedy's invitation to help make lasting, positive differences in the world.

Alan Guskin, Peace Corps Volunteer, Bangkok, Thailand

Guskin was a graduate student at the University of Michigan attending a student rally for Kennedy when JFK first voiced the idea of the Peace Corps. Over the years he has frequently served as the spokesperson at reunions of Peace Corps members and later became President of Antioch College.

When Kennedy was killed on November 22, 1963, I was in Bangkok, Thailand, serving as a Peace Corps volunteer in the first group to go to that country. As happened to many volunteers, the local people, especially those in cities, made a clear connection between President Kennedy and "his" Peace Corps volunteers. It was not uncommon for the early groups of volunteers to be referred to in the local media as "Kennedy's children." Kennedy was extraordinarily popular in Thailand and that helped us in our work. His death was devastating to the volunteers. American presidents just don't get assassinated; that happens in other countries.

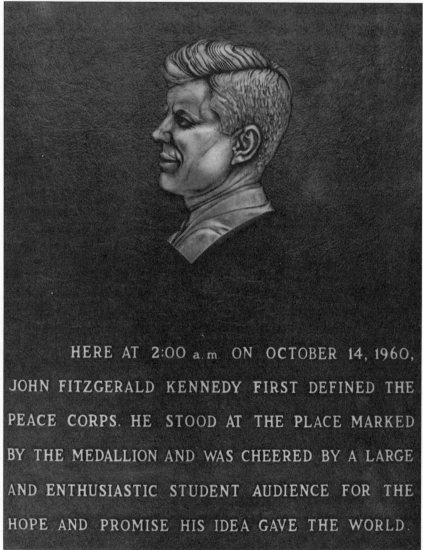

HERE AT 2:00 a.m. ON OCTOBER 14, 1960, JOHN FITZGERALD KENNEDY FIRST DEFINED THE PEACE CORPS. HE STOOD AT THE PLACE MARKED BY THE MEDALLION AND WAS CHEERED BY A LARGE AND ENTHUSIASTIC STUDENT AUDIENCE FOR THE HOPE AND PROMISE HIS IDEA GAVE THE WORLD.

Plaque at the site of the Peace Corps speech at the University of Michigan.

It took a few hours for me to learn of his assassination. I first heard that something strange had happened from a Chinese pharmacist whose store I was in. He didn't speak Thai very well and I didn't speak any Chinese, but he pointed to his head and used the word "shot" in Thai. I couldn't figure out what he was saying. The thought that something terrible happened stayed with me, even the thought that something had happened to the President. But no, the President couldn't have been killed.

An hour or so later a student of mine, who was living with me, rushed home and said that Kennedy was shot, possibly killed. I experienced disbelief, shock and then a strange reaction. I had been in Bangkok for almost a year and had studiously avoided other Americans except Peace Corps volunteers. But now I felt I needed to be with other Americans. I went to a restaurant where I knew they would be and I spent most of my free time in the next few days with other Americans, mostly Peace Corps volunteers.

The terrible loss of our President caused me to think back to a happier day in 1960. The Peace Corps began four decades ago, on a dark drizzling night in Ann Arbor, Michigan where I was a doctoral student in social psychology. It was October 14, 1960, and John Kennedy was coming to the University of Michigan Student Union to spend the night before starting a whistle-stop campaign trek through Michigan. I had watched the third Nixon-Kennedy debate and decided to go to the Union and wait for him. It was 2 A.M. before he arrived. He wasn't expecting a crowd, but 10,000 students were waiting for him. The press was not there because they were told "nothing" was going to happen. After all, he was just going to sleep.

Kennedy stood on the steps of the Student Union, stuck his arm out and pointing his finger at the crowd, challenged the students: were they willing to serve overseas to help the developing countries, many of them newly independent? We were told he really had no prepared speech. Maybe that's why it didn't sound political. He was a youthful presidential candidate who represented a new generation. He was asking us to dream with him.

That extemporaneous speech is thought by many to be the founding of the Peace Corps. Some even attribute Kennedy's election victory to his commitment to create a Peace Corps. The Peace Corps surely represents one of the high points of his abbreviated administration, and it is probably the program with which he remains most identified.

A few vivid memories remain about Kennedy and the Peace Corps. One is the reactions of the Thais to the death of President Kennedy; it was intense and immediate. People would stop me and say how sad they were. Faculty, students and others at the university would say how sorry they were for me. It was for them as if a member of my family had died. They not only paid their condolences to my colleagues and me, but they also wore clothes of mourning, mostly all black. Volunteers outside of Bangkok experienced similar reactions; people in villages with transistor radios heard the news and paid their respects to volunteers. Thailand was in mourning for President Kennedy. In fact, I was shocked when their Premier, a military dictator, died not long after Kennedy and there was much less grieving. While the Premier was not a beloved person, even the most unobservant couldn't miss the difference; love had poured out for Kennedy.

I have a second memory that surrounds Kennedy's death. Because of my involvement and that of my ex-wife in the founding of the Peace Corps and our service overseas, we were accorded a special honor during the 25th anniversary of the founding of the Peace Corps. We led the march of thousands of former volunteers to Kennedy's grave, and then on to a memorial service for the 199 volunteers who died in service. At the gravesite we carried a special wreath on behalf of all the volunteers and placed it in front of the eternal flame that marks Kennedy's grave.

The 25th anniversary celebration was focused on those who entered service in 1961-1962. About two-thirds of the total group was there. Thousands of people from other groups were there as well. There were numerous speeches and cultural celebrations. Amidst all this were the numerous reunions of people who served together, the reaching out across three decades to see friends and colleagues—all grayer, some heavier, some lighter, some divorced, others still married, but all surprisingly recognizable, and intensely devoted to reconnecting, as if to feel once again that special bond created decades earlier. People cried. In one or another corner of the great tent in which the events took place, there were tears shed without reason. "What was it," asked one volunteer, "that tore loose from our guts and provoked the most unabashed weeping I have ever witnessed?"

Courtesy of the Peace Corps

Laying a wreath at JFK's gravesite in memory of 25 years of the Peace Corps, September 21, 1986. Shown from left to right: Sargent Shriver, Judy Guskin, Alan Guskin, and Loret Miller Ruppe.

The emotions were real and deep because we were relieving these most powerful experiences with those who really understood. One volunteer described the feeling: "We could be free with each other in ways we don't regularly experience at home. For that weekend (in 1986) it was perfectly fine to be idealistic; perfectly fine to value commitment, to be moved to tears. For that weekend, cynicism retreated or was converted."

Senator Ted Kennedy addressed the first groups of volunteers in a breakfast gathering of about 500 people in a Congressional dining room. At the end of the speech he said: "You have reminded us once again of (America's) priceless ideas and enduring values. You have kept President Kennedy's dream alive, and I only wish he were here today to share the pride of your achievement."

After saying these words, he choked back tears and left abruptly. There were few dry eyes in the room full of "Kennedy's Children."

Chapter Twelve

International Community Reactions

The worldwide response to Kennedy's death was dramatic. The depth and breadth of the grief of the general public was unanticipated. A common scene found in many countries was to hold some form of religious service honoring JFK with a casket covered by an American flag representing his presence. Also, frequently, the reaction was for large numbers of people coming to United States consulates to express their loss for Kennedy's death and seek some remembrance of him. Another response was for parents to name their newly born son after JFK.

In this collection of vignettes, we find contributors offering examples of the sorrow of people around them. The one exception is Communist China. In China, a total dictatorship held absolute control of the media, and so residents there had very little information about the outside world. Communist China was the only nation in the world that exalted over the death of "the most cunning, cruel and warmongering" President. An account from a college professor of physics in China opens a window into life in China in 1963.

Nowhere was grief more deeply felt than in Ireland, ancestral home of JFK. Nicholas Furlong recalls JFK's death and his triumphal visit to Ireland in June 1963. Cathal O'Shannon, a reporter with the *Irish Times*, offers additional insights into the Kennedy visit and includes coverage of the funeral in Washington. He cites a classic refrain in Ireland concerning Kennedy heard throughout the world, "Ah, if only he could have lived."

In other parts of the world including the USSR, both leaders of government and large numbers of common people seemed deeply affected by the loss of JFK. A high school student, Marina Tempkina, from the USSR offers her account of these events. Others presenting sketches range from United States officials abroad, such as Bill Battle, Ambassador to Australia and good friend of JFK, and a housewife in South Africa.

American author, James A. Michener was in Israel when Kennedy died. Michener brings the unique reaction of the Israelis to his account. Another vignette of particular significance is by Lucian Heichler, a United States Foreign Service officer in Berlin. Heichler not only gives an excellent description of Berlin's sorrow at JFK's death, but also recalls the joyful visit by Kennedy to Berlin in the spring of 1963. A second United States Foreign Service officer, Robert Funseth, relates a touching anecdote on his description of the events in Bordeaux, France, and a special personal gift for the Kennedy children to close the book.

Nicholas Furlong, Author, Playwright, Dairyman, Wexford, Ireland

The excitement and joy generated by Kennedy's visit to his ancestral home is lovingly described here by Furlong.

My hometown is Wexford, Ireland. Wexford's origins are buried in the mist of antiquity. It bears four names: "Menapia" from Ptolemy in the second century A.D., "Loch Garman" from the Gaelic occupants, "Waesfjord" from the Norsemen and "Wexford" in English. Wexford has long experienced calm and ferocity. It has hosted Irish kings, French kings, English kings, murderous enemies, Irish patriots and rebels. Yet, for all the centuries that Wexford has existed, no happier and sadder times could be found than two days in 1963.

World history is not short on frightfulness to appall the memory. I was in the same old prehistoric core of Wexford on that November evening as an old horseman, Joe Reck, clenching his pipe burst past me. "Have you heard the news? They have shot Kennedy!" That was all he said. By the anguish in his own wide eyes I knew it could be no other. Nothing remained to be said. The shock, the grief and rage inflicted a very deep wound on me and everyone of my generation. Much more than a world political figure was cut down. Hope, prom-

ise, inspiration, style, pride, wit and uncommon ability were mutilat-
ed and a brother lay dead, shot down by a shabby bandit in a Texas
street. To this day I cannot bear to look at the books, films or news-
reel footage of that week of ghastliness.

But too much time is spent on the melancholy. Instead let me
share the brightest moment in the history of Wexford, a visit to my
town by President John F. Kennedy. I well knew that the presence of
President John F. Kennedy in Wexford would supersede all others in
rank, stature, and connection, and, for that matter, all previous occasions as well. The news that President Kennedy intended to visit
Wexford generated almost unbearable excitement. Because of his
ancestral roots, County Wexford people had watched the progress of
the Boston Kennedys with fascination and were well aware of their
progress. Nevertheless no one in our world had succeeded with such
dazzling effect as the new United States President. He uplifted the
downhearted, emboldened the dispirited, created irreversible courage,
added mirth to *gravitas* and instilled bold resolve with enterprise into
a generation across all boundaries of race, creed and geographical ori-
gin. That was our perception as we struggled with growing anticipa-
tion, excitement and some apprehension before John F. Kennedy
came home to the soil of his forebears.

We had been made well aware that where the President of the
United States was at any given moment was the site of his ultimate
executive power. In short the White House would be figuratively in
Wexford for a time. Streets and roads were broken to install communication cables before he arrived. Security was razor sharp and new to
us. The President's route was fine-combed to ensure that not a hair on
his head would be harmed or inconvenienced. Dunganstown had a
new road laid to the old Kennedy dwelling, which was still intact in a
modern farm homestead. There was an obsession that nothing would
be allowed to go wrong.

Along with thousands of others with routine chores my wife,
Mairead, and I along with our neighbours were up at the crack of
dawn to get the family business of dairying completed. We joined the
throngs in Wexford town at about 10 A.M. Instead of the tense atmos-

phere involved in the security of the most precious human in the hemisphere, there was an air of unrelieved celebration. The unbelievable was happening. Jack Kennedy was coming home as Jack Kennedy, not as the possessor of awesome power but rather as a neighbour's child who had achieved immortality and incredible fame. This man was ours, our own sinew, flesh, blood and instinct.

As I drove into the south end of Wexford port, a sequence took place that cemented the atmosphere in my mind. I drove toward the Military Base in Barrack street. I was made to halt as lorry loads of Irish Naval Service men were driving out the gates, rifles in hands. Two things startled me. My cousin, Captain Ray Roche of the Irish Army, was in the rear of one lorry, incongruous amongst the naval uniforms, yet he and all the naval men were cheering and laughing at the bystanders as if they were off to a carnival. As I rounded the block, I saw hundreds of Garda (Police) recruits in uniform disgorging from special trains at the South Station, all equally in festive mood. Was there, I asked myself, ever anything like this day in two thousand years? The sun itself was contributing glee from a cloudless sky.

I waited for the President with a friend of mine, Paddy Doris, at Redmond Square where the greatest civic honours that could be mustered would be bestowed. Even though the crowds were spread throughout the town, Redmond Square, itself, near the prehistoric nucleus of the town, was packed. The Abbey tower and the town's old fortified West Gate fringing the square certified centuries of moment and colour, but they had not sheltered anything to equal this unprecedented day.

As we waited in Redmond Square we could hear in the distance the bands playing the Irish and American national anthems. John F. Kennedy was laying a wreath at the bronze memorial to his hero, Commodore John Barry, near the spot where Barry embarked for the New World in 1757. Then quite suddenly the motorcade with outriders and swarms of white-coated security men swept into the square. Standing up in the presidential car was the young man, upon whom our eyes, intellects and warm curiosity had been focused for so long. I thought at first I was looking at a colour film. His suit was blue, his

President Kennedy lays a wreath at the statue to naval hero John Barry in Wexford, Ireland, June 27, 1963.

shirt was white, his face was sunburnt, his hair was the colour of wheat. It was as if the figure we had seen so often before the eyes of the world had stepped into our streets from the film screens and magazines. There was no question but that he was enjoying himself as in a homecoming and at ease. The flashing grin of teeth, the brushing back of hair, the rapport of instant effect confirmed all of that. My father had seen him and declared later in sustained astonishment, "But what a young man he is!"

The President, his two sisters and sister-in-law, Princess Lee Radziwill, joined the platform party where, unconsciously perhaps, strands of ages had been woven. The robed Mayor, Alderman T.F. Byrne, created John F. Kennedy a "Freeman of Wexford." Behind the Kennedy sisters stood the Superior of the Franciscans, a medieval Church order in Wexford since 1242 A.D. Alongside the Franciscan stood the cousin of Oscar Wilde, Richard Elgee. (Wilde's mother, Francesca Elgee, was born and raised close by the square.) Behind him was the President of St. Peters College, Fr. Thomas Rossiter of an old

Wexford lineage. At Jack Kennedy's elbow was the Wexford man who was Ireland's Labour leader, Brendan Corish.

JFK's visit and that time's remarkable niche in world history were articulated by Wexford County Councils patriarch, James Bowe. It was he who emphasized the recent triumph, awesome in peril and potential, called the "Cuban Missile Crisis." When John F. Kennedy rose to speak himself, his serious intent intermingled with his contagious outflow of wit provoked applause and shared laughter in waves. It may seem remarkable against the background of world affairs and sufferings to suggest what might be estimated as a trivial development that followed Jack Kennedy's stay in Wexford and Ireland. It may have been imperceptible, but Ireland and Wexford were changed utterly in morale, in courage and in confirmed pride. When he left us after four days, Ireland's atmosphere had been irrevocably changed for the better.

With formalities over, the President seemed unable to tear himself away from the outpouring of affection. He went down to the front of the crowd to shake hands of men, women, boys and girls. It was like an intense communion of feeling between the families of the history-drenched port and the exile "returned from years of pain." When time dictated his moment of farewell, it was in order to visit his mother's cousin, Mother Clement Ward, who was Superior of the Loreto Convent along his Spawell Road Route. Then it was a drive through the streets on the way to Wexford Park, the helicopters and the most emotional visit of all, that to the old Kennedy homestead and his cousins at Dunganstown.

And now some 40 years later, the stature of John F. Kennedy still grows. His place in world history is and will remain undiminished. No one has obliterated the scope of his creation of hope, inspiration, selfless help, and sacrifice for mankind's betterment he set in train with such unparalleled good humour. No statesman on the world scene has yet equaled his infectious charisma to the same extent. His real influence and effect on our evolution, our life and our times may not be fully assessed until the sum of his visible and unapparent contributions can be gathered. His promise will never be calculated. As

for my perspective, I can only speak for myself and the ancient seaport on the fringe of Europe where I was born. John F. Kennedy
spent but a forenoon in Wexford. The significance of that visit has
consolidated. It was Wexford's greatest day in over fifteen and a half
centuries of recorded history.

Cathal O'Shannon, Newspaper Reporter, Irish Times, Dublin, Ireland

*O'Shannon follows the events from Kennedy's visit to Ireland in 1963
to his attendance as an Irish journalist to the funeral in Washington, D.C.*

President Kennedy's proposed visit to Ireland in June of 1963
brought on a near frenzy of activities throughout all the places he was
scheduled to visit. He was, after all, what any of *them* might have
been. He was the American cousin that we all had in Boston or
Philadelphia or on what we knew was called the West Coast, a sort of
American Connemara where the sun always shone. He was heaven-
blessed, good-looking with a lot of hair and white, white teeth, a
Catholic, a bright, instant, sparkling intellect. And above all, he was
the most powerful man in the world, one of us.

On reflection, all these years later, what Kennedy did for Ireland
was happening anyway in the 1960s. This country was at last coming
into the 20th century after the political isolation of the neutral 1940s
and the austere 1950s. Dev was gone as Taoiseach and the modern
Sean Lemass had succeeded him. Television had arrived, and the tight
grip of the Catholic hierarchy was loosening just that little bit.

JFK, by choosing to come here, by acknowledging that he was
one of us Irish who had clawed their way to the pinnacle of power
somehow confirmed to us that we were part of the modern world, that
we *mattered.* As a reporter with the *Irish Times,* I covered various
aspects of the Kennedy visit to Ireland and the runup to it. Our first
real feel for the story was when a group of U. S. Secret Service men
came to Ireland as an advance guard some weeks before the visit to set
up security. With them came some White House press relations staff,
an expansive, helpful bunch of laid-back men. They fixed it up for

myself and Sean Cryan, a reporter for the *Irish Press,* to get seats on the White House Press Plane, a Pan Am 707, that was to fly out to Germany ahead of *Air Force One.* JFK was, of course, spending three days in West Germany before he flew to Ireland. By the time the group did fly to Ireland from West Germany, we had become familiar with the U.S. press, the White House staff, and the Kennedy entourage.

The Secret Service men had not made themselves particularly popular in Dublin. One of them had actually pulled a gun on a drunk in the Inter-Continental Hotel who had referred to them as "the New Romans." This was before Kennedy arrived but it helped to set one part of the scene.

In Germany we went to Mass with JFK at Cologne Cathedral, attended a press conference where the most important subject for the U.S. press seemed to be the state of the chicken industry in the United States and its export potential. We also heard JFK's "*Ich bin ein Berliner*" speech.

When *Air Force One* and JFK arrived at Dublin Airport, no Pope ever had such a welcome. Kennedy came down the steps of the aircraft, carrying that trilby hat, which he never seemed to wear. As the aged Dev greeted him there was a roar going on for what seemed minutes. Women and men crying at the joy of being able to greet the man who had chosen to visit the land of his forebears and to acknowledge a debt to this land.

There were near stampedes wherever he went. On a muggy June evening at Arus an Uachtarain, Ireland's White House in Dublin and the residence of President de Valera at that time, Dublin's *beau monde,* anyone with social pretensions and enough political pull to get an invitation, crowded the lawns for a presidential garden party, my parents among them. My father told me later: "The high heels were sinking into the lawn, the women pushing their way and knocking others out of the presentation line to get a look at Kennedy. You took your life in your hands if you got in the way. They were mad with excitement." They broke the security ranks and crowded round JFK till he had to break and run for the house.

When Kennedy visited New Ross, County Wexford, he almost became overpowered by the excitement and hysteria of the crowd. He pointed across the river at a warehouse and said, "I might have been working there if my grandparents hadn't gone to America." Roars of approval greeted this statement. Andy Minahin, a local politician and bigwig (and a great character), found that the power for the public address system had failed. "Oh, God, we're all ruined now," he screams. "We're disgraced. Some bloody pressman must be standing on the cable." A smiling JFK pointed out to him that he had kicked the electrical plug out of its socket. That, and the fact that the Secret Service men are getting nervous about the crowds, drove Kennedy off to see his relatives at Dunganstown.

He visited the small farmhouse where the Ryans, the Kennedy relatives, live in Dunganstown and the ruined byre that was the home of the Kennedy who went to America. He was welcomed by modest decent women in summer frocks, cheeks bright with pride and excitement at having their distinguished cousin in their home. Kennedy played a blinder. He's relaxed, at ease, but with an eye for the press and the occasion. Not all the press can get into the tiny place. There was a good deal of bad-tempered scrabbling outside among those who hadn't made it inside.

Kennedy's departure from Ireland was dignified, emotional, and in retrospect very sad. He flew out from Shannon Airport which is, as you know, on the shores of the River Shannon. Before he left he quoted a poem which, he said, had been given to him by old Sinead de Valera, our President's wife, for whom he had developed a great fondness. The poem ended with the line: " To see old Shannon's face again." Kennedy raised his head: "And I will come back. I *will* see old Shannon's face again." Of course, he never did.

So, to some extent, the Irish would see that departure as the going-away of the hero who was never to return. The Golden Boy who many people somehow felt would do so much for Ireland never came back. In November of that year he was shot dead in Dallas. The shock in Ireland was palpable. Disbelief! There were instant prayers that he was only hurt, that the radio reports were wrong.

Hysteria! Churches were crowded that night and early the next morning. All sports meetings were canceled. A terrible sadness!

President de Valera would represent Ireland at the funeral, it was announced. I was one of the reporters on the plane out to New York and Washington with him. When we landed at New York, we were told that JFK's assassin, Lee Harvey Oswald, had been shot.

In Washington we went with Dev and Ireland's foreign minister, Frank Aiken, to see Kennedy's coffin under the great cupola of the Senate Building. Andy Minahin, the man from New Ross, was with us, determined to pay his last respects to Kennedy. He brought with him a hired morning suit and tails, and a top hat. Suitably clad in black he headed for Arlington, his white socks contrasting with the sober black. I lent him a dark pair so he wouldn't make a show of himself.

It's nearly 40 years since Kennedy was in Ireland and since he died. Later another Kennedy came to us from America. One of his sisters became the new American Ambassador. It's a mark of what Ireland still feels about the Kennedys that she was welcomed. We are a more cynical nation nowadays, certainly not as naive as we were, and we know that the event was part of a Clinton-Ted Kennedy deal, but that doesn't matter. She was welcomed here as JFK's sister. It doesn't matter that the family had personal problems and that Ted himself is no saint. She was part of the Kennedy-Ireland legend. She has known suffering, like all the Kennedys and all the Irish.

Most Irishmen and women, if asked what Kennedy meant in a world that's gone, might be inclined to say: "Ah, if only he had lived!" To them, he is the "Lost Leader," the "Patrick Sarsfield," the "Michael Collins," the "Might-Have-Been." They would say that he gave us, the Irish, pride. They would have a muddled idea that he did a lot for the integration of the blacks in the United States, and that, had he lived, Vietnam would not have been the mess it was or the defeat it was.

In the newish Galway Cathedral, there is a huge terrazzo of Christ crucified. Underneath one of his armpits is a little roundel with the profile of a man and the letters PP. It is a poor representation of Patrick Pearse, one of the Commandants of the Rising of 1916, executed for rebellion. Under the other, there is another profile with the letters JFK. In houses all over Ireland, pictures of Kennedy stood under Sacred Heart lamps, sometimes with a picture of the Pope or Blessed Martin de Porres or Mother Theresa, depending on the mood and the piety of the householder. For people like these, and there are tens of thousands of them, Kennedy did spell hope.

Li-Zhi Fang, Lecturer in Physics, University of Science and Technology of China, Peking, China

Dr. Li-Zhi Fang received accolades for his activities as one of the inspirational leaders of the student pro-democracy demonstrations in the spring of 1989 in Tiananmen Square in Beijing. He gained further fame as a symbol of democracy when he was offered sanctuary in the U. S. Embassy in Beijing. In 1989 he came to the United States and in 1991 he was presented the Robert F. Kennedy Human Rights Award. Dr. Fang describes his response to Kennedy's death on November 22, 1963, living in the totalitarian state of China. He later became a professor at Arizona State University.

In November of 1963, the rest of the world may have found it difficult to believe how isolated the people of China were from news from outside the country. The Chinese government had complete control of the media and our educational systems. When I was in school, we studied American history and about famous Americans, such as Washington, Jefferson and Lincoln, but we heard very little about modern leaders. For example I never read or heard any speeches by Kennedy by 1963. What we did hear about him in the press was very negative. As a result of the constant drumbeat of anti-Americanism presented by Chinese propagandists, I and the rest of the population knew very little about President John F. Kennedy.

When he was killed, the papers only gave very small coverage to the event and as a result, the public, even intellectuals such as myself, were generally indifferent to the news. When you are completely shut off from the rest of the world and lack information, it is virtually impossible to make judgments on things you know little about. We were aware at the university level that the government was constantly propagandizing the public, but as a scientist I kept my distance from the Communist Party as much as possible. Later, when I became Vice-President of the University, it was despite party wishes, but at that point in time in the early 1980s, the faculty and students were supporting me and the party went along.

As a result of the news blackout in China, the death of President Kennedy meant very little to me at the time. Only in recent years have I learned about his call for freedom around the world as stated in his famous inaugural address. I also have been very impressed by the love and admiration so many of the ordinary American people still seem to have for former President Kennedy.

Marina Tempkina, High School Student, Leningrad (St. Petersburg), USSR

In the midst of the Cold War, many if not most Americans lumped China and the Soviet Union together as common enemies of our nation. However, the account of Kennedy's death presented by Marina Tempkin contrasts substantially with the reaction in China, particularly relating to access to information from the outside world.

I lived in a communal apartment with my mother and 40 other people in Leningrad in 1963. We all shared one bath and one kitchen and the prospects for the future for a high school student from a Jewish family were rather bleak. At the beginning of the Russian Revolution, my family had high hopes for the ideals of the movement. After the purges and many anti-Jewish actions by the government, we had given up hope. We were well aware that we were living in a huge communal grave that had subsumed millions of victims.

Because of our location in Leningrad on the eastern edge of the USSR, we had access by radio to programs broadcast from the West, including the BBC and the Voice of America. Much of my social studies I learned from these two sources, particularly the BBC. I also was well read for my age.

I had a great liking for President Kennedy and his beautiful wife. Both were young, charming and quite elegant, in stark contrast with Chairman Khrushchev and his wife. The events of the Cuban missile crisis in the fall of 1962 made President Kennedy a heroic figure in my eyes. I thought of him as a big person for causing Khrushchev to back down. Symbolically the Kennedys represented everything that was the opposite of our gray and depressing lives in the USSR. Of course I was living in an anti-Communist household. Although my mother would rarely ever say anything for fear of getting into trouble, I remember her calling our leaders, "those bandits" in the closed circle of our family.

We had a radio, and I learned of Kennedy's death and the days afterward from both radio and a neighbor's television. When we learned of Oswald's Russia connection, we assumed that Kennedy's assassination was a KGB plot. The father of a friend of mine was the coach of the women's volleyball team for Leningrad and often traveled in Europe. He was near Kennedy's age and had empathy for Kennedy. He was able to smuggle in magazines from the West and I saw pictures of the Kennedys in *Life* magazine.

The Soviet newspapers expressed sadness over Kennedy's death and our general culture under Khrushchev opposed murder. I was deeply saddened by Kennedy's death because I liked him personally and even more because he seemed to offer hope for a better world. When he died, I thought we had lost much of such hope. He brought a new look to my world as a teenager. I believed him to be the right person to counter our terrible government. Looking back I realize anything would be better. President Kennedy represented to me what I wished our leaders could become. These were my opinions but we rarely ever discussed such thoughts beyond our closest friends and family. In school, no mention was made of Kennedy's death and no discussion was allowed in school of this or any other topic. While many other Russians might share my positive views of the American President, none dared to voice such thoughts for fear of retribution by the government.

Josiah Tlou, Principal of a Church-Related Central Primary Boarding School, Masase, Southern Rhodesia

Kennedy was popular in Africa. Dr. Tlou recalls the reaction of his students to his death and the loss of hope expressed by black Africans.

When President John F. Kennedy was shot, it was 8:30 P.M. that evening in Southern Rhodesia. I was a principal of a private boarding school at the time. The all black school of 300 pupils was located in Masase on a small farm owned by the Lutheran Church 20 miles from West Nicholson the nearest small town in the southwest of Southern Rhodesia. In the 1960s, Rhodesia was in the midst of a political struggle between a small white minority government representing the British colonial administration in complete control of the country and a large black majority wanting independence from Britain. I spent that same Friday night in my office working until very late, and I did not catch the evening news on the radio. (We did not have TV). I woke up early in the morning to drive to Gwelo in the Midland Province of Southern Rhodesia for the Rhodesian African Teachers Association (RATA) regional meeting for which I was the treasurer. We drove to Gwelo with three other teachers and half-way to our destination, we stopped for gas at the small mining town of Shabani.

As we filled the car with gas, the gas attendant said "Have you heard that the "King" of America was shot?" I said, "what?" A cold feeling of utter helplessness gripped me. I went to my car and told my friends what I had heard. I quickly made a remark that Americans were notoriously known for assassinating their presidents. A similar mood seized all in the car, and everyone felt angry and upset.

As we drove into Gwelo we were greeted by posters announcing the death of President Kennedy on every corner of the streets. A dark cloud seemed to have descended on the whole city of 60,000 inhabitants. The talk of the town was about how great a leader John F. Kennedy was. At the time, most speculated, especially the white establishment in Southern Rhodesia, speculated that he was killed by the KGB or Cuban "hit men." But some politically astute people thought it might have been the work of his enemies in the South. At the meeting of the Teachers' Association we all took a moment of silence to remember and reflect on what the world would be like without his leadership. He was highly respected by many as a great leader and statesman.

Numerous people from our colonial background saw the Kennedy administration as one that provided world leadership in social justice. We perceived Kennedy as putting some sense into the British colonial policy and, hence, helping us to achieve our own liberation and independence. Kennedy had challenged the policies of the South by sending federal marshals into Alabama and Mississippi to enforce the laws of the United States. He attacked organized crime syndicates, like the Mafia and the Teamsters Union, and spoke out for human dignity in supporting the civil rights movement, quite often an unpopular subject at home and abroad.

In international affairs, he stood up against Khruschev during the Cuban missile crisis and aborted the Bay of Pigs invasion, the latter action making him very unpopular among certain quarters of society in the United States. To outsiders, especially the oppressed such as we were in Rhodesia, he was seen as a great moral leader who stood for principles of justice and fairness and was a true statesman.

Upon my return to my school, the students in my 8th grade class were equally depressed. They also held President Kennedy in high regard and viewed him as a new hope for the blacks in Rhodesia and elsewhere in Africa. They asked me in our history class what I thought would happen. Would the Russians go to Cuba and then invade the United States from there since Kennedy was gone? I told them that Lyndon Johnson, as the new President of the United States would not allow the Russians to develop a military base in Cuba either. They asked me about President Johnson. Was he was going to carry out the unfinished agenda of the late President Kennedy? Of course, I did not know a whole lot about President Johnson.

It was evident from our point of view, that with the loss of John F. Kennedy the world would be set back for many years to come. The independence of third world countries, especially in our part of Africa, was terribly affected. In retrospect, the work he started continued. The work of Peace Corps volunteers is a test to the efficacy of his administration policies. The civil rights movement in the United States resulted in a whole series of legislation that Congress passed to fulfill his dream. President Johnson seemed to have understood Kennedy's call for justice and human rights and carried out his goals.

Margot Sebba, Housewife, Johannesburg, South Africa

In neighboring South Africa, burdened by problems with apartheid, there were those who also grieved over Kennedy's death such as Margot Sebba, who later moved to the United States.

While the United States in 1963 was embroiled in a hotbed of controversy over the integration of colleges in their southern states, in South Africa the wide gap of views between the small, white minority and large black minority found us a nation increasingly concerned over the hostility between races. The small number of white caring families, such as mine, who supported policy changes to offer basic civil rights to blacks found themselves caught in the middle.

As we gazed across the Atlantic to the United States, a democratic nation built on the premise that all men are created equal, yet one facing turmoil over civil rights, we realized how difficult it would be for us to achieve racial equality and harmony. We were greatly sympathetic to the efforts of President Kennedy in the very difficult task of achieving civil right reforms and viewed him as a hope to bring new thinking to the world stage.

In the fall of 1963, I was a busy housewife with a seven-year-old son and was also actively involved as a volunteer in various community projects. My husband, Felix, was a professor in the Chemistry Department of the University of the Witwatersrand, Johannesburg, the largest English-speaking University in South Africa. On that soon-to-be grief-stricken Friday, I had been busy most of the day making arrangements for the joint celebration of our son and my husband's birthdays on Saturday, the 23rd of November. In the early evening of Friday, as a special treat, we had decided to go to a drive-in movie (which was very popular in South Africa at the time) and therefore missed the first announcements of the assassination "attempt" in Dallas. Later, unfortunately, it was confirmed as successful.

I can remember as if it were today, where I was and what I was doing when I heard the terrible news. It was Saturday, 6 A.M., in the morning. Our early morning tea had just arrived and our son had just entered our bedroom to greet "daddy" and wish him "Happy Birthday." So the three of us were somewhat companionably sitting up in bed when my husband switched on the radio as usual (no television was available to us until 1976) to hear the first news of the day. To our great consternation we heard the shocking news of President Kennedy's death! Our first reaction was one of horror, quickly followed by disbelief. As the bulletin continued, we began to feel deep sorrow and sympathy for Mrs. Kennedy and the children and, in fact, the whole Kennedy family. The South African press widely publicized Kennedy's death and was very consoling over the event.

A little later on we called friends and exchanged views on why it had happened and who could be responsible. The main feeling amongst our friends and acquaintances was a feeling of dreadful loss combined with feelings of anxiety for the greatest country on earth, America, and its people. Also undeniably we felt that in the passing of such a champion for the underdog of fairness and equality, our hopes in South Africa for a solution to our own terrible black/white problems had received a tremendous setback. We also feared that African-American people would most likely be adversely affected.

On Sunday, church services of all denominations contained reference to the death of President Kennedy and certainly South African people who were engaged in the political struggle for democracy felt very sad and fearful. All in all, a great American tragedy!

S. Wali Abdi, Fifth Grade Student, Kabul, Afghanistan

Even in the remote land of Afghanistan, the Kennedy death was noteworthy as described by young Wali Abdi. Dr. Abdi followed his dream of living in America and became a university professor in Tennessee.

I was only a ten-year-old fifth grader in elementary school when John F. Kennedy was assassinated. I was living with my parents and older brothers and sisters in Kabul, Afghanistan. One bright and sunny Saturday morning, I arose from bed and, upon entering the living room, I found my parents and brother in an agitated state as they listened to the morning news transmitted by Radio Afghanistan. The troubling news was that President Kennedy had been killed. This was a shock to me as I greatly admired him, and my family was upset and very sad as well.

As an elementary student, I had a rare hobby. I used to cut out pictures of famous people (kings, emperors, presidents, movie stars, etc.) from newspapers and magazines and keep them in my scrapbook. I thought JFK's photos showed him to be ebullient and gallant, and someone who would stand his ground with admirable aplomb. In fact, I kept duplicates of his pictures.

I used to think that a president like de Gaulle or an emperor like Hirohito had to be an older person with gray hair. Well, JFK changed all that for me. His photo cutouts were my favorites because he looked so different from the rest of the world leaders of the time. He looked so youthful and so brilliant. My lasting impression of JFK was the wonder of how one could be so young and still so accomplished. Given the fact that I was growing up in a culture where sagacity and erudition come with old age, JFK was a paradox. He was my intrepid hero.

One day early in the school year at the Sayed Jamaluddin Elementary School in Kabul, we fifth graders had to line up outside the principal's office. We were told that every child in the school would be given a sack of flour, courtesy of the United States, to take home. My teacher helped me find a porter to carry my sack of flour to the house. My parents were surprised and delighted when the porter entered the house with a sack of flour on his back. My father paid the man for his service. I still remember that day. I felt that JFK was worried about the hungry children of the world, so he made sure that my classmates and I had something to eat. He was my friend. He gave me a sack of flour.

But on November 22, 1963, I was a very sad ten-year-old when I heard that JFK had been shot. I thought it was a nefarious crime. I was befuddled. I was angry that someone had killed the man I admired. As a child, I thought someone was trying to foment trouble.

In one of his speeches, President Kennedy urged that America must land a man on the moon before the decade was out. Inspired by his dream and his schedule, I found my own "moon" to strive for. I made plans to come to JFK's country. I reached my moon in 1969. I came to America after winning a scholarship, to live and study here for one year as a senior in an American high school.

President Kennedy remains in my memories. He was my child-hood mentor and hero. I suppose everyone needs a mentor at certain stages of their lives. I have been to the Arlington National Cemetery on several occasions and have paid my respects to JFK. Invariably, it is an emotional experience for me. Several years ago, on my last visit, I looked around at the verdant hillside and I gazed at the eternal flame on JFK's grave. I had teary eyes. I thought he surely deserved such a remembrance for eternity. Suddenly, my thoughts went back to my admiration of JFK when I was a ten-year-old boy.

To this day, my heart aches at the unfairness of this world and for the fallen leader. Now, as an adult, I am glad I can finally speak a pane-gyric for the loss of JFK and say what he meant to me. One of my for-mer university professors still refers to JFK as "my president." Yes, indeed! JFK is my president, too, and he will always be. As a child, he inspired me to reach my summit, and I will never forget him.

James A. Michener, Author, Haifa, Israel

Despite all his fame as an author, the late James Michener never found greater excitement than when he worked as a Kennedy campaign worker. He shares the reaction to Kennedy's death in Israel and recalls working to elect him President in 1960.

That Friday I was in Haifa, the northern seaport for Jerusalem, and in accordance with my invariable custom during the years I worked on the manuscript for my 1965 novel, *The Source*.[24] I had spent the holy

James Michener at work.

evening at the synagogue for Friday prayers. Afterward I walked to the home of a Jewish family, who had befriended me, and with whom I often spent Friday nights at simple meals and good talk.

On this night I noticed that the three families who awaited me were more than usually sober, as if it had been they, and not me, who had attended the synagogue. During the quiet dinner they lacked their usual vivacity for customarily they were a lively lot. I noticed this without commenting on it or even trying to fathom what had caused this curious behavior.

You must understand that the clock-time in Israel was hours ahead of clock-time in the United States, so that when it was eight or nine at night in Haifa it was only early afternoon in Washington. As our congenial dinner ended, two adult men engineered it so that they could move me off to one side, and there they said: "We didn't want to alarm you before we ate, but just as you entered downstairs and rang our bell we heard on the radio that your President has been shot by an assassin."

"Dead?" I asked.

"We don't know, but let's turn on the radio," and although the extreme orthodox couple who had been dining with us protested this use of electricity on Friday night (forbidden till sunset on Saturday), they allowed us to activate the radio and there we heard the fatal news: "President John F. Kennedy was killed by an assassin's bullet in Dallas, Texas. Vice-President Lyndon B. Johnson, who was present in the city, has been sworn in as the next President of the United States."

It was the Israelis who started to weep, for they had come to think of Kennedy as a trusted friend, and to lose him in this way was both intolerable and dangerous. "What will happen now?" they asked me, and for the first time, I heard the comment that would be uttered frequently that night: "I hope to God the assassin wasn't a Jew." And they told of the terrible retaliations that the Nazis had visited on any village in which a Jew had insulted or killed a German. Terror was in the air that dark night.

When the two men who had revealed the assassination walked me to my quarters, I could not sleep, so I went to my typewriter and wrote a detailed account of what had transpired that night, ending with a speculation that powerful forces whom I knew to be opposed to all that Kennedy had stood for had somehow engineered his death! "There must have been, I reasoned a conspiracy, to remove him," and during the long, painful night I even speculated on who might have been engaged in the conspiracy, and for what reasons.

On Saturday morning, a Sabbath holiday of quiet in Israel, I breakfasted with a dear friend, Willem Van Leer, a brilliant cinematographer, with whom I listened for news from New York. When a bulletin announced that the assassin had been identified and captured and that his name was known, Lee Harvey Oswald, Wim covered his face, dropped his head and softly wept. Finally he whispered: "Thank God it wasn't a Jew."

In no other foreign country could the death of Kennedy have caused such deep emotionalism as in Israel, where he had been thought of not as a sentimental pro-Jewish sympathizer but rather as a stable influence in a writhing international snake pit. To the Israelis his death was a tragedy, and when, a day later, it was learned that Oswald had also been murdered, this time by a half-crazed Jew, Jack

Ruby, Wim laughed sardonically: "How these things crowd in upon us. Insane, there is no use in trying to sort them out."

In the days that followed I had to try to sort them out, for I had been an ardent supporter of Jack Kennedy and had, indeed, served as his 1960 election manager in a critical suburban county north of Philadelphia. Although my large district was certain to vote Republican our strategy was simple: "Get every Democratic vote we can, so as to hold the Republicans to a limited victory. Then pray that the big cities, Philadelphia and Pittsburgh get out enough Democrats to carry the state."

Our plan worked. We lost every district in which I worked, but by such diminished margins that our big vote in the cities kept Pennsylvania in Kennedy's column and helped him win the presidency. As a reward he appointed me his Director of Food for Peace, in which job I strove to move our huge agricultural surpluses to starving nations that hungered for them. I accomplished little, because the recipient nations allowed our gifts to be lost in internal thievery and red tape.

I was allowed to gain a constant insight into some of the ideas that motivated Jack Kennedy. He was willing to make bold moves in an effort to reach new solutions to old problems. He spoke for humanity, both at home and abroad. He was cut down before he had adequate time to bring into fulfillment the ambitions I knew he had. Also, he became so preoccupied with the inescapable problems of the Soviet Union and Cuba that he could not attend to purely national problems. His limited tenure as president could not be assessed a political triumph; the hard work of bringing his ideals into practical manifestation had to be left to Lyndon Johnson, who discharged that task brilliantly at home but less than adequately in international affairs.

What Kennedy did accomplish was the inspiration of the nation at a time when change of direction and commitment was absolutely necessary. FDR had held the nation together during a great war. Truman had consolidated peace. Eisenhower had effectively eased the nation into tranquil ways, quashing the McCarthy aberration and establishing patterns for prosperity. By 1960 the nation really needed a shot in the arm, intellectual ferment, a facing of new challenges. Jack Kennedy, with his gift for the happy phrase and his personal magnetism, started his nation along new paths and with a burgeoning excitement. Leadership contributes mightily to a democracy. At certain critical points, as Winston Churchill proved, personal example is worth a battalion in the field. Perhaps his brilliant leadership could have only a short life, perhaps his words were doomed to lose their power to inspire, but during the brief period when they were needed they accomplished wonders. I remember Kennedy as that sort of man, a flaming beacon shining in a somewhat murky night when his guidance was needed, extinguished far too soon, but leaving behind embers that still glow.

To have lost him, that strange night in Haifa when I saw his significance through the eyes of citizens from another nation, was a tragedy of such dimension that it still aches when I recall those anguished words of my friends and the tortured ones I wrote when trying to solve the mystery of his assassination. That night and the days that followed left an indelible impression on me, one whose tangled webs I have not even yet untwined.

Tharsella Sevareid, Housewife, Bangkok, Thailand
Mrs. Sevareid is the sister-in-law of the late news correspondent, Eric Sevareid.

My family and I were living in Bangkok in November 1963. My husband, John, was a Lieutenant Colonel in the army and was serving as a military advisor to the Thai army. I had just come home from the hospital after giving birth to our third child. On Saturday morning, November 23, my husband came into our bedroom and his face was ashen; he was agitated and visibly disturbed. He had clutched in his hands the morning paper, a local edition published in English, and the headlines announced that both President Kennedy and Governor John Connally of Texas had been killed in Dallas.

We were flabbergasted by the news. My husband dressed at once and hurried to the office. The news we received was somewhat fragmentary as we had no television and depended heavily on the local press and radio for information. It was many weeks before we saw the pictures and learned the specific details of the days of mourning and the funeral in Washington.

The embassy organized tributes to President Kennedy, and everyone from the United States connected to the government wore black armbands for several days. The military wives such as myself also were requested to wear black dresses when we were in public and we did. Families including ours also went to the embassy to register in a book placed before a large picture of President Kennedy draped in black. We were asked to bring the children over six years of age with us as well. Many Thais came to the embassy to express their sympathy and were given a copy of President Kennedy's inaugural address with his picture at the top.

We were somewhat caught off-guard at the depth of feeling and sorrow engendered by Kennedy's death among the Thai people. They were clearly deeply affected by his death, even at the working-class level. He was perceived by the Thais as a positive agent of change for the world. Our servants, for example, were very upset over his death and I didn't realize until that moment that they even knew he existed. It was a difficult time for all of us being so far removed from the United States and not to be a closer part of a great national calamity.

Kusum Singh, College Student, Meerut, India

Singh reports how many of the people in the world's largest democracy reacted to the death of Kennedy. In what may be surprising to some, she reports their strong feeling of loss.

On that fateful day in November, I was traveling by train from my hometown where I attended Meerut College to visit the home of my uncle living in Agra. I was riding in the second-class compartment that was fairly crowded but not jammed. In third class people virtually hung out the windows. The train slowly meandered from station to station and it was a beautiful, sunny and cool day.

As we pulled into one of the local stops, a young man rushed in and, in a high state of excitement and a loud voice, he told us that President Kennedy had been shot. Everyone in the compartment fell silent. Some on board said it could not be true and went outside to confirm the news. Unfortunately new passengers came on board and repeated the tragic news, including the news that the President was dead. Everyone seemed visibly moved. One old man commented how good men are taken before their time comparing Kennedy's assassination with that of our great leader, Mahatma Gandhi, who like Kennedy died by the hands of an assassin.

As the train continued on its journey, there was a strange sadness in the air. People talked in hushed tones and shared their grief and dismay with each other. As we rode along, I could not take my mind off this horrible event. Only a year or so earlier, Mrs. Kennedy had made a visit to India. One of her stops had been in Agra where I was heading. I recalled pictures I had seen of her during that visit and they kept flashing in my mind, particularly one where she rode an elephant. My heart was filled with deep regret and sympathy over the loss of her husband The Indian people were quite mesmerized by her charm and were taken by her youth and beauty.

When I arrived at my uncle's house in Agra, everyone was in an uproar and in a state of depression over the death of President Kennedy. We felt someone dear and close to us had been removed. That event certainly cast a shadow over my visit.

President Kennedy was tremendously popular in India as there was high expectations and new hopes raised for better relations between the United States and India. With his death, these hopes were dashed. People were concerned over what impact his passing would have on our country.

After this, because President Kennedy was so very highly regarded, it was not unusual to see a large framed picture of him hanging beside our national heroes, Nehru, Gandhi and even Buddha in the homes of people and in shops. This occurred even in very small towns in remote parts of India. It might seem strange to Americans, but even today in India, you can often find his picture enshrined as it was years ago.

It is difficult to explain this phenomenon, but President Kennedy somehow captured the imagination of the people of India. To us, he symbolized hope, good will and a fresh course of direction for all people. No American President since Kennedy has come close to matching him in popularity in India.

William C. Battle, Ambassador to Australia, Canberra, Australia

Bill Battle was an old friend of JFK. He recalls the reactions of Americans abroad, in particular, the Davis Cup team.

I was appointed the American Ambassador to Australia in the spring of 1962. On November 22, 1963, I was living in the Australian capitol of Canberra. My relationship with President Kennedy dated back to World War II when we were both young officers in the Navy serving together in PT boats. We first met when we were stationed at the PT boat base at Tulagi in the Solomon Islands. Lt. Kennedy had the nickname of "Shafty," and I carried the sobriquet of "Bitter" Bill.

In the spring of 1960 I worked actively for Senator Kennedy in the Democratic primaries and in the general election of the fall, and I served as Kennedy's campaign chairman for the state of Virginia. He narrowly lost in Virginia, even though he gained tremendous ground in the closing days of the campaign. I was also campaign coordinator for the southeastern states.

On the early morning of Saturday, November 23 (Australia is a day ahead), I was up very early preparing to go trout fishing with my two boys and Malcolm Fraser, than a back-bench member of Parliament, who later became Prime Minister. Around 5:00 A.M. I received a telephone call from a newspaper reporter in Sydney, who was appalled to learn I hadn't heard the news that Kennedy had been shot. We then hung by the international radio and thus learned the news. I went to my office and had an unbelievably empty feeling. My staff trickled by. None could even open their mouths; they were so distraught.

Around midmorning I received a call from the nonplaying captain of the Davis Cup team, Bob Kelleher. I knew his son well when he attended law school at the University of Virginia while living in our cottage. Bob was a card-carrying Republican, but was absolutely distraught. His major problem was what should the Davis Cup team do. Dennis Ralston was to play that day in the finals of the South Australia Open and didn't want to play as he was totally destroyed by the news. Knowing the Kennedy family the way I did, and after much conversation, I urged that Ralston should go ahead and play. He did so and got wiped out in a match he was expected to win.

We then began a period of official mourning, and the Davis Cup team came to Canberra to be with other Americans. Some stayed with us at the embassy and others with staff members. It was really sort of a gathering of the clan of Americans in mourning in support of each other. For a week or more the team stayed with us until they went on to Adelaide to compete in the Davis Cup.

In Canberra, we had a memorial ceremony and the church was packed. The diplomatic staff and the Davis Cup team were seated in the front row. The reaction of the Australians to Kennedy's death was one of total dismay and disbelief. In fact, the entire nation seemed to have ground to a halt. Kennedy was viewed in Australia and all over the globe as a great young man that the world could follow.

As I think back, not in my time can I recall a President that stirred the enthusiasm and spirit of change that Kennedy fostered. He also was a man of action as he demonstrated in the Cuban missile crisis when we were brought to the brink of war. I believe absolutely that if he had continued in office, he would have been reelected by an overwhelming margin.

David M. L. Farr, Acting Dean of Faculty of Arts, Carleton University, Ottawa, Canada

In his tribute to JFK, Dean Farr offers a thoughtful and thorough overview of the Kennedy Presidency from the Canadian perspective.

In regarding the American political scene, most Canadians prefer presidents from the Democratic party. This attitude goes back, I think, to the enormous popularity President Franklin Roosevelt

enjoyed in Canada. Roosevelt was admired as the president who nego-
tiated the 1935 trade agreement that helped lift Canada out of the
great depression; he was also applauded as the president who favored
Britain and France during the first two years of World War II when
Canada was a belligerent and the United States a neutral. Roosevelt's
successors, Truman and Eisenhower, did not gain the same level of
appreciation in Canada as FDR.

Then in 1960, John F. Kennedy emerged. Canadians took to him
with enthusiasm. He was young, energetic, intelligent. He was exciting, full of promise. He appealed to idealism when he urged us to
engage with him in the struggle against "the common enemies of man:
tyranny, poverty, disease, war itself." He stood on the side of the
oppressed in the civil rights crisis. He was prepared to bear the costly
burden of the "long twilight struggle" of the Cold War, giving the
West a sense of high purpose in the contest.

During the fall term of 1960 I taught as a visiting lecturer at
Duke University in North Carolina. The Duke students whom I met
were wild about Kennedy, even though Richard Nixon had been a
graduate of the Duke Law School. The Kennedy-Nixon debates were
the topic of conversation in every student lounge. Most students, I
believe, judged Kennedy as the victor in these contests and were overjoyed when he was elected to the presidency. I did not follow
American politics as closely when I returned to Canada, but it was my
impression that the commitment among the young to Kennedy and
his ideals remained strong.

Thus the news of his assassination came as a dramatic shock to
Canadians as well as Americans. At the time I was serving as Dean of
the Faculty of Arts at Carleton University in Ottawa, Canada's capital. I remember vividly hearing of the event at a meeting where we
were planning future space requirements for the faculty. The next day
the university's president called me and asked me to arrange, in his
absence, a memorial service for the late President Kennedy. The model
was to be services we held annually on November 11, in memory of
the dead in the two World Wars. I was honored by the president's
request but nervous at the prospect of a formal public occasion. I had

occupied the post of dean for only three or four months and had never presided over such a solemn gathering. Nevertheless, I took on the task and spent part of the weekend that followed organizing the event and preparing some remarks. During those two days there were memorial services in Ottawa's churches and hours of grave television coverage of the removal of the late President's body from the White House to the Capitol.

Our service at Carleton University took place at 1:45 P.M. on the Monday following the president's death. There were about 70 faculty members present, a large proportion of our permanent faculty, as well as hundreds of students. The faculty, wearing academic costume, walked slowly from one building to a large foyer in an adjoining building. Here the half-hour service was held before a hushed, standing audience. I uttered my brief eulogy. One of the professors from the Political Science Department read extracts from some of Kennedy's speeches, and a professor of English, speaking on behalf of members of the faculty from the United States, recited a 1942 poem by Robert Frost, "The Gift Outright," that was read by Frost at Kennedy's inauguration. I also gave a tribute as well where I warned against the use of violence.

Looking back on Kennedy and his times, I see him as the icon of a simpler, more optimistic age than that of today. Compared to our decade, the years of his presidency represent something of an age of innocence. Kennedy has come to be regarded as a martyr for the faith and the hope that we, who were his contemporaries, possessed. Thus my tribute of November 25, 1963, to him is also a lament for my own generation.

Lucian Heichler, U.S. Foreign Service Officer, Berlin, West Germany

Next to Ireland, there was no stronger demonstration of grief in any area of the world than in Berlin at the death of Kennedy. He had visited Berlin earlier that year where he was greeted with open arms. Lucian Heichler offers a detailed and moving account of the reaction of Berliners to the assassination and recalls the great joy of the earlier visit to Berlin.

Lucian Heichler greets Berlin Mayor Willy Brandt.

In the evening of November 22, 1963, the cultural affairs officer of the U.S. Mission in Berlin hosted a reception for young Fulbright scholarship students just returned from the United States. When I arrived at his home, a few minutes before 8:00 P.M., someone had turned on the radio to catch the AFN (Armed Forces Network) news. We heard the fateful words, "The President has been shot." Within minutes the announcer confirmed the worst: "The President is dead." The reception ended immediately. The guests left quietly. The same thing was happening all over the city, but I did not know that yet; I only learned later that everywhere in West Berlin, stage, film and concert performances ended abruptly, bars and restaurants closed, private dinners and parties broke up.

Trained to respond like a homing pigeon, I headed straight for my office at the U.S. Mission on Clay-Allee. As a young Foreign Service officer assigned to the Mission's Political Section, I held the special position of liaison officer to the West Berlin City government, then headed by Mayor Willy Brandt. Without being summoned, a number of the Foreign Service and military officers on the staff of the

U.S. Commander Berlin, the Berlin Brigade, and the U.S. (State Department) Mission gathered at U.S. Headquarters for what turned into an all-night working session in the "bunker," the rarely used emergency operations center.

Almost eagerly we turned our attention to mundane, practical matters, partly because it was necessary, partly because it helped us to deal with our own emotions. Once persuaded that there was no international crisis, no need to move to a high stage of a military alert, we became absorbed in questions of protocol: What needed to be done? None of us knew the procedures to be followed when a president dies in office. Manuals were consulted, cables were fired off to Washington, requesting instructions.

We arranged to buy a number of so-called "condolence books" from Berlin stationery stores, books that would be placed in various locations around the American sector for people who might want to sign their names. No one dreamed that in the days to follow, more than a quarter of a million people would stand in block-long queues, patiently waiting to sign these books. Our military colleagues frantically searched for what army protocol required under these circumstances. They came up with a number of answers, including a special military review to mourn and honor the slain Commander in Chief. This review would be held on the parade ground at Andrews Barracks with German and Allied dignitaries invited.

By coincidence, the student councils of West Berlin's Free University and Technical University met in joint session that evening. On learning the sad news, they adjourned their meeting and immediately organized a torchlight procession of students to march to the Rathaus, West Berlin's provisional city hall in the Borough of Schoeneberg. As the students marched, thousands of ordinary citizens joined the procession. By midnight, about 75,000 people stood in Rudolf-Wilde-Platz (soon to be renamed John F. Kennedy Platz) in front of the Rathaus, waiting for their mayor to say some words of comfort and reassurance to them.

Willy Brandt had returned only that afternoon from an exhausting two-week swing around West Africa. He was asleep. My boss and

I made frantic phone calls trying to contact Brandt at home to convey to him the terrible news. At one o'clock in the morning of November 23, Brandt appeared before the huge crowd assembled at city hall and announced that he would go himself to Washington to represent Berlin at the funeral of the American President. Deputy Mayor Heinrich Albertz would preside over a commemorative rally to be held in front of the Rathaus in the same spot where Kennedy had addressed the Berliners only five months earlier at the same hour as the funeral in the evening of November 25 (Berlin time).

The American military review to honor the fallen Commander in Chief was deeply moving. Never before or since have I witnessed the quiet, measured step—more loping stride than march step, of infantrymen marching to the beat of muffled drums. The ceremony concluded with the playing of taps rendered exceptionally haunting by an echo effect achieved by two buglers posted at opposite ends of the parade ground as they echoed the melody back and forth between them. Brandt was so taken with this that he turned to me to ask that I make exactly the same arrangements for the Rathaus memorial service. I transmitted the Mayor's request, and Berlin Brigade sent the same two buglers downtown: one stood on the Rathaus roof, the other atop an office building across the square. The effect was every bit as beautiful and moving there as it had been at Andrews Barracks.

For Monday, the day of the funeral in Washington, U.S. military protocol prescribed that guns should be fired every minute on the minute, all through the long day, until evening. For this purpose Berlin Brigade drew up six 105-mm self-propelled howitzers in the courtyard of U.S. Headquarters, three on each side of the central flag pole. These guns fired in rotation, like clockwork thunder, every minute on the minute, all day long, providing somber punctuation to our work in the building.

About four-thirty in the afternoon that day, a bugler and a platoon of infantry came marching up to the flagpole to conduct a simple retreat ceremony. Along with one or two others still in the building, I went downstairs to attend. I watched as the flag was slowly lowered; I listened to the bugler play taps against the background of the guns booming away with sullen, somber regularity. In that moment, I was finally overcome by emotion and gave way to tears.

That weekend, and in the days and weeks to follow, we Americans in Berlin received condolence calls and notes from many Berlin friends and neighbors, and, most movingly, from total strangers. Waitresses we had hired for one dinner or reception called and wrote to express their sympathy and sorrow. It dawned on us only gradually what John F. Kennedy had really meant to these people, and especially to the youth of Germany and the world. To them he had been a symbol of hope, at last one leader in whom they could place their confidence and their faith.

The hour of the "*Trauerfeier*" literally the "festival of mourning," at the city hall drew near. Once again, as on that beautiful, sunny summer day in June, hundreds of thousands of Berliners filled the square in front of the Rathaus on Monday evening. But what a contrast: in place of bright sunshine, a dark, cold drizzle; instead of cheering, chanting crowds, a sad and largely silent throng.

For the first time ever, the city government had requested that an Allied military honor guard be posted on its territory: a platoon of American soldiers stood at attention, presenting arms in front of the Rathaus. Mayor Albertz and other high officials delivered their eulogies with Albertz calling Mr. Kennedy a "brother of Berliners." Albertz ended by renaming City Hall Square for the late President as the new street signs were undraped. As I sat among the other invited guests on the hastily erected bleachers, I reflected on the stark and painful contrast between this sad hour and the electrifying moment when John Kennedy had stood here and told the cheering crowd, "*Ich bin ein Berliner!*"

Then two American soldiers played taps, one answering the other as the lights in the square were dimmed. Thousands of candles glimmered in the windows of houses around the square. Finally the Freedom Bell, a gift of the American people to Berlin, tolled for one minute while the crowd gazed upon the huge picture of President Kennedy suspended over the place where he spoke earlier in June.

What a joyful day the visit by Kennedy earlier in the year had been. Kennedy won not only the hearts of the Berliners, he succeeded also in charming the rather cynical men who had worked for two solid months to prepare every detail of his eight-hour triumph in Berlin. I recalled every moment of that day and of our preparations for it, with their crises and frustrations, their bickering among Allies, their funny, even ludicrous moments.

Air Force One, a Boeing 707 four-engine jet, was too large to land at Tempelhof Airport in the American sector. Only Tegel Airport, then just a French military air base in their sector of the city, had runways long enough. The American Commandant, naturally enough, wanted to be first in line to shake the hand of *his* president. But the French commandant argued that Tegel lay in *his* sector; therefore, . . . And Willy Brandt argued that it was, after all, *his* city; he was the host, and therefore . . .

Then there was the problem of the appropriate music for the arrival ceremony: the Americans wanted the Allied military bands to play the three Allied national anthems, but the British said it was not British protocol to play "God Save the Queen" on such an occasion; however, they'd be glad to play the "Star-Spangled Banner" if we would play the British anthem. The Germans wanted, naturally enough, to play *"Deutschland, Deutschland uber Alles"* but the Allies did not like that, especially the French, who suggested that the Berlin police band play *"Das ist die Berliner Luft,"* a popular Berlin ditty. The Germans, naturally enough, considered this an insult to their national pride, and so it went. In the end, of course, everything worked perfectly.

John F. Kennedy came and took the city by storm. He solved our protocol problems by seeming to shake all proffered hands simultaneously. The route in from the airport, like all routes taken in the course of his visit program, were lined with wildly cheering people. Berlin celebrated a holiday, the like of which had not been seen in many, many years. A few poignant details stand out in my memory. By dint of my special position, I was deeply involved in Kennedy's visit to the Rathaus and his great speech on that occasion (for which I had written the initial draft). I was also involved in the state dinner given in his honor by the city authorities.

When President Kennedy spoke from the balcony of the city hall to the approximately one million people filling the square below, I stood behind him as a member of his entourage. Chancellor Adenauer had made available his best English-German interpreter, a Herr Weber, who stood next to the President at the railing and interpreted his speech consecutively, sentence by sentence. When Kennedy reached the climax of his speech, his dramatic pronouncement, "*Ich bin ein Berliner,*" Weber quite automatically repeated the phrase in German.

The applause was thunderous and lasted for several minutes of wild cheers, chants and clapping. During this interval, Kennedy, with his pixieish sense of humor, leaned over to Weber and commented in an undertone, "Thank you for correcting my pronunciation." Only a few of us on the balcony were able to overhear this footnote to one of Kennedy's most famous lines.

Now, a mere five months later, John F. Kennedy lay dead in the Rotunda of the U.S. Capitol in Washington. None of us could really comprehend the senseless tragedy that had befallen us. How have the myth, the hope, the promise fared in Germany in the years since November 22, 1963? To a certain extent, inevitably, the image has been tarnished by revelations from Kennedy's private life and his handling of U.S. involvement in Vietnam. Yet, to a remarkable extent, the myth lives on, especially among the newly liberated Germany east of the Elbe River, and perhaps eastern Europe generally. To certain friends I now have among former German citizens, the name Kennedy retains its magic.

Robert Funseth, American Consul, Bordeaux, France

The reaction in southern France to the President's death was surprisingly poignant, a testimony to the common bonds that many of the French still have with the American people. Funseth recalls two separate memorial services for JFK, one formal, the other, quite simple, in a small village. He also offers a touching story of a Frenchman who sent his dearest possession to cheer up the children of the fallen President.

I shall never forget the fateful day that President Kennedy was killed. It was around 8 o'clock on a Friday evening. My wife, Marilyn, and I had just tucked our three-year old son, Eric, in for the night and had come downstairs to have dinner when I received a frantic telephone call informing me of a report from America that President Kennedy had been shot. I turned on the radio and on the 8 o'clock broadcast, we heard the awful news that the President was dead.

I returned at once to the American Consulate on Rue Esprit des Lois in downtown Bordeaux, believing that I should be at my post at such a tragic and uncertain moment. As I went up the broad circling staircase to our second floor office, I was met by the French manager of the Barclay's Bank with whom we shared the 18th century building. He grasped my arms and, with his eyes glistening with tears, exclaimed his great sadness and shock. This was only the first of thousands of such expressions of condolence we would receive from the people of Bordeaux over the next several days and weeks. Their reaction was one of intense and heartfelt grief over President Kennedy's violent death and the loss it meant for America and the American people for whom they had great admiration.

Saturday morning was an unusually quiet day in Bordeaux. There seemed to be a subdued atmosphere hanging over the city. I sent a French member of our staff to a nearby department store to buy black crepe to drape our office and flag during the period of mourning. She told me that when the sales clerk recognized her as an employee of the consulate, she gasped and, when she learned that the black crepe was for President Kennedy, tears streamed down her cheeks as she carefully measured and cut the black cloth.

In conversations with the Archbishop of Bordeaux, we arranged to have a Requiem High Mass celebrated in honor of the President late in the afternoon of Monday, November 25, to coincide with the state funeral at Saint Matthew's Cathedral in Washington where President de Gaulle would be present, representing France and the French people. It was to be held in the historic Cathedral of Saint Andre where Eleanor of Aquitaine had been married centuries earlier and where the most important religious events in the history of Bordeaux, the

Aquitaine, and France were solemnized. The Archbishop at first expressed concern that the mammoth cathedral would be half-empty at that time of day as people headed home from work for their evening family meal and would thus not accurately reflect the truly deep feelings of Bordeaux over the death of the President. It was finally decided, however, that only the Cathedral of Saint Andre was the place to memorialize the fallen American President who, with his wife and young daughter and son, was so beloved by the people of Bordeaux.

When we arrived at the end of that fateful day, we found the cathedral square packed with people. Before entering the cathedral, we reviewed and greeted the flag bearers of French war veterans, principally from World War I, whose black berets and medals and flags with streaming, fading campaign ribbons from Verdun and other battles were a familiar sight at the annual Armistice Day commemorations. They stood erect, if a bit bowed by age and old wounds, as we slowly walked down their long line. At the entrance of the cathedral, a very large American flag hung in the majestic arched portals. Over the centuries, the cathedral had slowly settled below street level, so it was now necessary to descend into the nave. It was crowded from side to side with more than 3,000 mourners. From the organ, I heard a familiar melody. Because it was being played so slowly, I did not recognize at first that it was the "Star Spangled Banner!" As we made our way down the center aisle, I could see in the distance before the chancel, four ten-foot high candelabra whose flickering flames softly illuminated each of the corners of a giant black-draped catafalque. It hovered over a coffin draped in the new American flag that had flown half-mast from the consulate's flag staff following the President's death and which we had sent to the cathedral that afternoon. In the shadows of the chancel, circling behind the main altar, I could make out the Archbishop, surrounded by the bishops and priests of the archdiocese. The officers of the consulate and their wives were seated alongside the catafalque with the coffin resting there above at shoulder-height. During the Mass, I sensed the presence of President Kennedy and found it difficult to believe that his remains were not really inside the flag-draped coffin beside us. It was an indescribable, unforgettable and profound experience.

Later that evening after dinner, I drove out into the countryside where I had been invited by a local parish priest to attend a Mass he was celebrating in honor of President Kennedy at his small rural church. Though the setting was completely different, it was no less majestic. Here too was a catafalque with its coffin draped in an American flag from the consulate. The church was crowded with townspeople and farmers whose respect and sorrow for the dead American President were no less eloquent than those at the cathedral Mass.

A final memory remains in my mind from that very sorrowful time when a few days after the memorial services a Frenchman, standing in line with hundreds of others to sign the consulate book of condolences, asked to see me so that he could personally express his grief. He walked slowly into my office and, as I stood to greet him, I recognized him as the region's most celebrated puppeteer. In his Bordeaux French accent, he slowly related to me how he had devoted his entire life to making children laugh. Since the President's death, he had become increasingly worried about the terrible effect on Caroline and John over the loss of their father and had wept over their tragic plight. He placed on the table in front of us a simply wrapped package and said he had a small gift for the children. Although he was only an ordinary Frenchman, he too wanted to do something that might bring some happiness into the lives of Caroline and John. The puppeteer's father had also been a puppeteer and had hand-crafted puppets still used in his performances. The gift he unwrapped before me contained two of the favorite members of his puppet "family," conceived and created by his father a half-century earlier. With tears streaming down his face, he placed the priceless puppets into my hands—a man and a woman—and told me that the couple had never failed to make French boys and girls laugh. He hoped they would some day do the same for Caroline and John. I sent them in the next diplomatic pouch to the State Department for presentation to Mrs. Kennedy and to Caroline and John.

Recalling these days many years later, I remember these poignant events as if they had been experienced only last week or last month, certainly not decades ago. These recollections reinforced my memory of the profound admiration and affection by the people of Bordeaux and southwestern France for Americans and America. These bonds were formed over more than two centuries of association, from the establishment of the American Consulate in Bordeaux during our Revolutionary War through the two World Wars and the Marshall Plan. During my time in Bordeaux, the United States was the only foreign country honored by the citizenry on its Independence Day, when American flags flew from government and office buildings and from homes all over the city on the Fourth of July. In the evening there was a Fourth of July celebration in the city park, capped by fireworks. On this day, the American flag always flew over Bordeaux City Hall, facing the Cathedral of Saint Andre. The flag of no other country was so honored except, of course, the French Tricolor.

Postscript

Nearly 40 years after the death of John F. Kennedy, it is quite apparent that he has taken his place among the legendary figures of American history. Based on accounts from all parts of the world, no other American President has ever captured the heart of the people of the world to the degree of a youthful and dashing Kennedy.

One common thread running throughout these recollections was the hope and aspirations held by people everywhere that Kennedy in some way would better their lives. No political figure could possibly live up to such expectations, but because Kennedy was struck down so tragically at a time when he seemed to be peaking in office, the refrain is repeatedly heard in the accounts, "What if?"

JFK was the first President to serve in the age of television, and he met the needs of the new medium admirably. The drama of his death and subsequent funeral further enhanced his place in history and became one of the great television events of all time, only paralleled by the tragic destruction of the World Trade Center in New York.

Finally there is little doubt that his greatest contribution has been his call for public service as was illustrated throughout these vignettes. Caroline Kennedy declared her father's idealistic and enthusiastic inspiration of public service for young people to be "the shining message of his life."[25] This is the living legacy of John F. Kennedy that will continue into the future so well encompassed in his classic statement, "...ask what you can do for your country."

Sources

Personal vignettes from individuals provided the key ingredients for this book. The vignettes included: on-site interviews of the contributor by the author, telephone interviews between the author and the contributor, and written accounts from the contributor. In numerous cases, a combination of written accounts and telephone conversations between the author and contributor were utilized. Other sources provided by contributors included personal letters, excerpts from diaries, speeches and sermons.

Several difficult tasks faced the author. First, what contributors should be contacted? The potential here was unlimited. Next was determining where key people were located several decades after Kennedy's assassination. This created a problem in a number of cases. Finally, people had to be persuaded to participate in the project. Surprisingly, only a relatively few people that were contacted declined to take part.

One of the more unique features of the interview process was the desire of nearly all those interviewed, whether Democrats or Republicans, to focus on their positive recollections of John F. Kennedy. A example of this response was that of the late Senator Barry Goldwater, always known for his frankness. Goldwater commented about the charges made against Kennedy by revisionists over the years, "I'm tired of having this stuff brought up, over and over again."

There were thousands of people that could have made legitimate contributions to this book. An effort was made to obtain a cross-section of people that knew Kennedy personally as well those from the general public viewing him from a distance. Many people that were interviewed had excellent stories to relate, but, because of space limitations and topic overlap, their accounts were eliminated.

Presented below are the contributors of vignettes in the book. The name of the contributor is listed followed by the date that the contributor was interviewed or contacted. The only vignette not a result of a personal contact, was that of President Jimmy Carter, drawn from a speech he made at the dedication of the John F. Kennedy Presidential Library.

Names and Contact Dates for Contributors

Wali Abdi, February 3, 1992
William C. Battle, June 2, 1992
James J. Bausch, September 9, 1992
Susan Burho-Hensley, July 2, 1993
James MacGregor Burns, August 10, 1992
John Burton, April 2, 1993
Mike Burton, June 19, 1992
Jimmy Carter, Speech in Boston, October 20, 1979
Ned Chalker, September 3, 1992
Keith Clark, November 27, 1992
Darrel Clowes, January 23,1993
John M. Crowell, July 8, 1992
Richard M. Daley, August 5, 1992
Margaret Truman Daniel, May 11, 1993
Jerry David, August 4, 1992
Robert Davis, February 26, 1993
Jeane Dixon, May 7, 1993
Robert J. Donovan, November, 10, 1992
Rowland Evans,Jr., September 30, 1993
Myrlie Evers-Williams, April 26, 1992
Fang Li-zhii-Fang, June 23, 1992
James Farmer, September 1, 1992
David M. L. Farr, August 26, 1992
Paul B. Fay, Jr., February 2, 1992
Gerald R. Ford, March 3, 1993
Robert W. Foster, January 6, 1993

Charlene Freeman-Coker, September 15, 1992
Orville F. Freeman, July 20, 1992
Robert L. Funseth, September 30, 1992
Nicholas Furlong, August 4, 1993
J. William Fulbright, September 28, 1992
Richard Gaudreau, July 24, 1992
Graham Gilmer, Jr., October 27, 1992
John Glenn, September 3, 1993
Barry Goldwater, June 29, 1993
Thomas Goodale, June 17, 1993
Terry Graham, April 12, 1993
Alan Guskin, October 29, 1992
Paul H. Guzzi, July 2, 1992
Elizabeth F. Harris, November 1, 1992
Ken Hechler, July 28, 1992
Lucian Heichler, October 23, 1992
Theodore M. Hesburgh, June 23, 1992
Homer H. Hickam, Jr. January 20, 2002
Lena Horne, August 18, 1992
Jeanne Howard-Roper, April 27, 1992
Sam Huff, June 2, 1992
Christopher C. Kraft, Jr, May 11, 1993
Lucy Kroll, December 9, 1992
Paul Landis, August 15, 1993
William M. Landis. August 16, 1993
Evelyn Lincoln, April 2, 1993
G. Robert Lucas, February 23, 1992
Carl McDaniels, April 7, 1993
Vivian J. Malone-Jones, March 8, 1993
Romeo M. Massey, June 4, 1992
James A. Michener, September 7, 1992
Melody Miller, February 8, 1993
Janet R. Murrow, February 26, 1993
James Nightingale, June 22, 1992
Kathleen O'Connell, November 16, 1992

Thomas P. O'Neill III, August 15, 1992
Cathal O'Shannon, June 1, 1993
Nelson C. Pierce, Jr., September 10, 1992
George E. Reedy, December 3, 1993
George R. Riley, June 24, 1992
Mario Rivas, February 29, 1992
Cliff Robertson, June 23, 1992
James I. Robertson, Jr., June 4, 1992
Mary Ross, October 25, 1993
Richard M. Scammon, July 19, 1992
Thomas J. Scanlon, June 18, 1992
Margot Sebba, January 18, 1992
Tharsella Sevareid, July 16, 1993
Thomas Sherman, April 14, 1993
Kusum Singh, April 20, 1992
George A. Smathers, October 14, 1992
Margaret Chase Smith, February 3, 1993
Yvonne Snyder-Farley, June 8, 1992
Robert L. Steiner, August 14, 1992
James Stephens, July 24, 1992
Jeff Stewart, April 20, 1992
James B. Swindal, March 9, 1993
Marina Tempkina, July 19, 1992
Josiah Tlou, February 10, 1992
Albert F. Turner, June 9, 1992
Richard W. Weber, June 18, 1992
Peter A. Weng, August 3, 1992
Bernestine Williams, April 25, 1993
Bob Wright, October 5, 1992

Notes

1. John F. Kennedy, *Profiles in Courage* (New York: Harper and Brothers, 1956).
2. Theodore H. White, *In Search of History* (New York: Warner Books, 1778), 513.
3. William Manchester, *The Death of a President* (Harper and Row, 1967),189.
4. Ralph G. Martin, *A Hero For Our Times* (New York: A Fawcett Crest Book, 1983), 522.
5. Telephone interview with Robert J. Donovan, November 10, 1992.
6. Robert J. Donovan, *PT 109: John F. Kennedy in World War II* (New York: McGraw-Hill, 2001).
7. Ibid.
8. John Hershey, "Survival," *New Yorker*, 1944.
9. Donovan, *PT 109*.
10. Arthur M. Schlesinger, Jr., *A Thousand Days* (Boston: Houghton Mifflin Company, 1965), 612.
11. Fletcher Knebel and Charles W. Bailey, Jr., *Seven Days in May* (Harper and Row,1962).
12. Manchester, *Death of a President*, 600.
13. Kennedy, *Profiles in Courage*.
14. John W. Gardner, *To Turn the Tide* (New York: Harper,1961).
15. From Eulogy to JFK by Senator Mike Mansfield, November 24,1963.
16. Jimmy Carter, Speech in Boston, October 20,1979,
17. James MacGregor Burns, *John Kennedy: A Political Profile* (New York: Harcourt, Brace and Company, 1959).
18. *Scholastic* (The student weekly of the University of Notre Dame) November 26,1963.

19. Kennedy, *Profiles in Courage.*
20. Ibid.
21. Homer H. Hickam, Jr., *Rocket Boys* (New York: Delacorte Press, 1998) .
22. Ibid.
23. Thomas J. Scanlon, *The Waiting for the Snow* (Chevy Chase, Md. Posterity Press, 1997).
24. James A. Michener, *The Source* (1965: Random House).
25. Caroline Kennedy, "My Father's Legacy." *Newsweek*, June 1, 1992, 49.

Index